by Michael Sanchez

Fiddle For Dummies®

Published by: **John Wiley & Sons, Inc.,** 111 River Street, Hoboken, NJ 07030-5774, www.wiley.com

Copyright © 2015 by John Wiley & Sons, Inc., Hoboken, New Jersey

Media and software compilation copyright © 2015 by John Wiley & Sons, Inc. All rights reserved.

Published simultaneously in Canada

For general information on our other products and services, please contact our Customer Care Department within the U.S. at 877-762-2974, outside the U.S. at 317-572-3993, or fax 317-572-4002. For technical support, please visit www.wiley.com/techsupport.

Wiley publishes in a variety of print and electronic formats and by print-on-demand. Some material included with standard print versions of this book may not be included in e-books or in print-on-demand. If this book refers to media such as a CD or DVD that is not included in the version you purchased, you may download this material at http://booksupport.wiley.com. For more information about Wiley products, visit www.wiley.com.

Library of Congress Control Number: 2014940491

ISBN 978-1-118-93022-9 (pbk); ISBN 978-1-118-93024-3 (ebk); ISBN 978-1-118-93023-6 (ebk)

Manufactured in the United States of America

10 9 8 7 6 5 4 3 2 1

Contents at a Glance

Table of Contents

Introduction

. . . .

Over the years, I've come in contact with some great people who were interested in learning how to play the fiddle. Some of them heard a popular song on the radio with a great fiddle solo, and others stumbled upon the music played live in a local venue. Wherever they first heard fiddle music, all became interested in the beautiful sounds that the fiddle makes.

I was classically trained as a violinist, but somewhere along the line, I fell in love with the sound of the fiddle and had to learn it. I had an advantage because I already knew the fundamentals of the instrument (the violin and the fiddle are the same instrument but differ in the style of music they play). So when people come to me and are interested in learning to play the fiddle, I always cover the fundamentals of the instrument first. Whether they want to learn Charlie Daniels or Beethoven, it all comes down to starting off with the proper fundamentals.

Because some of the best fiddle players in the world are classically trained, I'm excited to take my approach to learning how to play and show you how to apply it to some of the most popular fiddle genres in the world. My approach to teaching may be a classical approach, but it's also mixed with my years of experience playing the fiddle and also as a Nashville fiddle player. I hope to build passion in you that will continue to grow for a lifetime.

About This Book

This book aims to explain everything you need to know about playing the fiddle properly. Even if you have no musical experience, this book teaches you what you need to know in detail. It's the closest thing to having a private fiddle lesson with me!

There are many great songs associated with the fiddle, including "The Irish Washerwoman," "Turkey in the Straw," "Arkansas Traveler," "Mississippi Sawyer," "Cripple Creek," and more. This book teaches you not only how to play the notes for these songs but also how to apply various techniques to make the songs sound even better.

Instead of jumping right into learning songs on the fiddle, the first half of the book starts with the basics, including what type of instruments I recommend. I cover everything you need to know about what to do with your right and left hands, and I teach you how to read music. These chapters give you the perfect foundation for learning to play various styles of songs.

In the second half of the book, I start by showing you some of the popular styles of fiddle, including Scottish, Irish, old-time, and bluegrass music. I include many song examples for you to try out, and I give you suggestions of various fiddle techniques to apply. As you progress through these styles, I give you tips and point out spots in the songs that are important to practice. Tips related to specific songs help you get the best sound out of each and every song. This is very similar to what I'd do in a private lesson with you. You'll find it helpful to hear the songs as well, so I include many audio clips throughout the book.

Toward the end of the book, I cover some of the more advanced concepts of playing the fiddle, including how to play double-stops and how to get a great sounding vibrato. I also cover improvisation and working with an electric fiddle system.

This book focuses on the practicality of playing various songs rather than the history and background of styles, although there is a little of that too! The goal of this book is to get you to the point where you can pick up a fiddle music book and know exactly what to do to play a song properly. To do that, you need to understand music theory, know how to produce a good tone, know how to play properly in rhythm, and much more. This is all covered throughout the book and taught in a progressive format.

Foolish Assumptions

The only assumptions I make about you are that you're interested in discovering more about playing the fiddle, that you're using standard tuning (G, D, A, E), and that you're playing with a bow. I don't assume that you can read music, that I know what style of music you want to play, or that you're interested in only one style of music. I don't even assume that you own a fiddle yet.

I also don't assume to know your level of experience. See which one of the following categories you think you fit into, and read some of my suggestions for you.

✔ **Total beginner with no musical background:** I recommend taking your time through this book and spending a good two months on Chapters 3 through 6. These chapters teach you how to create a good sound. If you can tolerate not playing songs right away, this is the best road to create a solid fundamental foundation. Because you don't have experience reading music, you can also take those two months and work on Chapters 7 and 8 at the same time.

After you get through Chapter 8, you should take another month going through Chapter 9. This chapter was written to follow a progressive format, and it should take you at least a few months before getting to Chapter 10. I wouldn't start Chapters 11 to 14 until you feel confident with the fundamentals of playing. This can happen as soon as three months, but the average length of time (if you practice about two hours per week) should be about six months. I don't recommend you start Chapter 15 for at least a year if you're a total beginner. Everything after that you can certainly read, but I wouldn't recommend trying anything in those chapters until you have a solid understanding of the instrument.

✔ **Total beginner with musical background:** I recommend taking the same track as a beginner with no musical background, but you don't have to spend as much time on Chapters 7 and 8. You may want to start Chapter 9 after about a month, but you can take longer; there's no rush to go through the beginning Chapters 2 through 8.

✔ **Some experience playing violin, but now you want to play the fiddle:** In this case, you may want to just briefly touch on Chapter 5, but everything else before Chapter 8 may be repetitive knowledge. You'll want to get to Chapter 9 as soon as possible after you review the beginning chapters. You'll want to focus on Chapters 9 through 14 for the first six months and then progress to later chapters when you feel you're ready.

Remember, with any new technique you learn after Chapter 9 (things that are unique to learning fiddle), you may want to look back at Chapter 5 to make sure you're doing the new technique fundamentally correct. For example, when you start doing the drone technique in Chapter 13, you may be holding the bow tighter than you should. Going back to Chapter 5 and doing the drills can be very effective to create a clean sounding drone.

✔ **Intermediate/advanced violinist interested in fiddle:** Chapters 1 through 8 won't be that helpful to you, although you may like some of my suggestions on technique in Chapter 5. Chapters 9 and 10 may be too easy for you, so you may want to start at the end of Chapter 10 and then go to Chapter 11. After a month (or sooner), you can get into Chapter 15, which covers vibrato, shifting, and double-stops. There are plenty of songs to learn, but remember that it's not just about playing the notes but the technique you're putting into the tunes. Listen to the audio clips to see the difference between the way you may be playing it and the way it should sound.

✔ **Fiddler who doesn't have interest in the fundamentals:** This isn't the best road to take, but I know there are many of you out there. You aren't going to like Chapters 1 through 8, so you may want to just start at Chapter 9 or Chapter 11 to get into the heart of the different fiddle styles. If you don't have interest in reading music and have more knowledge of chord structures, you'll get a lot out of Chapter 17 on improvisation.

Icons Used in This Book

To highlight different types of information throughout the book, I've marked certain paragraphs with the following icons:

This icon points out tips, tricks, shortcuts, and more that make your life as a fiddle player a little easier.

This icon points out especially important concepts that you don't want to miss or forget.

This icon highlights common mistakes and pitfalls you want to avoid.

This icon highlights technical information that you can skip if you're short on time (or if you just want to focus on the need-to-know stuff).

This icon points out the audio tracks and video clips I've recorded to supplement the text and figures.

Beyond the Book

As if all the great information in this book weren't enough, you can go beyond the book for even more!

I've recorded numerous audio tracks and video clips so that you can view and listen to various scale patterns, songs, techniques, and musical styles. Go to www.dummies.com/go/fiddle to download these files.

Also be sure to check out the free Cheat Sheet at www.dummies.com/cheatsheet/fiddle for all sorts of super-handy info, including a checklist to help you make sure your fiddle fundamentals and technique are solid.

Where to Go from Here

I've written the chapters in *Fiddle For Dummies* so that they're as self-contained as possible. This approach allows you to devise your own personal course through the book, depending on your interests and skill level. Here are a few suggestions to get you started:

- ✔ If you haven't played in a while and want to get a refresher course on technique and important aspects of playing, start with Chapter 1.

- ✔ If you're interested in starting as a beginner but don't have a fiddle yet, begin with Chapter 2.

- ✔ If you already know the basics of playing fiddle or maybe have played the violin for a span of time, you may want to kick things off with Chapter 4, which covers all basic fundamentals.

- ✔ If you don't know anything about reading music and are interested in learning how, skip to Chapter 7.

- ✔ If you have some experience and are ready to start learning songs in a progressive format, check out Chapter 9.

- ✔ If you'd rather get right down to the specifics of styles of fiddle that you haven't learned before, start with Chapter 10.

- ✔ If you're an intermediate player and want to get into some more advanced techniques like vibrato, shifting, and double-stops, go to Chapter 15.

- ✔ If you have some basic knowledge and just want to learn how to jam with a guitarist, skip to Chapter 17.

However you decide to use this book, the thing to do now is relax, read on, and enjoy the ride with the greatest instrument in the world: the fiddle!

Part I
Getting Started Playing Fiddle

In this part . . .

- Get an introduction to the fiddle and what goes into playing it.
- Find the right instrument, bow, and accessories for you.
- Know how to tune your fiddle, tighten or loosen your bow, and apply fiddle rosin properly.

Chapter 1

Getting Ready to Become a Fiddle Player

In This Chapter

▶ Defining a fiddle versus a violin

▶ Obtaining the right equipment

▶ Taking care of your bow and tuning your fiddle

▶ Starting out with good fiddle fundamentals

▶ Knowing the basics of reading music

▶ Getting acquainted with some fiddle techniques and styles

▶ Access the audio tracks in this chapter at www.dummies.com/go/fiddle

So, you want to play the fiddle? Well, you've come to the right place. This chapter gives you an overview of the basics you need to know about fiddle playing. I explain the difference between a fiddle and a violin, and I give you advice on how to choose a fiddle. You also get a crash course on fiddle fundamentals and reading music. Finally, you explore various techniques and take a look at a few of the styles of fiddle playing.

What's the Difference between a Fiddle and a Violin?

Did you know that the violin and fiddle are the same instrument? So if you purchase a violin, it's the exact same thing as purchasing a fiddle. They differ only in the style of music that's played on them and the techniques you apply to make unique sounds.

If you play music that was written by composers like Mozart, Bach, or Beethoven, you'd call your instrument a violin during that time. If you play music like bluegrass, Irish, or Scottish, you'd call your instrument a fiddle. I show you how to play these specific styles in Part IV of the book.

The wood piece on the fiddle that's arch-shaped is called the *bridge*. This piece isn't attached to the fiddle; it's held on by the tension of the strings. Fiddlers tend to like their bridge to be flatter (instead of more on the arched side) than violinists do. That's one difference in setup that's worth mentioning. So why does the bridge shape matter? Fiddlers find playing the technique of hitting two strings at once much easier if the bridge is flatter. This is certainly not a required thing, but more of a preference. One thing to note is that you don't have to change your bridge back and forth when you decide to play a classical or fiddle song. You can easily play fiddle music on a classical-style bridge, and vice versa. It's all about getting used to the bridge you're playing on.

So how does the technique of playing violin versus fiddle differ? If you were to put a piece of sheet music in front of a violinist (someone who plays a lot of classical music), she would play it much differently than a fiddler (someone who plays a lot of fiddle music) would. The violinist would take everything on the page literally and never create her own unique additions to make the piece into her own style. The fiddler may add sliding of the hand or changes in the direction of the bow that aren't technically on the page. These additions are called *ornamentation,* and I cover them in Part IV.

Another thing that's unique to fiddle playing is the concept of *improvisation*. This is when a fiddler understands chord structure and is able to create her own melodies based on the structure of the song. Even advanced violinists would have trouble improvising because they're not used to doing it. Learning improvisation is a lot of fun and allows you to jam and play in a band. I explore improvisation in Chapter 17.

Getting the Right Gear

How do you know exactly what you should look for when you start your search for a fiddle? What makes a fiddle sound good? How much should you spend for a decent fiddle? Is renting or buying best? Does the bow really make a difference in sound? I wish choosing a fiddle was as simple as walking into a store and picking the one you think looks the best, but it's not. There are a lot of variables to consider. The most expensive instrument and bow are not necessarily the best. There are pros and cons to buying versus renting, and yes, the bow really does make a difference in sound! You find answers to all these questions and more when you get to Chapter 2.

To start playing the fiddle, you need the fiddle itself, the fiddle bow, rosin, and a shoulder rest. I talk about these in Chapter 2, along with some other helpful accessories like a bow-right tool (which helps keep your bow straight across the strings), a dampit, a metronome/tuner, and more.

Chapter 2 also has some helpful videos that allow you to listen to the sounds of various quality fiddles and bows. You can also watch a video where I show you all the accessories and how they can help you improve your skills and take care of your fiddle.

Preparing to Play

Getting prepared to play the fiddle starts with understanding more about your bow and strings. The bow has horse hairs (yes, real horse hair!) that you can tighten by moving the screw at the bottom of the bow. You need to understand how tight the bow hair should be, both when you're ready to play and when you put the fiddle away. This is very important, as you can actually damage the bow if you don't do this properly!

Other important things that are necessary in preparing to play include making sure the fiddle hairs are sticky enough to grab the strings (applying rosin) and making sure the fiddle strings are tightened properly (tuning). I briefly walk you through these steps in this section, but you find more about each subject in Chapter 3.

Tightening your bow

Making sure your bow hair is tightened properly isn't optional for success — it's required. Your bow hair needs to be properly tightened to get the best response from the strings. If the hair is too loose or too tight, you'll run into trouble. A bow with hair that's too tight can lead to a bouncing bow (which can actually damage a delicate wood bow), and a bow with hair that's too loose will result in the bow stick making contact with the strings, which won't make a proper sound.

So, how do you loosen or tighten the bow? The bow has a screw at the bottom called a button. If you turn the screw to the left (counterclockwise) a few rotations, the hair will loosen and dangle, and the stick will slightly curve. This is how the bow should look when you place it in the case after you're done playing. This is *not* how it should look while you're playing your fiddle.

If you start turning the screw several rotations to the right, you'll notice that the bend of the stick changes. If you tighten the bow hair until the stick is perfectly straight, it's too tight. If you leave it like this, you can damage your bow.

Rosining your bow

Rosin is concentrated tree sap that's used to create a sticky film on the horse hairs of the fiddle bow. Without rosin, the fiddle's horse hairs wouldn't grab the strings at all.

To start rosining the bow, you have to scratch the surface with either the screw of the bow or another tool like a nail file. If you don't do this, the rosin will remain concentrated and won't be ready to be applied to the bow. After you scratch the surface, apply rosin on the bow hair with a motion similar to scrubbing a kitchen counter stain or shining your shoes. Take a second or two on each area of the bow, applying the rosin evenly, going up and down the bow to get a nice even coat. In Chapter 3, you find out how to tell whether you have too much rosin on your bow and how often to apply rosin. Remember: no rosin, no sound, or know rosin, know sound!

Tuning your fiddle

A fiddle will only sound as good as it's tuned. To start playing, you have to tighten (tune) each string properly to a specific note pitch. If you have new strings, you have to tune them at least three times each practice session for an entire week because when strings are new, they stretch (lower in pitch) while they're set in place. After that, you normally only have to tune once before each practice session. It takes time to master tuning (especially with the pegs), but the more you do it, the faster you'll get.

You tune the fiddle starting with any string: G, D, A, or E. The G string is the lowest/thickest string, and the E is the highest/thinnest string. Sometimes you have to tune all your strings, while other times you have to tune only one.

Initially, you'll probably use a digital tuner to tune your fiddle. When you pluck each of the strings on your fiddle, the digital screen on the tuner should display the corresponding letter for each string. To get your strings in tune, you have to use either the *fine tuners* — the screws located on the tail-piece of the fiddle — or the *pegs* — the knobs located below the scroll of the fiddle. You turn the pegs either forward or backward to slightly raise or lower the pitch of the string. I go over tuning in greater detail in Chapter 3.

Fiddle Fundamentals

"Garbage in, garbage out." This phrase applies to many things in life. What you hear, what you see, and everything you learn affect what you do. Starting off with bad fiddle habits affects how you play going forward. Everyone knows that bad habits are hard to break!

In this section, I cover the fundamentals you should start with to b
foundation for fiddle playing. Go to the various chapters mentione
details.

Holding your fiddle properly

It may seem like holding your fiddle should be simple. Slap it under your
chin, grab your bow, and you're good to go! Wrong. Holding your fiddle
improperly can lead to bad habits that are hard to fix later. You need to be
able to hold it comfortably with no hands, which may be uncomfortable at
first. Many people find that using a shoulder rest is best — I talk about shoulder rests in Chapter 4.

To hold the fiddle properly, bring the fiddle up to your left shoulder. Aim the
button at the bottom of the fiddle toward the center of your neck. Point the
scroll toward the left side of the music stand. Your fiddle should be pointing to your left about 45 degrees and parallel to the floor. Keep your back
and head straight, turn your head slightly to the left, and lower your left
jaw and chin over the chin rest, pressing down with your chin so that you
pinch your fiddle between the chin rest and your collarbone. This should
allow you to hold your fiddle with no hands. Don't let go unless you know for
sure you aren't going to drop it! I go into holding the fiddle in greater detail in
Chapter 4.

Bow stroke mechanics

The most important thing that can either make or break your fiddle progress
is how you decide to hold the bow. To start, follow these points:

- Your thumb should be curved and placed gently in the groove of
  the bow.
- The rest of your fingers should make an angle on the bow.
- Your pinkie should be curved at the button of the bow.

I cover these points in more detail in Chapter 4, and I include a video that
demonstrates how to do this correctly.

To get an idea of how you want to place your hand on the bow, drop your
hand to your side and relieve any sort of tension in your hand. Look at your
hand and see how naturally each finger is curved and how none of your fingers seem to naturally straighten out. That natural curve of each finger is the
position you want. I cover this in a helpful video in Chapter 4.

Do you tend to lift heavy objects? Do you lift weights? If so, you'll have a hard time at first with the lightness you need in your hand when holding the bow. Think about how you'd hold a baby bird that's very tender and fragile. The same concept applies to how you should barely hold on to the bow. The fiddle essentially holds the bow for you; it's just a matter of how you apply your index finger to guide it. To find out more about this concept and also to watch a great video on it, refer to Chapter 4.

The key to practicing fundamentals is to work on them one at a time. Some of the most successful new fiddlers are those that take the drills and fundamentals seriously. The more you do something physically, the quicker your brain can tell your muscles to carry it out. Muscle memory doesn't care whether you're doing well or poorly; it just repeats what it knows. If you practice your bow stroke incorrectly over and over, you'll always do it incorrectly.

I'm sure it seems as if there are so many things to remember, and there are! Chapter 5 has more details on bow stroke mechanics and some drills to help you achieve the proper bow stroke.

Knuckles up and angles back

Placing your left hand properly on the fiddle starts with understanding how to hold the instrument. Chapter 4 covers this in detail. You definitely want to make sure you understand that your chin and shoulder should hold the fiddle and not your left hand. Keeping your wrist straight is also very important to left-hand placement. I discuss this in Chapter 6.

Understanding how to place your fingers down on the fingerboard is the next important point to consider. Mastering these fundamentals can lead to great fiddle playing; failing to execute them can lead to struggles finding the correct notes. I refer to these fundamentals as keeping your knuckles up high and keeping your angles back.

Keeping your knuckles up means you need to have your hand high enough to be able to find every note on the fiddle without having to reach with your hand. Your hand should stay still as your fingers move. When you start to put fingers down on the D and A strings, you may find it easy to reach notes with your fingers. Don't lower your knuckles because of this, though; eventually, you'll have to play notes way over on the G string and then jump to the E string.

You also have to be sure to keep your fingers angled back. Point all your fingers at your left shoulder. Place your middle finger down (pointing at your left shoulder) and see how far your ring finger can stretch. This is the proper way to angle your fingers.

Both of these concepts can seem complicated. I spend more time talking about them in Chapter 6.

Reading Music

Learning to read music, although scary for many people at first, isn't that difficult after you learn the fundamentals. There's nothing like being able to read the thousands of fiddle tunes out there when you understand the basics of reading music.

In this section, I cover those basics, which you can then carry over to many other instruments. Of course, I also show you how music-reading fundamentals relate specifically to the fiddle, which will allow you to start playing basic tunes. Eventually, you'll be playing songs you thought you'd never be able to play!

Getting to know the notes

So how do you know what fingers to put down on the fiddle to play some of your first fiddle tunes? Understanding how to read music is the answer. A good place to start is the music *staff,* the lines that music notes are placed on. The positions of the notes on the staff tell you what type of note you need to create on the fiddle. I go into detail about the staff and what it means when notes are placed in different spots on the lines in Chapter 7.

There are five lines on the staff, and the letters associated with those lines are E-G-B-D-F, starting with the bottom line. An easy way to remember the letters is by remembering the phrase *every-good-boy-deserves-fudge.*

In between the lines on the staff are blank spaces, which also have notes assigned to them. The four spaces (F-A-C-E) conveniently spell the word *face.*

When you play the fiddle, you encounter many different types of musical notes. The most common is the *quarter note,* which is considered one musical bow stroke or beat. A quarter note is represented by a black note with just a single stem. I cover more types of rhythms (and their symbols) like whole notes, half notes, and eighth notes in Chapter 8.

Unfortunately, not every fiddle piece has the same finger placements. Getting to know key signatures is a huge part of reading music and will make your songs sound the way they should. The *key signature* consists of symbols that define how many *sharps* (higher in pitch) and *flats* (lower in pitch) are played in a musical piece, thereby determining your finger placements. I cover these concepts in detail in Chapter 7.

Understanding rhythm

Aspiring musicians are at different levels regarding how well they can count in a song. By counting, I mean how many beats you hold each note and how fast you play the notes. Doing this properly leads to a fiddle song that sounds more musical. Even if you think you're counting properly, you may not always be, so understanding what you need to work on is key.

If you're unsure where you're at regarding rhythm, take the quiz I put together for you in Chapter 8. This will give you insight into how much work you need to do.

When it comes to rhythm, you have to allot each note its proper amount of time, or number of beats. When you start playing a piece, you set a certain tempo, and if you stray from that tempo and one note is too short and another too long, the piece won't sound very good. In Chapter 8, I explain in detail how long you have to count each note and how to find out whether you're counting it right.

Fiddle Techniques and Styles

After you get down the basics of how to read music and play some notes, you can start learning specific fiddle styles like Irish, Scottish, old-time music, and bluegrass. Each of these styles has a lot of techniques you can add (on top of just following the music) that will give your music flavor and personality. Each style has various bowing preferences, and I make suggestions of where to add various techniques that fit each style of music.

Two of the first techniques I suggest learning are sliding and slurs, as these are some of the easier techniques that you can start adding to playing the fiddle. After that, understanding how to use your 4th finger (pinkie) can be very useful. I cover these techniques in Chapter 9 while applying them to some famous fiddle tunes.

After you understand some basic techniques, you can start applying ornamentation to Irish and Scottish tunes. *Ornamentation* is basically the addition of various finger movements that add flavor to fiddle tunes. A couple types of ornamentation that I show you include grace notes (Chapter 11) and drones (Chapter 13). Then you can take your playing to another level by adding *vibrato,* which is shaking your left hand a certain way to create an even more beautiful sound on select notes. See Chapter 15 for more on vibrato.

The last and most difficult fiddle technique I talk about in the book is double-stops, which require you to place multiple fingers down while playing two strings at once. Learning how to do double-stops properly opens up a lot of possibilities to add more depth to fiddle tunes.

Sliding and slurring

Sliding creates a certain "droopy" sound that makes any song sound more like a fiddle tune. It's a simple technique that you can add to any note and do a few different ways. There are *upslides* and *downslides.* You do them by basically "sliding" your finger between two notes that are a half step apart while drawing the bow. This is a simplified explanation, but I go into more detail in Chapter 9. Sliding creates a uniquely different sound from just playing one note by itself.

Listen to Audio Track 1 to hear an upslide and Audio Track 2 to hear a downslide.

4th finger

The 4th finger is your pinkie, and it's probably the weakest and, thus, the hardest finger to use. However, using it isn't as difficult as you may think — it's all about following some basic rules. Making sure you place your 4th finger the proper distance from your 3rd finger is important, and this normally takes a few weeks to master.

It's very easy to want to grab the fingerboard too tightly when using your 4th finger, which actually makes the finger more difficult to extend. Following the tips I cover earlier in the chapter about keeping your knuckles up and angles back also contributes to reaching the 4th finger spot properly.

Ultimately, you need to know how to use the 4th finger because it will help you get a better sound on some songs. Also, some fiddle songs aren't possible to play without using the 4th finger. I go over how to use the 4th finger in more detail in Chapter 9.

Grace notes

A *grace note* is a very quick little note that's played right before a base note. It's an added little flourish that the fiddler puts in, and it almost sounds like a mistake, but it's not. Utilizing this technique is key to creating the unique sound of Irish and Scottish music.

It's very important to learn notes and rhythms first before attempting the grace note technique. It's also important to keep your hand close to the fingerboard because if it's too far away, you'll have difficulty playing grace notes fast enough.

You see many grace note examples in songs I've written, starting with Chapter 11 on Irish music.

Drones

Playing a fiddle tune with all single notes is nice, but you can take your fiddle playing to the next level by adding drones. Basically, a *drone* is when you play one note on the fiddle in combination with an open string, meaning that you play a string that you aren't pressing with your finger. I cover drones in more detail in Chapter 13.

Playing drones cleanly takes a certain technique with both the right and left hands. With the right hand, it's all about not tensing up. You'll find that when you start doing new techniques on the fiddle, you'll start grabbing the bow harder and doing things you may not have done with an easier piece. It's important to use your right-hand index finger when doing a drone and to focus on contacting the strings evenly with the bow.

Regarding your left hand, you can easily do some things incorrectly. If you have to play a drone that requires your 1st finger on the D string played in combination with an open A, and your 1st finger hits the A string at all during this process, it'll cause your drone to sound horrible! Make sure you put your 1st finger more on the side of the G string instead of the A string to get a nice clean sound.

Vibrato

After you get the hang of hitting the right notes on the fiddle, you can add some *vibrato*. This is a technique where you move your left hand back and forth on the strings (almost like you're vibrating your hand) to create a more beautiful sound.

Achieving good vibrato technique involves many steps, and an important one is consistency. Instead of just trying to make your hand move, you must work on making your hand do the exact same movement every time. This takes practice and a whole lot of patience.

I have an organized and detailed system for you to learn vibrato in Chapter 15 that you'll want to check out. If you follow the system step by step, you'll be doing vibrato before you know it.

Double-stops

Another technique that's similar to droning is the *double-stop.* This is when you play two notes at the same time, with your fingers down on both notes on the fingerboard. Because the fiddle is a fretless instrument (no metal bars on the neck, like on a guitar), having a good left-hand technique for this is very important.

In fiddle, you'll see many situations where adding in a double-stop may be challenging, but doing so will add a lot to the overall sound. Listen to the piece played on Audio Track 3. You'll hear just single notes first and then double-stops.

In Chapter 15, I cover double-stops in more detail and give you some song examples that contain them.

Styles of music

Fiddle music encompasses many different styles: Irish, Scottish, old-time, and bluegrass, just to name a few.

- ✔ **Irish fiddling** is one of the most well-known fiddle styles in the world. It's all about *ornamentation* — little elements that are added to a fiddle piece that make it sound unique from just the base melody. Irish fiddle is known for *jigs* and *reels,* which are upbeat songs that are great for dancing, with lots of accents and grace notes.

- ✔ **Scottish fiddling** is different from other fiddling styles because of the lively and vibrant delivery of the notes and rhythms. The style is heavier sounding (some refer to it as "dirtier") and much more rhythmic than the Irish style. While Scottish fiddling has jigs and reels, it also has marches, slow airs, and *Scottish snaps* (sixteenth-dotted eighth-note rhythms, done with only a flick of the wrist and fingers). Because the rhythm in Scottish fiddling is quick, it's important to keep your bow hand relaxed and not tense.

✔ **Old-time fiddling** is actually not that old; it's traditional American music that got its name in the 1920s. The fiddle is often tuned differently in old-time music to give it a unique sound. A lot of old-time music has an off-beat rhythm pattern called *syncopation,* which is when notes deviate from a typical beat pattern. There's a certain pulse that drives old-time music that's unlike other styles.

✔ **Bluegrass fiddling** is a distinct American style. Musicians take turns playing the melody and improvising around it while the other musicians play accompaniment. Some bluegrass and old-time fiddlers tend to disregard the standard rules; they hold the fiddle on the chest and don't use chin rests and shoulder rests. This style is very sophisticated though and has a lot of difficult elements involving soloing and backups. Bluegrass also features various unique bowings, such as *shuffling,* which are characteristic of the music's style.

Chapter 2

Selecting the Right Instrument and Accessories

In This Chapter

▶ Considering various factors to help you find the right fiddle

▶ Purchasing a fiddle that fits your playing abilities

▶ Choosing a bow

▶ Buying some necessary accessories

▶ Exploring some optional tools that can help your playing

▶ Access the video clips in this chapter at www.dummies.com/go/fiddle

Did you know that over 75 percent of people who decide to start playing fiddle quit after just one month? The main reason people quit is because they buy the cheapest fiddle they can find and have no idea that there are accessories that can help them learn to play!

Making the right purchases in the beginning is very important. Your choices can lead to either forward or backward momentum when learning the fiddle. Trust me, any ol' fiddle isn't going to do the trick! Throughout this chapter, I guide you through the process of finding the perfect fiddle and accessories to improve your chances of success.

Finding the Perfect Fiddle

How do you know exactly what you should look for when you start your search for a fiddle? What makes a fiddle sound good? How much should you spend for a decent fiddle? Is renting or buying best? Does the bow really make a difference in sound? I answer all these questions throughout this chapter, so don't worry if you're confused at this point!

Here are some reasons why selecting the right instrument and accessories is important:

- A high-quality fiddle will sound better to you and others.

- The better the quality of your bow, the easier it is to get a clean sound. Fifty percent of a fiddle player's sound has to do with the quality of the bow!

- Choosing the right accessories can help with your technique and help prevent bad habits on the instrument. The lack of certain accessories can make playing very difficult and even impossible. For example, no rosin — no sound!

Many people acquire fiddles through inheritance (like their great-grandpa's fiddle that has sat in the attic for 100 years) or at flea markets and garage sales (for $20). Everyone who has shown me one of these is convinced that he possesses a very fine instrument, either because of age or because grandpa was a "professional." I have yet to be shown one that is even of intermediate quality. Obviously they've remained in the attic all these years with good reason.

Getting familiar with the different fiddle sizes

Many different sizes of fiddles are on the market, as shown in Figure 2-1. Players should choose fiddles based on their *reach* — meaning how far they can stretch their arm horizontally. This section is mainly to help determine the correct size fiddle for kids younger than 13. Most people over this age use a full-size (4/4/adult) instrument.

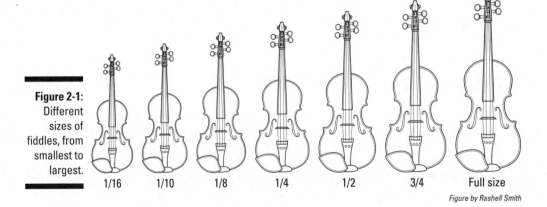

Figure 2-1: Different sizes of fiddles, from smallest to largest.

1/16   1/10   1/8   1/4   1/2   3/4   Full size

Figure by Rashell Smith

TIP

To know exactly what size fiddle you (or your child or student) need, measure the distance from the center of the shoulder blade to the very tip of the middle finger. Write down the distance in inches. Based on the distance, you can see in Table 2-1 what instrument to get.

Another method of finding the right-size fiddle is to hold the fiddle under your chin, stretch your arm as far as possible, and wrap your hand around the scroll of the fiddle. If your fingers curl all the way around the scroll, the size is correct. If they don't, you should drop to a smaller size.

Table 2-1 Fiddle Sizes Based on Arm Reach

Length of Arm Reach	*Fiddle Size*
Under 14"	1/32 size
14"–15⅜"	1/16 size
15⅜"–16⅞"	1/10 size
16⅞"–18½"	1/8 size
18½"–20⅜"	1/4 size
20⅜"–22¼"	1/2 size
22¼"–23⅝"	3/4 size
Over 23⅝"	4/4 or full size

TIP

An instrument that's too small is better than an instrument that's too big. A fiddle that's too big can cause you to form bad habits such as not reaching the tip of the bow, positioning your fingers incorrectly, or holding the instrument wrong. Having the correct size instrument is very important!

REMEMBER

Every fiddle size has a matching-sized bow to go along with it; the bow gets bigger as the fiddle gets bigger. Whenever you purchase a fiddle, it should come with the appropriate-sized bow and case. If you purchase a bow separately (like a replacement), make sure you ask for the appropriate-sized bow.

Understanding fiddle sound qualities

Fiddles have many sound qualities. Here are a few of them:

- **Cleanliness of tone:** A fiddle is only as good as its capability to make a clean/pleasant tone. As you see in Chapter 5, bad techniques cause a lot of unclean sounds, but a cheap fiddle can also make creating clean sounds much harder.

✔ **Instrument projection:** An important sound quality of a fiddle is its *projection* — the capability it has to play loud. Compare this to hearing a singer's voice. The better a singer's *projection,* the louder he is able to sing. Good projection always goes hand and hand with clean sound.

✔ **Richness and depth:** *Richness* and *depth* refer to how beautiful each note sounds coming out of the instrument. Compare this to singing again. If you were to hold your nose while singing a song, the noise coming out of your month would sound nasally or thin. This unpleasant sound is similar to the sound of many low-quality fiddles found on the market.

Exploring factors of quality in fiddle pricing

It would be nice to be able to rely solely on price to determine the quality of a violin, but price is only relative to quality. Many fiddles that cost $500 may not sound as good as a fiddle that only costs $250. The following sections explain the factors used in pricing a fiddle.

Quality of wood

The quality of wood used to make a fiddle carries the most weight in determining the price. Although many fiddles look very similar and may even have similar colors, the quality of wood can be very different from one fiddle to the next. The value of a fiddle that's *handcrafted* (each piece of wood carved by hand) is much higher than a fiddle that's manufactured in a factory. Handcrafting can take over three months of full-time work! The result is always a better projection from the instrument and a richer, deeper sound. A manufactured fiddle is much less valuable because it's easier to make, which always results in a lower asking price.

Every fiddle that costs less than $1,000 is, more than likely, manufactured — I've yet to see an exception to this. That doesn't mean that you can't find a good-sounding beginner fiddle that's factory-manufactured.

It's not uncommon for a well-known fiddle maker to charge more than $10,000 for a well-made, handcrafted instrument. Fiddles in this price range tend to be for people who decide to make fiddle playing a profession.

Who made it?

A prestigious *luthier* (someone who makes and repairs stringed instruments) can charge higher prices for her finished instruments — upwards of $10,000. A luthier who's unknown to the industry may only charge somewhere in the range of $1,000 to $2,000 for a finished fiddle. An *appraiser* (someone who decides the price) takes into consideration the prestige of the instrument maker.

If you look inside the F-hole on a fiddle, you may see the name of the person who made it, which can influence the price. Alternatively, you may only see the year and place the violin was manufactured.

Many labels are fakes. During the early 1900s, thousands of Stradivarius copies were made in Europe, so they're very common instruments to come across. "Copy of Stradivarius" is a common label especially found on fiddles on sale at places like flea markets. Unless you're extraordinarily fortunate (lottery-winner lucky), the instrument is definitely not made by Stradivarius. However, these instruments still have value and can sometimes be worth up to $2,000 if they're in great condition (not like a Stradivarius, which can be worth more than $20 million!).

What country was it made in?

The country where a fiddle is made is a big factor when considering the fiddle's quality. For example, you can find yourself tripping over the number of fiddles that are made in China (75 percent of all the fiddles in the world!), resulting in much lower prices. Because the quality of Chinese fiddles varies from very bad to outstanding, it's important to only buy a violin from China that you know sounds good or is highly recommended — do your research!

Europe makes some of the best fiddles in the world, but they're often over-priced and not worth purchasing as a beginner. After you exceed the $5,000 price range, you'll want to strongly consider a European-made instrument over a Chinese-made instrument. Examples of countries with high reputations for making violins are Germany, Italy, Romania, the United States, and the Czech Republic.

How old is the fiddle?

It's surprising to many people that a fiddle's value actually increases over time — about a 1 percent increase each year. Many fiddles made before 1900 are worth twice as much as newer fiddles of the same quality made with the same type of wood. Fiddles also sound much better over time as the wood becomes more and more *resonant* (responsive) to sound. Luthiers today, however, are capable of creating very high-quality contemporary instruments that are worth the price.

The condition of the fiddle

An old fiddle may be more valuable and potentially sound better than a newer fiddle. But the older a fiddle gets, the more prone it is to things like cracking of the wood and open seams — places where one piece of wood comes unglued from another. You can definitely maintain your fiddle with the proper tools; I talk more about these later in the chapter.

Cracks can be repaired, but if they're severe, they can be costly to fix. Cracks or broken parts can cost thousands of dollars to fix, and although sometimes fixing them is worth it on an old fiddle, many times it's not. If you notice any sort of cracking on a fiddle, don't buy it unless you feel you're getting an extremely good deal. A severe crack can diminish the value of a fiddle by more than 50 percent and can negatively affect how the fiddle sounds.

So why isn't sound on this list?

As I said in the beginning of this chapter, the price of a fiddle is relative to the sound quality, but it's not a direct factor. Many appraisers aren't violinists, and they honestly don't have to be. A fiddle's price is solely dependent on the five factors I explain in the previous sections, and that doesn't include sound!

Buying a Fiddle

Sound should be the number one thing you look for when buying a fiddle because the sound is what keeps you wanting to play. However, you have to take other factors into consideration, such as whether to buy a left- or right-handed fiddle and what level fiddle to buy in terms of your goals, playing ability, and interest level. I cover these points in the following sections.

Choosing between a left- or right-handed fiddle

The most common way to play the fiddle is with your left hand holding the instrument and your right hand holding the bow. This is considered playing fiddle right-handed. So, which way should you learn how to play? Don't base your decision on whether you're better left- or right-handed in other areas. It doesn't make a difference when first learning the fiddle; your left- or right-handedness gives you no advantage whatsoever.

The only time you should consider learning left-handed style over right is if you have any issues with your arms or hands. If you have trouble moving your right arm up and down and feel that crossing strings will be tedious, then learning left-handed may be better for you. Another example would be if you feel you'd have trouble pressing down with your left-hand fingers (or you're missing a finger on your left hand). In that case, a left-handed fiddle may be what you need.

Left-handed fiddles are rarer but are available online and in select music shops. You can request that any right-handed fiddle be changed into a left-handed fiddle by flipping the bridge around and putting the strings on the opposite side from where they originally were.

Fiddle versus violin buying

It's important to note once again that a fiddle and a violin are the same instrument; they differ only in the way they're played. You should expand your web search to "fiddles and violins" when searching for an instrument. Many fiddle players prefer a slightly lower bridge than violinists, but this really doesn't matter to the pure beginner because this preference only helps advanced players. Even if you buy a violin with a high arched bridge, you can get the bridge shaved at a music store, so don't let this be a factor in your decision.

Choosing a beginner-level fiddle

I consider any fiddle under $1,000 a beginner-level fiddle. You can purchase many instruments both online and in stores in this price range, and the quality among them can vary a lot.

If you see a fiddle in this price range with a lightly grained top and back, this is a good sign. This typically means that the quality of wood is better, which improves the sound. A fiddle without a grained top or back may be made out of plastic, which isn't uncommon, especially in fiddles priced lower than $200.

When purchasing a beginner fiddle, watch out for the following warning signs of low quality:

- **Cheap bow/case:** A poor-quality bow is a bad sign. Also, if the fiddle case is made out of cheap foam and is falling apart, the quality of the fiddle isn't going to be very good either.

✔ **Cheap strings:** Ask the seller what kind of strings are on the fiddle. If the seller doesn't know or you find the strings for under $20 online, this isn't a good sign. String quality makes a difference in the quality of sound, and if the seller doesn't care what strings are on the fiddle, chances are good she doesn't care about much else.

✔ **Flimsy fingerboard:** Push down on the fingerboard on the side closest to the bridge. If there's any flimsiness, the fingerboard is made out of plastic and not ebony (which is much better quality).

✔ **Low-quality parts:** Many cheap fiddles are made out of plastic parts, including the peg fittings, tailpiece, and chin rest.

If a fiddle sounds unpleasant and you're a beginner, the sound may not be due to poor quality. Getting a good sound, even out of a high-quality premium fiddle, takes time. Try to judge the quality of the fiddle based on the points in the previous list. Another way to judge quality is to hear the fiddle played by an experienced player. Squeaks and bounces aren't usually caused by the fiddle but by bad technique and potentially by the bow.

Instruments on eBay, Amazon, and Craigslist can sometimes be of good quality but can have many issues, especially in the beginner-level price range. Avoid considering instruments from these sites until you reach the intermediate-level price range. Even then you really have to be careful, so make sure you consider all red flags!

Just because you're a beginner to the fiddle doesn't mean you have to purchase a beginner-level instrument. If you can afford it (and you feel committed enough to sticking with your fiddle hobby), a better quality fiddle will help you tremendously, even in the short term. Same goes for the bow.

Typically, fiddles in the beginner price range will satisfy you for a short period of time (one to two years) before you want to upgrade. The amount of time varies depending on how quickly you progress, your standard of sound, and how well you take care of the instrument. The longer you play the fiddle, the more you'll find it necessary to have a better quality instrument.

Going with an intermediate-level fiddle

I consider any fiddle between $1,000 and $2,000 an intermediate-level fiddle. This price range is filled with great instruments, but be careful — not every fiddle in this price range is good. Remember, sound is relative to the price of a fiddle, meaning you can find many fiddles in the intermediate price range that sound like premium-level fiddles.

The richness and depth of the fiddle sound increase in this price range. If you find any of the negative traits I mention in the previous section on beginner fiddles to be true of an intermediate-level fiddle, run for the hills!

Following are some of the characteristics of a high-quality intermediate fiddle:

✔ **Clean sound:** If you find it easy to get a good sound out of your fiddle, that's a good sign.

✔ **Good-quality wood:** If the wood looks pretty generic or standard, the fiddle may be more in the beginner category. An example of an intermediate-quality wood would be a handcrafted, bird's-eye maple back. The more unique the wood feels and looks, usually the better the sound.

✔ **No cracks/chips:** An intermediate-level fiddle shouldn't have anything wrong with it. No cracks, chips, or bad glue jobs!

✔ **Premium setup:** If the fiddle has strings that are priced over $50 retail, that's a good sign.

Here's a list of some good places to start looking for intermediate-level fiddles:

✔ **Craigslist:** This is totally hit-or-miss, so make sure you do your research! I'd estimate that 85 percent of instruments on this site aren't ideal, but that leaves 15 percent that are great buys! Typically, these are parents selling their kid's instrument because the kid doesn't want to play anymore.

✔ **eBay/Amazon:** This is also hit-or-miss, so do your research and make sure there's a return policy in place just in case.

✔ **Local shops:** Small mom-and-pop shops that deal primarily in stringed instruments can be great places to look.

✔ **Online stores that deal primarily in stringed instruments:** Examples include Superior Violins (www.superiorviolins.com) and Johnson String Instrument (www.johnsonstring.com).

Investing in a premium-level fiddle

Buying your first premium fiddle is like buying a new car. The price isn't cheap, but owning it is so rewarding and fun! Consider going this route if you can, but price is usually an issue when it comes to buying a premium-quality fiddle.

If you're positive you'll stick with playing the fiddle and you want to sound the best you possibly can, a premium fiddle will get you to that point the quickest. If you've been playing the fiddle for a while and you're looking for an improvement in sound, a premium-quality fiddle will do the trick.

Following is a list of some of the characteristics of premium-level fiddles:

- ✔ **Beautiful handcrafted wood:** In my book, a fiddle is only considered premium if it has beautiful wood and is handcrafted. These types of fiddles take longer to make but ultimately make the best sound.

- ✔ **Clean and full projection:** The fiddle should have a very clean sound all the way across the strings. You should also notice many unique and beautiful tones.

- ✔ **Fancy parts:** Premium fiddles typically have beautifully shaped pegs, parts made from ebony, and high-quality strings.

- ✔ **Rich tone:** Always strive to get a rich/pure sound out of any instrument. This should be possible with any premium-level fiddle you're considering buying.

Talking about the different qualities of fiddles and what makes them valuable is one thing, but actually hearing the differences is another. Most people who are looking for a better-quality fiddle are interested in an improvement in sound and not necessarily the look of the instrument. Check out Video Clip 1 for the different visual and sound comparisons among beginner, intermediate, and premium fiddles.

Here's a list of some good places to start looking for premium-level fiddles:

- ✔ **Forums:** You can learn a lot about your next instrument purchase on forums and websites like Violinist.com (www.violinist.com). Definitely worth checking out!

- ✔ **Instrument maker shops:** Shops that make instruments have many nice quality instruments to choose from. When you do your research, ask the shop if it has luthiers who make the fiddles.

- ✔ **Local universities:** It doesn't hurt to call your local university to see what type of instruments it would recommend. Ask to talk to the school's violin/fiddle professor and see what the teacher recommends. This is usually a good way to find those mom-and-pop shops that I was talking about.

- ✔ ***Strings* magazine:** Many times you can find great reviews on instruments in *Strings* magazine. You can also find a lot of great information on the magazine's website (www.allthingsstrings.com).

If you go to a local shop, ask whether the fiddle you're looking at is on *consignment* — an instrument owned by a third party. These fiddles are always priced higher because the shop has to make something from the purchase as well. On average, these fiddles are priced 25 percent higher than they should be.

If your first reaction to a fiddle doesn't wow you in some way, don't buy it. You should be inspired to practice and learn more. If you don't feel that way right away, don't waste your time trying to make yourself like the fiddle.

Most online websites that deal in higher-end fiddles, such as Superior Violins and Shar Music, have payment plans. You can usually find a payment structure that fits your budget, even if you can't afford the entire payment upfront. Always ask the company you're working with if it has payment plans available. Many times they don't even charge interest!

Opting to rent instead of buy

Should you rent or buy an instrument? Typically, the quality of a rental instrument isn't as good as one that you buy, but there are definite advantages to renting over buying.

Many online and local shops have rent-to-own options that include everything you need to get started. After you make a certain number of payments toward the instrument, you'll own it. The time it takes to own an instrument is generally between 12 and 24 months, and a typical monthly payment is between $18 and $30 per month.

Rent-to-own is a great option for child-size fiddles because you can turn in the fiddle for a larger one as the child grows rather than purchasing each child-size instrument outright and trying to sell it after the child outgrows it.

If possible, avoid any sort of long-term contract. You want to be able to return the fiddle if you don't want to spend the money anymore or if you (or your child) decide to quit playing.

Some shops put all the equity you pay toward the purchase of a higher-quality instrument in the future. This gives you the ability to upgrade at a much lower price later on. You may be better off spending a little more on a beginner instrument if you're planning on upgrading because any equity will go into the new fiddle. Ask about the return policy and the system in place if the instrument gets damaged.

Considering the Bow

Did you know that the quality of your fiddle bow is just as important as the quality of your instrument? In this section, I go over everything you should consider when buying a fiddle bow and how to find the best one for you.

Many people are satisfied with whatever bow is given to them in a package deal. Most of the time a *fiddle outfit* — the combination of a fiddle, bow, and case — comes with a bow that must be good, right? Not usually!

If you pay less than $100 for a fiddle, the quality of the bow that comes with it will be poor, and that's going to hurt your playing. This is frequently why many beginners end up quitting so early. It's difficult to create a decent sound without decent equipment — you're setting yourself up for failure.

Having a nice quality bow you can grow into and learn with helps you stay motivated and encouraged. A good bow helps you tremendously in getting a better sound along the way.

Getting familiar with the different types of bows

Low-quality bows are pretty easy to make, and quality varies significantly from one bow to the next. In this section, I talk about the number one factor that makes a bow sound good: quality of material.

Standard fiberglass fiddle bows

The most common type of fiddle bow is made of standard fiberglass material, similar to plastic. These types of bows are typically found in many cheaper quality fiddle packages because they're the least expensive to make. Fiberglass bows are very stiff and are the hardest to get a good sound out of. I wouldn't pay more than $30 for this type of bow.

Brazilwood fiddle bows

An upgrade from fiberglass is a brazilwood fiddle bow. These bows are better quality than fiberglass and can make a significant difference in sound. There are cheaply made brazilwood bows out there, but you can typically weed these out by not paying bottom dollar for them. A good price range to purchase a brazilwood bow is between $50 and $100.

One way to tell a quality brazilwood bow is by the tip. If you see any sort of inconsistency in how the tip is made and how the hair is attached to the tip, this is usually a bad sign.

Carbon fiber fiddle bows

Carbon fiber bows are very good quality bows that many players use. Carbon fiber material is very durable and has a nice flexible feel to it. Although these bows won't improve your sound quite as much as pernambuco wood (see the next section), they're definitely the next best thing. Carbon fiber bows can range from $150 to $2,000. I wouldn't pay more than $400 though, as the quality after that doesn't significantly improve.

Here's an example of a high-quality carbon fiber bow: www.superior violins.com/teresa-angelo-carbon-fiber-violin-bow-49.html.

Pernambuco fiddle bows

Pernambuco wood is regarded as the best quality wood for bow-making in the world. The improvement of sound you can get from a pernambuco bow is striking. These bows have a way of adjusting to the strings, making it easier to create a clear, beautiful sound. The sky is the limit when it comes to the price of these bows, but the starting price is normally around $200. Pernambuco bows ranging between $300 and $500 are usually good bows.

Here's an example of a starter-quality pernambuco wood bow: www.superiorviolins.com/leandro-pernambucco-bow-51.html. And here's my favorite high-quality pernambuco wood bow: http://superiorviolins.com/carmela-pietro-pernambucco-violin-bow-2099.html.

If a pernambuco bow is priced below $100, I'd be very cautious in purchasing it. Most likely it's either not really pernambuco (pernambuco and brazilwood can look similar because they're from the same tree) or not very good quality.

The type of hair associated with various bows has nothing to do with value or quality. Bow hair should be replaced every so often, and it's important to note that losing bow hairs is pretty common. I cover when and how to rehair a bow in Chapter 3. For now, just consider the quality of the stick and not the hair.

Some bows can have slight defects to them, such as an imperfection in the frog, for example, but if the defect doesn't have to do with the stick itself, it doesn't affect the bow's quality. The stick of the fiddle bow is what's important.

So what exactly will a better bow do?

A better-quality bow makes a huge difference in the quality of sound, even for a beginner fiddler. Check out Video Clip 2 to hear and see the comparisons among fiberglass, brazilwood, carbon fiber, and pernambuco bows.

A good-quality bow can help create cleaner sounds, avoid bow bouncing, refine sound accuracy, improve sound depth and richness, and create world peace. Okay, it won't create world peace, but I can't stress enough how much a quality bow can improve the sound of your fiddle!

Testing out bows

A great way to find the best bow for you is to try out different ones. Many shops around the world (both local and online) let you try out bows for a period of time and only charge you to ship the bow back to them.

Call around your area to see whether any local shops have bows you can try. I suggest only dealing with shops that specialize in violins/fiddles/strings, and not just general music. Any shop that actually creates violins/fiddles is a great shop to try bows from.

Have a price range in mind when calling companies. They'll ship you a selection based on your budget and what they have available.

After you receive the bows, here's the trial process I'd suggest to you:

1. **Put a small sticky note or a colored sticker on the end of each bow to keep track of which company it came from.**

    Eventually, you'll need to ship the ones you don't want back.

2. **Make sure there is rosin on each of the bows.**

    Go to Chapter 3 to find out about applying rosin on the bow hairs.

3. **Play each bow for at least 30 seconds on the G and D strings.**

    You'll be amazed how each bow changes the tone of the fiddle! If you don't know how to play yet, have a teacher or friend who plays fiddle or violin do this for you.

4. **Note one or two bows that you feel are best and one or two that you feel aren't as good.**

5. **Repeat Steps 1 through 4 for the A and E strings.**

6. **If you find a trend where one bow doesn't sound as good, eliminate it from the bunch.**

7. **Continue this process over the next few days until you're down to two or three bows.**

8. **Spend time testing these "finalists" for the next couple of days/weeks.**

   Consider price in your decision and call the companies to find out more about the bows before you make a final decision.

Here are some additional points to consider when trying out a bow:

- ✔ How does it feel in your hand? Do you find it easy to do certain techniques? Do you prefer a lighter or heavier bow?

- ✔ Does the bow feel easy to balance at the frog? At the tip?

- ✔ What kind of sound does it bring out of your fiddle?

- ✔ Is there anything on this bow that makes it look different from the others? If so, you should ask the company about it.

- ✔ What do your teacher or friends who play fiddle think of this bow?

Don't feel rushed through this process. Sometimes you'll have different opinions on different days. Always write down your observations and then note them for making future decisions.

Because every fiddle player has a different technique (how he pulls the bow across the strings and many other factors), you shouldn't rely on someone else's opinion as much as your own. It's good to hear how another fiddle sounds with a bow you really like, but don't let other players totally change your opinion. This is ultimately the bow you're going to be playing with for a while, so it has to be comfortable for you!

If you're more of a beginner player and are interested in a bow upgrade, you may not be able to tell a drastic difference in bow quality. My suggestion in this case is to find an advanced player and see what he thinks of the bow's quality. Have the person demonstrate various passages and give his feedback to help you in making a decision.

Building Your Accessories Kit

Now that you have your fiddle bow, it's time to get equipped with your accessories kit. In this section, I tell you the things you definitely need to get and some things that are optional to improve your skill.

Buying a shoulder rest

A *shoulder rest* is a tool that you put on the back of your fiddle to help you hold it better. In my opinion, this is a necessary tool to play the fiddle properly, but some instructors disagree. The reason I feel that a shoulder rest is important is that it helps you support the fiddle between your chin and shoulder; otherwise, you may hold it improperly with your left hand.

There are many different types of shoulder rests, including the most popular brand, Kun. This is a nice shoulder rest that fits well into your shoulder and chin, but you can also use a foam pad or even a cloth strapped on with a rubber band. Any of these will help you support the fiddle better. In Chapter 4, I show you how to put on the shoulder rest, so don't worry if you don't know how to do this yet!

Finding the right shoulder rest is like finding the perfect bow. Everyone is going to have a different preference, so you may find yourself trying out a few different ones over the years. If you feel like your shoulder rest doesn't fit well with your neck, try some others.

Buying rosin

When learning to play the fiddle, you must have some sort of *rosin* — sticky chalk that helps the fiddle bow hairs grab the strings. Without rosin, you'll have no sound. My only recommendation is that you stay away from rectangular rosin that's in a box, as the rosin isn't quite as concentrated. This type of rosin will work, but it will be very flaky and put a lot of rosin dust on your violin and strings. (In Chapter 3, I show you how to apply rosin.) Jade is my personal favorite. You can find hundreds of different options by doing a simple Google search for "rosin."

Finding a metronome/tuner

A *metronome* is used to help keep rhythm by making a clicking noise, and a *tuner* helps you tune your instrument. Many times you can find devices that serve both functions by searching Google for "metronome tuner." I wouldn't suggest anything fancy because many of the more expensive ones have functions that can be more confusing than helpful. Anything under $30 is a good price for a metronome/tuner.

You can also use any smartphone to download both metronome and tuning apps. My personal favorites are the Pro Metronome app and the insTuner Lite app. Both are very easy to use, but there are many other ones out there!

Getting a music stand

As you find out in Chapter 4, having your fiddle level when you play is important. A music stand helps you keep your fiddle level because it adjusts according to your height. Also, having a place to put your music when you play is helpful.

There are many different music stands out there, but I wouldn't worry about getting anything fancy. You can find music stands on Amazon for less than $15.

Watch Video Clip 3, which shows you some specific accessories that I talk about in this section, as well as more tools that I discuss in the following section.

Examining Other Helpful Tools

In this section, I give you some suggestions for tools that will help improve your ability to play fiddle. All these tools are optional, but they can really help your technique.

You can find all the tools mentioned in this section without ever leaving your house! Online stores such as Shar Music, Johnson String Instrument, and my own store, Superior Violins, carry these tools.

The "Don't Fret" Tool

The "Don't Fret" tool can help you feel confident about where on the strings you should put your fingers. The tool is a long sticker that fits perfectly on the fingerboard (for the appropriate size) and is a nice alternative to putting multiple stickers on the fingerboard. If you don't want to use this tool, flip to Chapter 6, where I show you how to put finger placement stickers on your fiddle.

The "Bow Right" Tool

As you find out in Chapter 5, it's very important to keep your bow straight when going back and forth across the strings. The "Bow Right" tool gives you an exact place to put your bow on the strings and forces you to stay straight.

If you watch yourself play in the mirror (see Chapter 5 for more on this) and find that you aren't having trouble keeping the bow straight, this tool isn't necessary. I'd say about 50 percent of people who start playing need this tool to help them achieve proper *bow straightness* — keeping the bow exactly straight and perpendicular across the strings. After using this tool for a while (usually a few months), you'll be able to take it off and, hopefully, see improvement!

The "Finger Finder" Tool

Because reading music isn't easy, the "Finger Finder" tool serves as a great aid to help you with everything you need to know about reading music. As you find out in Chapter 7, different songs require different finger placements. This tool tells you exactly where to place your fingers in each of those songs, in all the major and minor keys of music.

Chapter 3

Tuning, Rosining, and Taking Care of Your Fiddle

In This Chapter

▶ Using a tuning device, the fine tuners, and the pegs to tune your fiddle

▶ Making sure your bow is tightened properly and rosined

▶ Keeping your fiddle and bow in tip-top shape

▶ Rehairing your bow, replacing your strings, and storing your fiddle

▶ Access the audio tracks and video clips in this chapter at `www.dummies.com/go/ fiddle`

*T*hink about something you're really good at and how long it took you to learn the fundamentals before you started doing it well. For example, if you fancy yourself a chef, you had to learn the ins and outs of a kitchen and all about various foods before you could cook well. Or if you own your own business, you had to learn dozens of things about how to get it started before making your first sale.

In this chapter, you discover what you need to know about tuning your fiddle, tightening and rosining the bow, and exercising general care and maintenance.

Staying patient through this learning process will go a long way in your journey to become a good fiddle player. Skip it and you'll have a hard time playing a good tune because of things you didn't take the time to learn before playing your first note.

Tuning Your Fiddle

Now that you're ready to start playing, you need to know how to tune your fiddle. Each of the four strings on the fiddle produces a certain sound when you pull or pluck it. Before you can start playing, you need to make sure that the strings are in the proper position.

Take your finger and lightly grab one of the four strings on your fiddle. Notice a certain tension or tightness? This tightness needs to be just right or the fiddle is *out of tune.* It takes practice to learn what "just right" is, but that'll come in time . . . honest!

The following sections take you through the steps of tuning your fiddle.

Using a tuning device

Every musical instrument, including the fiddle, has the capability to create various types of *pitches* — sound highs or lows — that your ear picks up on. These pitches are different musical sounds, and you can be way off pitch, slightly off pitch, or in perfect pitch, which is what everybody strives for!

In this section, I show you how to get the right pitch on your *open strings* — the way the four strings sound with no fingers down. Then you can create the proper sounds when you actually start putting fingers down in Chapter 6. The open strings are also notes you can play, but if these notes are slightly off pitch, your fiddle is out of tune.

A *tuning device* is a tool that tells you whether your strings are on pitch or not. It's very useful for formatting the proper pitches on your open strings. A digital tuner is a modern way to tune your instrument, although there are alternatives, like a pitch-pipe or tuning fork. If you're just starting, I highly recommend using a digital tuner, as it doesn't require having a good ear.

If one of your open strings is slightly out of tune, then all the notes you play on that string (when you start putting fingers down) will be out of tune — it's a domino effect.

Here's how to use a basic tuner:

1. **If you have a clip-on tuner, clip it onto the scroll of the fiddle.**

   The *scroll* is the part of the fiddle farthest away from you when you're holding it on your shoulder.

2. **Turn on your tuner and position it so that you can see the digital display.**

3. **Take your finger and pull the string.**

This basically means to strum or pluck the string, which makes the string vibrate slightly and produce a sound.

4. **Do this with each of your strings and notice the changes in the display.**

A tuner functions based on the sound frequency it picks up. It's more accurate when clipped right onto the fiddle than sitting next to it. If you don't have other distracting sounds in a room though, non-attachable (stand-alone) tuners work just fine.

You can also download apps for your smartphone to use for tuning. Because tuning is universal, even guitar tuning apps or other instrument apps will work. My favorite is the insTuner Lite app, which is free and easy to use.

Some tuners have adjustable settings that can cause confusion. You have to make sure your default settings are on or you won't get a proper reading. Make sure the number on the tuner reads 440. If you see any flat symbols (♭), adjust the tuner until you erase them from the display or the tuner will give an incorrect reading.

Finding string pitches

The fiddle can be tuned in any order, starting with any string: G, D, A, or E. The G string is the thickest string, while the E is the thinnest string. When you pick each of those strings, you should see the corresponding letter for each string on the tuner's digital screen. You'll likely need to make some adjustments to the strings; I show you how to do this in the next section.

On Audio Track 4, you can hear what each string is supposed to sound like.

In addition to the letters A through G, you may notice the symbols ♭ or ♯ to the right of some of the readings on the tuner screen. If you pick your G string and it says G♭ or G♯, it's either an entire pitch too low (G♭) or an entire pitch too high (G♯). If you see just a straight G reading, you're in tune.

You'll also notice a pointer leaning toward the left or the right on the tuner display. This indicates even more precisely whether the string pitch is too low (pointing left), too high (pointing right), or just right (in the middle). You want the point to be as close to perfectly in the middle as possible, but a little bit to the left or right is okay (plus or minus 15 degrees is good). Figure 3-1 shows the range I like to be in when I tune.

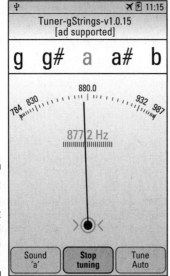

Figure 3-1:
Tuning range that I would consider "in tune."

Tuning with the fine tuners

To get your strings in tune, you have to use either the *fine tuners* — the screws on the fiddle's tailpiece — or the *pegs* — the four knobs in the peg box, which is just below the fiddle's scroll. Figure 3-2 shows where the fine tuners are and what string each one is associated with.

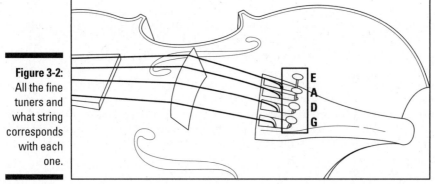

Figure 3-2:
All the fine tuners and what string corresponds with each one.

Tuning with the fine tuners is pretty simple — all you have to do is turn them either left or right to slightly change the string's tightness. An entire turn to the left slightly lowers the pitch of any string, while turning to the right slightly raises the string's pitch.

If you run out of room with how much you can turn the fine tuner, or if your strings are very loose and don't make any sound at all, you'll have to tighten them using the pegs (see the next section).

So how do you know whether you should use the fine tuners or pegs? You use the pegs if your strings are way out of tune (see the next section) and the fine tuners if your strings are relatively close. The following list shows when to use either the fine tuners or pegs to reach desired pitch:

✔ **Tuning G**

- F♯/G♭: Twist G fine tuner about two full rotations to the right

- G: Twist G fine tuner until you see the tuner pointer right in the middle

- G♯/A♭: Twist G fine tuner about one full rotation to the left

- Anything else, use the peg

✔ **Tuning D**

- C♯/D♭: Twist D fine tuner about two full rotations to the right

- D: Twist D fine tuner until you see the tuner pointer right in the middle

- D♯/E♭: Twist D fine tuner about one full rotation to the left

- Anything else, use the peg

✔ **Tuning A**

- G♯/A♭: Twist A fine tuner about one to two full rotations to the right

- A: Twist A fine tuner until you see the tuner pointer right in the middle

- A♯/B♭: Twist A fine tuner about half a rotation to the left

✔ **Tuning E**

- D♯/E♭: Twist E fine tuner about one full rotation to the right

- E: Twist E fine tuner until you see the tuner pointer right in the middle

- F: Twist E fine tuner about half a rotation to the left

Some fine tuners are based in sharps (♯), while others are based in flats (♭). Many notes in music can be called two different things; for example, F♯ and G♭ are the exact same pitch (both a half step below G).

Beginner fiddles typically have the fine tuners on them, but if you don't have all the fine tuners, you can always have them installed on any fiddle. Take the fiddle to your local music store, where you can get fine tuners installed on the rest of your strings.

Over-rotating a peg can break a string easily, but don't worry about breaking a string when turning the fine tuner. Don't be afraid to crank the fine tuner screws quickly and then check the pitches.

Tuning with the pegs

Perhaps your strings are very loose and need some attention, or maybe they're just way out of tune and need to be tightened up. Follow these steps to tune with the pegs:

1. **Turn your tuner on.**

2. **See Figure 3-3 to find what string matches up with each peg.**

   For example, if your D string needs to be tightened, you use the peg in the top-left corner.

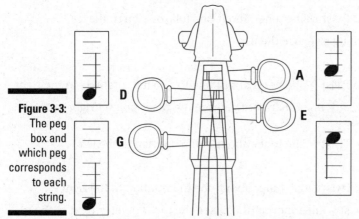

Figure 3-3: The peg box and which peg corresponds to each string.

Figure by Rashell Smith

3. **Turn the peg a half turn toward you to loosen it.**

   Don't totally let go of the peg, because it will unwind from the string. If this happens, follow the steps I outline for you later in this chapter on how to replace a string.

4. **Twist the peg back and forth to get a feel for how it's sticking to the** *peg box* **— the rectangular area that the pegs fit into.**

   Every peg is different in how tight or loose it fits into the peg box, so getting a feel for this is important.

Some pegs may be very hard to turn. In this case, you may have to work them away from the peg box slightly (pull out). Some pegs, on the other hand, may be very loose and easily turn back and forth. Still others may be too loose, and you'll need to push them tightly into the peg box.

If you can't get the peg to turn at all, you may want to use *peg lubricant/ compound.* You can find this online or at most music stores. If you're having trouble getting pegs to stick, you can use *peg glue,* which is very easy to apply to the peg. Because peg glue is in liquid form, all you have to do is squeeze out a drop of it on the pegs, and they'll stick much better than before.

The following steps will set up your fiddle for fine tuning:

1. **Hold the fiddle in between your legs to get a nice support.**

   Grab the neck with your spare hand that you're not using to turn the peg.

2. **Practice pushing the peg into the peg box and making it stick.**

   The amount of force you use to make the peg stick is important when trying to find the correct pitch. You may have to really push in to make the peg stay in the right place.

3. **Use the hand that's holding the neck to pluck the string to get a reading on the tuner.**

   The goal is to put your peg in the exact place to get the same sound as those string pitches.

4. **If you have trouble finding the spot after a few attempts of adjusting, loosen the peg a little and try again.**

   You have to have the perfect balance of tightening the peg and pushing in to get it to stay.

5. **When you're close to the note pitch (and get it to stick), you can start using the fine tuner.**

If you go too far over the pitch of the note, you'll break the string. Sometimes you may think you're too loose when actually you're too tight, so listening to the string pitches is important.

If you're tuning a string for the first time, it will take a while to break in because new strings tend to stretch. That means that even if you get it in the perfect spot, it will begin to lose its tuning within seconds. Tune above the pitch for the first couple of days, until you start to see the note pitch stick better.

Tightening the Bow

Your bow has to be properly tightened to get the best response from the strings. If your bow hair is too loose or too tight, you'll find yourself running into problems. A tight bow can lead to bow bouncing (and can actually damage a delicate wood bow), and a loose bow will cause the bow stick to hit the strings, which makes a weird, improper sound. So how do you change the tightness? The bow has a screw at the very bottom that can change the tightness. Figure 3-4 shows where the screw is located on the bow. You twist the screw to the left to loosen the hair and to the right to tighten the hair.

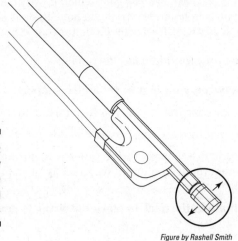

Figure 3-4:
The screw
of the fiddle
bow being
twisted.

Figure by Rashell Smith

Here's an exercise to show you both extremes of bow tightness and how to get it just right.

1. **Turn the screw to the left a few full rotations, until you see the hair loose and dangly.**

   Do you notice a slight curve in the stick? This is how loose it should be when you put it away after you're done playing.

   If you keep turning the screw to the left, it will eventually come off, and the frog of the bow will separate from the stick. This can frighten some people, but it can be easily reattached. It takes quite a few turns to the left, though, to get this screw to come off.

2. **Start tightening the bow several full rotations to the right and notice how the bend of the stick is changing.**

Tighten the bow until the stick is totally straight. This is too tight, and you'll notice about an inch of space between the hair and the stick. This needs to be adjusted so it's looser. If left in this position, the bow stick can actually become damaged.

3. Loosen the bow now to get a nice balance.

Take a look at the three bows in Figure 3-5 and try to get yours to look like the "just right" picture. This is about how tight you want the bow when you're ready to play.

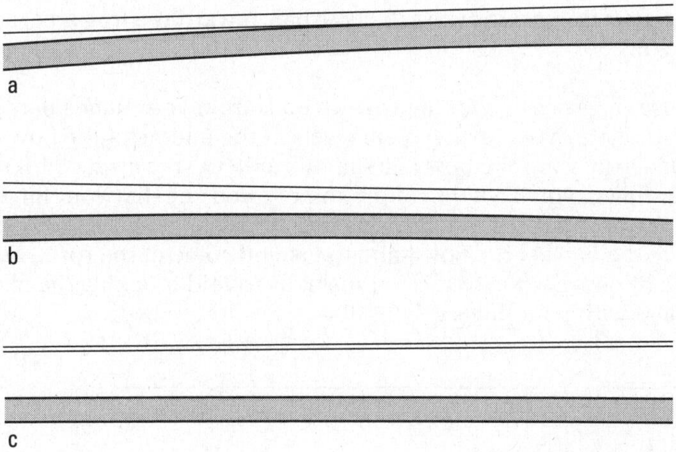

a

Figure 3-5:
Comparison of a too loose, too tight, and just right bow.

b

c

Figure by Rashell Smith

A good rule of thumb is to tighten the bow just enough so an average-sized pinkie finger barely fits in the space between the stick and the hair in the middle of the bow. When you actually start learning how to play, another rule of thumb is to get the bow hairs as close as you can to the stick when you're playing most aggressively. This means a more aggressive player will need a tighter bow, while a less aggressive player will need a looser bow.

Be sure you loosen your bow when you put it back into your case. Bow hair can tighten up in high humidity, which can cause the bow stick to warp (change camber). You never want your bow stick to be perfectly straight, and you should always loosen the hairs when you put it away.

In Video Clip 4, I show you how to tighten your bow to the correct tension. I also show you how to rosin your bow properly, which is covered in the next section.

Rosining the Bow

One very important part of playing the fiddle is knowing how to *rosin the bow* — the process of applying rosin to create a sticky film on the bow hair. Rosin comes in many different sizes and shapes and is universally used to help the bow hair grab the strings better. Without putting rosin on the bow, your fiddle will have a wispy, airy sound when you play.

If you've used a bow, chances are it still has a light coat of rosin on it. To start, you need to determine how much rosin is on your bow. Simply take the back of your finger and swipe the bow hair toward the frog area, as shown in Figure 3-6.

Don't use the front of your finger or the oils from your hands may get the bow hair dirty. Avoid testing rosin levels at the middle of the bow because you especially want the bow hairs in this area to stay clean. If there's no rosin on your finger, you'll need to apply some. If you see that your finger is pure white, the bow has too much rosin on it. If this is the case, take your finger and flick the back of the bow hairs to take off some of the rosin. You can also use a light paper towel to take off rosin, but avoid touching the front of the bow hairs with your fingers if possible.

Figure 3-6: Testing out rosin level using the back of your finger at the frog.

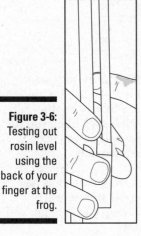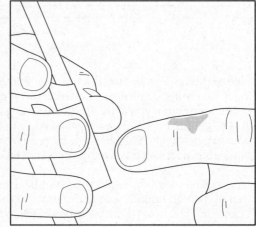

Figure by Rashell Smith

Here's how to apply rosin to your bow:

1. **Grab your rosin block (if you don't have any, refer to Chapter 2 for suggestions) and scratch it to bring rosin powder to the top.**

Scratch the rosin by using the screw of the bow or a nail file on the surface of the rosin. Figure 3-7 shows what a rosin block looks like after you scratch it and powder is shown on the surface.

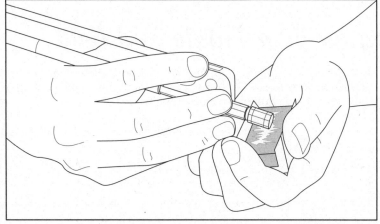

Figure 3-7:
Rosin block with powder on the surface from being scratched.

Figure by Rashell Smith

2. **Take your tightened bow (don't be afraid to tighten it a little more than normal) and start putting rosin on the bow hair.**

   The motion of this should be similar to scrubbing a counter stain or shining your shoes. Spend a few seconds in each area of the bow and apply rosin evenly throughout, going up and down the bow to get a nice even coat. Again, don't be afraid to dig into the rosin with your bow because you want the rosin to stick to the bow hairs.

3. **Test to see how much rosin is on the bow by carefully taking the back of your finger and testing it like you did before, but don't do this often.**

   If it's a new bow, you may not notice a lot of rosin in certain spots. It may take up to five minutes of rosining a new bow if you're being too delicate with it.

4. **After you have enough rosin on the bow, you have to reapply it every 60 minutes of practice.**

   This normally equates to once every other practice session. Each time you put more rosin on the bow, it usually only needs five to ten seconds' worth of application to be sufficient.

If you keep using the exact same area on the rosin block when applying rosin to the bow hairs, a groove will be created over time. You'll have to purchase a new block sooner if you don't avoid this groove. Each time you apply rosin, use a different part of the block so that you don't get any unwanted grooves.

If you've recently purchased a new fiddle, it probably came with a brand-new bow. This is great, but many people don't understand the amount of rosin that needs to go on new bows. Be sure to follow all the preceding steps to get enough rosin on the bow.

Caring for Your Fiddle and Bow

Just as things can happen to your car requiring maintenance, things can also happen to your fiddle. Following is a list of things that can happen to your fiddle/bow if you don't take care of them:

- Wood cracks can cause your fiddle to sound bad and lessen its value significantly.
- Open seams, or separations of different parts of the wood on the instrument, can also cause unpleasant sounds.
- The sound post inside your fiddle can collapse, causing the back and the top of the fiddle not to resonate properly.
- Rosin buildup on your strings and instrument can be very hard to clean. This can cause the varnish to deteriorate and/or the strings not to respond as well.
- Hair on your bow can deteriorate over time, making it hard to get the full projection out of your instrument.
- Bridges can collapse if bumped a certain way because they're not glued to your fiddle.
- Strings wear out and can sound dull over time, making it necessary to get your strings replaced to have the best resonation.
- Bow stick hair can condense in hot conditions, causing your bow stick to warp.

The following sections show you what you need to do to keep your fiddle and bow in good shape.

Polishing and cleaning the fiddle

Keeping your fiddle in good condition starts with understanding what it's made out of. Think of a really nice wood piece in your home. If you never clean it, the piece won't look as good or last as long.

Follow these steps to polish your fiddle correctly. You should do this at least once a week, but preferably each time you play:

1. **Take a dry cloth (never use a wet cloth) and wipe down the front and back of your fiddle to remove any dust that you see.**

2. **Take the cloth and fit it underneath the fingerboard, and then wipe this area because it's an easy place for rosin to build up.**

3. **Gently take your cloth and rub the spot right underneath the strings where you play because this is a prime spot for heavy rosin buildup.**

4. **Clean each string individually by pinching and wiping each string with an up-and-down motion.**

   If you haven't done this in a while, the cloth may not help you enough. The strings are the only place you can use rubbing alcohol if you have any sort of gunk buildup. I also use my nails to peel rosin off, but that isn't required.

There are polish cleaners that you can use on the instrument, but be sure they're designed for wood instruments! You can find these in any basic music store, but if you keep cleaning your fiddle with a dry cloth, you won't need the cleaners.

Preventing cracks and open seams

One of the worst things you can see on your fiddle is a crack. This drastically diminishes the fiddle's value and can be very costly to repair. A crack happens when the fiddle's wood is so dry it starts to break slightly. It can also happen if you don't keep your instrument out of harm's way or if it's the victim of an accident, like falling to the floor from a high place or being inadvertently banged against a hard surface. Cracks don't have to be huge to have an impact on the fiddle's sound, so try your best to prevent them!

When humidity (moisture) levels in an area are very low, wood is most vulnerable to cracking. Typically, dry conditions go along with cold conditions, but not always. If your fiddle is in a dry area, you want to invest in a *fiddle dampit* — a long sponge tube that holds water and is placed inside the fiddle's F-hole.

Directions on how to use dampits are clear when you order them, but here are some additional tips:

   ✔ Be sure you refill the dampit at least every two weeks.

   ✔ Don't put the dampit inside the fiddle until you dry off the outside of it. You don't want water dripping on your instrument!

   ✔ Sound isn't affected at all by the dampit staying in the F-hole. You don't need to do anything with it until you refill it.

Cracks typically require the top piece of wood on the fiddle to be taken off, depending on how deep the crack is. Anytime a luthier has to take the top off to repair a fiddle, it's going to cost a lot of money. Some shops charge as much as $500 to $1,000 just to take off the top. If you have a nice quality instrument, these repair fees should inspire you to take care of it with a dampit!

Instruments that aren't handcrafted aren't as sensitive to dry conditions. In fact, I wouldn't even worry about having a dampit unless your instrument is worth over $500. Instruments below this price range are typically manufactured and often aren't even made of wood.

Open seams are common in dry conditions and happen when the glue separates between two pieces of wood. Bring your fiddle to a shop to get it checked out every so often; these types of problems aren't always seen by the human eye. Fortunately, having an open seam fixed isn't very expensive.

Staying away from humid conditions

Fiddles are very sensitive to not only dry conditions but also wet (humid) conditions. If you leave your fiddle baking in your car for a long time on a hot day, the heat can damage it.

Many parts of the fiddle are glued together, such as the neck and body. They can actually break apart if enough moisture accumulates where these two parts are glued together. More commonly, I've seen fingerboards collapse from a fiddle being exposed to too much moisture. I'm sorry to make it sound like your fiddle has to be treated like a little baby, but it's true!

Overall, you want to try to keep your fiddle in an environment that's between 30 percent to 50 percent humidity, although major problems only happen when you're outside of these parameters for a long period of time. You can get a humidity tracker by buying the dampit that I mention in the preceding section, and many nice cases have a humidity control, called a *hygrometer,* built into them.

Fiddle strings often go out of tune because of moisture in the air. If you leave your fiddle in hot conditions for even a short amount of time (even just transporting it), you may find that you have to tune it more drastically than usual. Prepare to tune more in the hot seasons.

Understanding your sound post

If you look through your fiddle's F-hole, you'll find a post standing up connecting the top and back of the fiddle. This *sound post* is a very important part of the fiddle, as it connects the resonation of the top and back when you play.

The sound post isn't glued but held together by the pressure of the top and back of the fiddle. Having the sound post in exactly the right spot causes the fiddle to ring more and produce a more resonant sound. Over time, your fiddle will be bumped and bruised by all the accidental hits it takes. These bumps can sometimes cause the sound post to move very slightly or even collapse, making your fiddle sound hollow and unpleasant. It happens, but not often!

If your sound post does slip, take your fiddle in to get it adjusted. It's a quick fix and typically costs $15 to $20 to bump the sound post back to the ideal position. Don't try to do this yourself; honestly, I haven't even figured out exactly how to do it yet! This is money well spent to get the best sound out of your instrument.

If you hear something rattling in your instrument, it probably means your sound post has collapsed. It's pretty difficult to get the sound post out of the inside of the fiddle, so don't even try. A luthier will have the right tools to retrieve it and put it back into place. It's a good idea to get your sound post adjusted periodically (even if it hasn't collapsed) because it plays such a big part in the way your fiddle sounds.

Putting on new strings

You aren't a true fiddle player until you've broken at least one string! This happens sooner rather than later and can happen for several reasons:

- Drastic change in weather conditions
- Tightening the pegs too far
- Installing a string improperly

The following steps tell you how to change strings properly on your fiddle. You can also check out Video Clip 5 to see a demonstration.

1. **Completely remove the broken string from the peg and the tailpiece.**

2. **Grab a spare string that corresponds to the one you want to replace.**

   If you broke all the strings, you have to do this process for each one.

   Each string has its own thickness/color and will only work in the correct spot (G, D, A, E). Make sure you use the right string!

3. **Remove the peg completely from the peg box and find a small hole on the peg.**

This is where the string goes. Practice poking into this hole with your string. The correct side of the string has a unique color — the other side won't fit anyway.

4. **Make sure your bridge is in the proper location (not tilted) when you're about to put a string on.**

   You want the bridge to be totally vertical to the top of the violin. The bridge should be level with the center of the F-hole.

5. **Put the peg back into the peg box and then put the string into the hole, going only as far as the thickness of the peg.**

   Again, make sure you're dealing with the correct string and the proper peg.

   If you're replacing the G or D strings (pegs on the left side), you need to tilt the string slightly to the left before twisting in the next step. Doing so helps you wind the string up from right to left. The opposite is true if you're replacing strings A or E.

6. **Wind the string by twisting away from you.**

   You should be creating a nice, organized wind around the peg with your string. Use the skills you learned in the earlier section about tuning the pegs to make sure you keep the peg from slipping.

7. **Keep tension and wind the string up until you see the color match up with the nut of the fiddle.**

   This indicates when the string has been wound enough to be hooked on the other end.

8. **Hook the string on the tailpiece by attaching either the ball end or the loop end.**

   Different strings may have either one of these ends to attach the string to the tailpiece.

9. **Keep tension so that the wind on the peg remains the same, and start turning until you begin to close the gap between the string and the bridge.**

10. **Place the string over the nut and bridge.**

    The fiddle should have little grooves assigned to each of the strings on both of these areas. Match them up accordingly.

11. **Tune the strings, keeping in mind that they'll take time to stretch.**

    Keep pushing in as you adjust to keep the string from unwinding from the peg.

Always have a spare set of strings around just in case one breaks. I recommend brands like Dominant, Helicore, or Pirastro. Carry more E strings than usual because these are the easiest strings to break. If one breaks, you don't have to replace the whole set; strings from different brands can function together fine.

Replacing strings takes a bit of practice, so don't feel bad if it takes you a few times to get the hang of it. If you don't want to replace the strings yourself, you can always bring your fiddle to an experienced fiddler or shop to do it for you. String shops typically charge less than $10 to put strings on, but where they make their money is selling you more strings. If you want to save on that cost, buy the strings yourself online and then bring them to the shop to have them put on. If you've done business with the shop before, the shop shouldn't have a problem with this.

Dealing with a bridge collapse

A bridge doesn't collapse that often, but when it does, it can really scare you! Like the sound post, the bridge isn't glued to the top of the fiddle. This means that a severe bump to the fiddle can cause the bridge to collapse. It's really not that big of a deal and is something you can easily repair yourself.

The pressure of all four strings pressing down on the bridge is what causes it to stay in place. Don't loosen too many strings at once or you can cause the bridge to collapse because it relies on the strings to keep it standing up. I recommend loosening only one string at a time.

Follow these steps to put a bridge back into place if it does collapse:

1. **Evaluate how tight your strings are.**

   Do you think you can fit the bridge underneath the strings? If not, loosen the appropriate strings until you know for sure you can fit the bridge underneath.

2. **Take a close look at the bridge.**

   Notice that one side is higher than the other side. The lower side should correspond with the E string, and the higher side corresponds with the G string.

3. **Fit the bridge underneath the strings, making sure it stays even with the notches in the middle of both F-holes and is vertical, as I discuss in the preceding section.**

   Hold the bridge in place with your right hand. Also make sure the bridge is positioned correctly with the fingerboard tailpiece.

4. **Tighten one string at a time, making sure the peg and bridge stay in place properly.**

   Ideally, have someone hold the bridge in place for you, so you can focus on tightening the strings properly. Make sure the strings go over the grooves in the bridge as well.

Wear and Tear Guide

Just as a car wears and tears over time, the same goes for a fiddle and bow. Every once in a while, you may have to replace some parts on a car, like the tires or the windshield wipers. When it comes to the fiddle, the parts you'll need to replace are the bow hairs and the strings.

The bow hairs are one of the most unique parts of the fiddle compared to other musical instruments. Don't let people touch your bow because they may not know how to grab it properly! Bow hairs are very delicate and can build up dirt easily and easily dwindle away. I cover this in more detail in the next section.

Earlier in this chapter, I discuss how to replace strings when they break, but I haven't yet talked about when you should replace them based on wear and tear. I cover that in the later section "Replacing strings."

Rehairing the bow

As I mention in Chapter 2, the quality of a bow has nothing to do with the bow hair. Whether you have a $30 bow or a $1,000 bow, the hairs are generally going to be the same quality — the stick is what's valuable. Dirty bow hairs and loss of bow hairs contribute to the need to get your bow *rehaired*.

Dirty bow hair

Remember, touching the top of the bow hairs with the oily parts of your hands is a big no-no. The more oil that gets on the bow hairs, the faster you'll need to get it rehaired.

So how do you know whether your bow hair is dirty and needs to be replaced? Compare your bow with a new bow at a music store or with a spare bow you haven't used before. Put them side by side and compare color differences. If your bow hair is a brownish white (most of the time it may be this color in only one area), then you might consider getting your bow rehaired.

Dwindling hairs

Every player experiences the fright of opening up her case and seeing that bow hairs have popped off the bow. This is very common and will happen a bit over time.

You may be wondering why it even matters how many bow hairs you have. The more bow hairs you have hitting the strings of the fiddle, the better you'll be able to grab the strings and produce a good sound. Think about how your bow would look and sound if you only had one bow hair!

Here are three things that can cause bow hairs to fall off:

- ✔ Leaving your case in really hot conditions or dry conditions
- ✔ Bow hairs getting snagged on something and pulling off
- ✔ Tension from playing, causing a few to come off

There's no stopping tension from playing, and every fiddler has to get a rehair at some point. Here's a standard rate for getting your bow rehaired based on the amount of time you play:

- ✔ Practice/play less than 60 minutes/week: Rehair once every 3 to 4 years
- ✔ Practice/play 1 to 2 hours/week: Rehair once every 2 to 3 years
- ✔ Practice/play 2 to 4 hours/week: Rehair once every 1 to 2 years
- ✔ Practice/play 4 to 6 hours/week: Rehair once every 6 to 12 months
- ✔ Practice/play over 6 hours/week: Rehair once every 3 to 6 months

These are estimated figures, as the time period also has a lot to do with the climate you live in, how aggressively you play, and how many ceiling fans you hit — kidding! (Although this has actually happened to me before.)

A good way to tell whether you have enough bow hair is to compare your bow to a bow with a full rack of hair. If you have about ¾ less bow hair than a full rack of hair, you want to get it rehaired.

Warped stick

If the stick of the bow is severely warped, you'll have to get a new bow. Trying to play with a warped stick is kind of like trying to cut a steak with a spoon — it just won't work. A warped bow will cause you to have a bow tilt, which is terrible for building good solid tone and technique.

If you really love your warped bow and don't want to throw it away, you can bring it into a shop for a luthier to fix. This is possible if the bow is slightly warped but not extremely warped.

Here are some things that can cause a bow to warp:

- ✔ Playing with the bow way too tight. The stick will begin to slowly change shape because of the tension. Remember, you never want the stick to be totally straight when you play.
- ✔ Keeping the bow hair tight when you put it away. Over time, the bow takes a different form.

✔ Using your bow as a sword and hitting it up against something, causing it to bend.

I mention in Chapter 2 that the most delicate bows are made of pernambuco wood. These are the best quality, but they can warp easily because of how flexible they are. This flexibility is great for making a beautiful sound, but the bow can easily warp if you don't take care of it.

Carbon fiber bows are a good option if you're at all frightened of a wood bow warping. They're similar in feel to a wood bow but are unwarpable. They're great for outdoor playing and also for kids who may decide to play swords with their friends at school.

Bow hairs can retract or shrink in hot weather, causing them to slightly shorten over time. If your bow is already tight, the shrinking of the hairs can actually cause the bow to warp. Be careful to never leave your bow tight in the case and always loosen it whenever you're done playing. If you're dealing with cold conditions, the hairs can actually stretch, causing the opposite effect from shrinking. Because cold air creates dry conditions, the hair can also dry out, become more brittle, and break more easily. If you loosen your bow way too much and leave it in the case for a week in a cold environment, you may find it difficult to tighten the bow all the way. This doesn't cause the bow to warp, but it will need to be rehaired.

So how do I get my bow rehaired?

Rehairing a bow takes a certain skill that not everyone has, so you want to take it into a music store that deals specifically with stringed instruments. Because the violin and fiddle are the same instrument, a violin luthier shop is a great place to go. You can find these by searching on the Internet for "violin shop [your city]" or "stringed instrument shop [your city]."

Cost including labor for rehairing is in the range of $30 to $50 and typically takes a few days. If you paid $50 or less for a bow, you may as well skip rehairing it and just buy a new one. Most bows that come with beginner rental outfits are low quality, so you'll want to purchase a better bow instead of getting it rehaired.

Anybody who rehairs a bow at very low cost is probably not the best at it. Sometimes if a bow is not rehaired properly, the hairs may pop out easier than normal. It's better to pay a bit more to get a better quality rehair. A poorly rehaired bow can also affect the quality of sound because it can change the stick's camber.

If you should happen to drop the bow and it lands squarely on the point, a very drastic thing can happen. The wood will crack and break at the tip's end. If this occurs, there's no possible way to repair it. Your bow is finished.

Replacing strings

Fiddle strings are made a certain way to get the best resonance out of your instrument. Over time, you'll find that the strings start sounding dull, and you'll need to replace them, even if they haven't broken.

String types

Here are the different qualities of strings and their characteristics:

- **Synthetic:** This is the newest and most commonly used type of string. Synthetic strings take the longest to break in and don't last as long as steel strings, but they have a really nice sound. Common synthetic string brands are Dominant and Pirastro.

  Dominants are priced fairly, around $50 per set, while Pirastro strings are typically priced as high as $125 per set. I'd recommend starting with Dominant strings until you feel the need to expand into other types later on. Some synthetic strings last longer than others depending on the brand. One set that sounds really good when broken in is the Pirastro Obligatos, but these strings typically have half the life span of most strings.

  Keep in mind that it takes time to break in synthetic strings. The first day you get them, you'll have to tune them five to ten times, as they'll be stretching like crazy. Each day for a week you'll have to tune less and less, but the first day will be the worst for tuning.

- **Steel:** These types of strings take less time to break in but can often sound metallic. They work well on electric fiddles and some acoustics. Helicore makes some of the best steel strings.

  Don't get the cheapest quality strings because they can make even an expensive fiddle sound bad. Helicore strings are priced fairly at $30 per set. Stay away from anything you see priced lower than that. The low quality can really hurt you.

- **Gut:** These types of strings are more for classical violin playing. They were common before synthetic strings came out and have a very rich tone. They can be quite expensive, take a long time to break in, and are unnecessary for fiddle playing.

So how can you tell what type of strings you have? All string brands are characterized by their color. This resource will tell you exactly what kind of strings you have: www.thesoundpost.com/files/en/Colors_English_new_violin.pdf.

Here's another resource for telling what brands match with different types of strings (synthetic, steel, gut):

```
www.ifshinviolins.com/Articles/tabid/145/articleType/
ArticleView/articleId/411/Guide-To-Choosing-and-Using-
Strings-for-Violins-Violas-and-Cellos.aspx#gut
```

Many fiddlers prefer different types of E strings. For example, the Kaplan Solutions E string prevents bow whistling, where the E produces a high-pitched squeaky noise. This squeak is caused partially by bad technique but can actually be prevented by using this string. Another popular string that goes well with Dominants (it's considered better than the Dominant E) is the Pirastro Gold E string. Many fiddlers get Dominant strings for G, D, and A and get the Pirastro Gold for the E.

When to replace your strings

When to replace your strings depends on the amount of time you practice and the type of strings you have. Steel strings typically last longer than synthetic, and the more you play, the sooner you'll need to replace your strings.

Here's a test for when to consider replacing your strings:

1. **Take a tuner and tune up the string in question.**

   I cover how to do this earlier in this chapter.

2. **Put your 3rd finger down on the string in question and match with the appropriate pitch of the tuner.**

3. **If you notice that there isn't much of a ring sound (assuming you're providing good technique to the string), the string may be getting dull.**

You can also detect dead strings by simply plucking the open string and determining whether it's really ringing the way that it should. If you find that the sound stops very shortly after you pluck the string, the string may be dead. This method assumes that you're familiar with what a good, healthy string really sounds like.

If you're unsure whether your strings need to be replaced, bring your fiddle into a shop and have the shop take a look at the sound post, the strings, and the setup. The problem may not be with the strings; it may be something as simple as an open seam that just needs to be glued.

I recommend replacing strings every 12 to 18 months no matter what. It's better to change them sooner, but you won't build bad technique by not changing them right away. I always get my strings replaced a week before a performance, and it always gives my sound a boost compared to before.

If you want to replace your strings for a performance, do so at least a few days before to break the strings in, because the strings go out of tune often as they're breaking in.

Instead of throwing your used strings away, consider putting them into a string tube that often comes with many decent quality cases. If one of your new strings breaks, it's nice to have a backup, even if it's a used string.

Putting your fiddle away in your case

Now that you've learned everything there is to know about taking care of your instrument and bow, it's time to put the instrument away. Here are some different types of cases for storing your fiddle:

- **Basic quality case:** These cases are around $20 to $60 and are typically made of foam, which offers less protection than a better quality case. Some basic cases have a pocket to store music at the top, while others do not. Basic cases don't have a lot of room to store your fiddle playing accessories and typically only have one or two *bow holders* — the place where you latch the bow in the case.

- **Standard quality case:** These cases are made of either foam or plastic and offer moderate protection. They're typically priced between $60 and $200. You should be able to store your shoulder rest and rosin somewhere in a standard quality case, and they generally have at least two bow holders. Some standard quality cases have a nice outer and interior design.

- **Premium quality case:** These cases have a wood shell or carbon fiber frame, providing good protection for your instrument. If you own a fiddle priced over $500, you want to store it in a premium quality case. These cases frequently contain a hygrometer to measure humidity levels, up to four bow holders, a string tube, plenty of storage, a music pouch, and more. Half-moon cases weigh a little less and are good if you like a lighter-weight case.

The following steps describe how to put away your fiddle properly. This will allow you to transport it anywhere you like or pack it up safely so nobody can fiddle with it — no pun intended!

1. **Take your bow and loosen it to the point where the hairs start to dangle.**

2. **Put the tip of the bow into the pocket in the case.**

3. **Flip the bow up or down to accommodate fitting it entirely in the case.**

   In some basic cases, the bow needs to be in a certain position or it won't fit.

4. **Put the bow into the bow latch and then turn the latch to secure the bow from moving.**

5. **Remove the shoulder rest from your fiddle and put it into a pocket in the case (if it fits) or set it off to the side.**

   You can sometimes put the shoulder rest into the music pouch depending on what type of shoulder rest you have and the size of the pouch.

6. **Wipe off your strings with a dry cloth and then set the fiddle into the case where the shape fits the instrument.**

7. **Secure the neck by tying it into place.**

   Some cases have velcro ties but not all do.

8. **Close the case and zip it up.**

   Sometimes premium cases have a latch and lock on the case.

Store the fiddle case in a safe place where nobody can tamper with it. Keep it out of extreme conditions to avoid damaging the instrument and bow.

Do your best not to bump the fiddle, even when it's in the case. A wood shell case will protect the fiddle pretty well, but only so much. Always make it a habit to be as gentle with the case as you would be with the actual fiddle!

Part II
Working with Technique Basics and Fundamentals

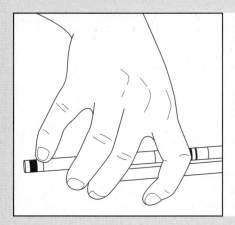 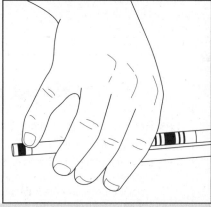

Head to www.dummies.com/cheatsheet/fiddle for a checklist that high-lights fundamentals for playing the fiddle properly.

In this part . . .

✔ Find out how to put a shoulder rest on properly and how to stand properly while playing.

✔ Discover all the important fundamentals of playing fiddle, including how to hold the bow, how to place your fingers, and what it takes to create a clean sound.

✔ Put all your newly acquired skills together to play some simple songs with detailed descriptions of how to move the bow across the strings.

Chapter 4

Holding the Fiddle and Bow

In This Chapter

▶ Making sure your shoulder rest and chin rest are put on correctly

▶ Going through the steps of a proper fiddle hold

▶ Paying special attention to your bow hold to get started right

▶ Access the video clip in this chapter at `www.dummies.com/go/fiddle`

Did you know that most of the mistakes fiddlers make at first has something to do with how they're holding the fiddle or bow? Terrible sounds can arise by skipping this chapter and assuming you know how to do everything right. The whole process is an art, and you need to understand and practice it from square one.

In this chapter, you make sure that your shoulder and chin rests are put on correctly and are comfortable. Then, you find out the correct way to hold the fiddle and the bow. I walk you through all the important steps and make sure you don't forget anything that you need to know!

First Things First: The Shoulder and Chin Rests

The shoulder rest and chin rest help you hold the fiddle properly, so it's important to have them on correctly before trying to hold the fiddle the right way. A shoulder rest is portable, and you put it on when playing the fiddle and take it off when putting the fiddle away. A chin rest, on the other hand, always stays on the fiddle until you decide you want to install a different one.

Choosing the right shoulder and chin rests is important, as certain combinations can either bring comfort while playing the fiddle or discomfort that makes it hard to play for a long period of time. In this section, I show you how to put the shoulder rest on and take it off and how to change your chin rest.

Putting on the shoulder rest

Think for a second how it feels to sit on a hard chair compared to a nice soft couch. Wouldn't you much rather spend your day sitting (or even sleeping) on a nice soft couch? This concept is similar to that of using a *shoulder rest* — a tool that helps you hold the fiddle properly. Without the use of a shoulder rest, you'd have to place the back of the fiddle (which is hard) against your collarbone, which may force you to want to use your left hand to support the fiddle (which you don't want).

Shoulder rests come in many different shapes and sizes. If you have a full-size fiddle, purchase a full-size shoulder rest (also known as 4/4 size). If you have a half-size fiddle, purchase a half-size shoulder rest. If you aren't sure what type of fiddle you own, refer to Chapter 2.

I suggest going with a *Kun* shoulder rest — I cover how to find one in Chapter 2. (You can also just use a cloth if you prefer. See the nearby sidebar to find out how to attach a cloth to your fiddle using a rubber band.)

Many stores don't have Kun-style shoulder rests for smaller instruments. Instead they'll offer you a small rectangular piece of foam that you can attach to the instrument with a rubber band.

The good thing about the Kun shoulder rest is that it adjusts to your shoulder and collarbone nicely. It also has padding that makes holding the fiddle more comfortable. To put on the Kun shoulder rest, follow these steps:

1. **If you get a brand-new Kun shoulder rest, you'll have to put the legs of the shoulder rest on.**

   Common brands have three different holes that you can screw the legs into. The hole you decide on will make the shoulder rest a certain width, which is something you'll have to play with. If you have trouble putting the shoulder rest on in the next step, you may have to readjust where the legs are installed.

2. **Point the feet of the shoulder rest (the rubber part) inward and grab on to the side that has the thinner-shaped pad with your left hand.**

3. **Take your left hand and hold the feet securely on the fiddle, about an inch from the bottom of the back.**

4. **Slide the feet on the other end of the shoulder rest securely on the right side of the fiddle, about the same distance as the other side.**

   If you find that both sides aren't securely attached or that the right side won't slide far enough, you have to adjust the legs.

5. **Hold your fiddle in either hand and test to see how secure the shoulder rest is with the other hand.**

   Does it feel like it would stay on with minor pressure up against it? If so, you're good to go! Figure 4-1 shows a picture of the final product after putting on your Kun shoulder rest.

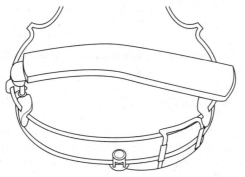

Figure 4-1:
Back view of the Kun shoulder rest when put on.

Figure by Rashell Smith

 Do not under any circumstances place the fiddle face down on a surface in order to attach the shoulder rest. This could result in tremendous pressure on the bridge (which already has enough pressure from the strings), and it may buckle or even break.

 If you don't find the Kun, many other options are out there. Go to a music store and ask for its shoulder rest selection. Try different ones out until you find one you feel has the best comfort. Because you're going to be practicing all the time (hopefully) and spending a lot of your time playing, you want to feel as comfortable as possible.

 A decent percentage of fiddlers don't use any sort of shoulder rest. There's some disagreement about whether to use one; some teachers think that you should never use a shoulder rest. Not using one is okay as long as you're exercising proper fundamentals, which I discuss later in the chapter. My opinion is to definitely use one if you're a beginner and then feel free to stop using it when you're sure you have the fundamentals down.

Who needs a shoulder rest? How to use a cloth instead

If you want to use a cloth, I suggest one that has a decent amount of padding (like a kitchen rag). You don't want something that's so thin that it doesn't provide you comfort at all when you put it on your collarbone. To put it on, follow these steps:

1. **Fold the cloth once or twice, until you have about a half inch of padding.**

2. **Put the cloth on the back of the fiddle on the bottom *bout* (this is the widest part of the fiddle).**

3. **Take a rubber band and attach the cloth by having the rubber band grab on to one of the corners of the fiddle and the bottom button.**

Use a thin rubber band, as sometimes a thicker rubber band won't stick on the bottom button. If you find the rubber band coming off all the time or want a potentially more comfortable option, try out the Kun shoulder rest.

Considering the chin rest

Chin rests are a big part of what's used to help hold the fiddle. The most common type of chin rest is toward the side of the fiddle. Most instruments come with a side chin rest installed.

With the side chin rest, you have to place your chin toward the right side, as placing it in the middle may be awkward for your neck. Because of this, I highly recommend a middle chin rest, which you can get online or at your local music store. Two types I recommend are the Flesch brand and the Wittner brand. Take a look at the Wittner brand in Figure 4-2.

Higher chin rests serve you better if you have a taller neck. Lower chin rests serve you better if you have a shorter neck. This same concept also applies to different types of shoulder rests.

Many chin rests are just plain uncomfortable. In general, the smaller the chin rest, the more uncomfortable it will feel.

Replacing a chin rest

So you want to try a new chin rest? The process of taking off your current chin rest and putting on a new one isn't that difficult. Just follow these steps (and have an Allen wrench handy):

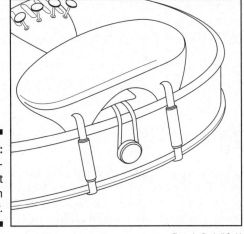

Figure 4-2:
Center-
mount
Wittner chin
rest.

Figure by Rashell Smith

1. **Take a look at what attaches the chin rest onto the fiddle — you should see two bars that can be adjusted.**

2. **Stick a small Allen wrench into one of the circular holes.**

3. **Turn the metal bar to the left to start loosening it from the fiddle.**

4. **Take out the Allen wrench and find the next hole that will allow you to continue to turn the bar.**

5. **Loosen the bar to the point where it's starting to come off the fiddle, and then do the same to the other side.**

6. **Take the chin rest off.**

7. **Loosen the bars of your new chin rest to the point where it will fit onto the fiddle.**

   If you're trying out a middle chin rest, make sure it goes in the center of the instrument.

8. **After you get the metal bars tightened on the fiddle with your fingers (as far as you can turn them), start using the Allen wrench to tighten the metal bars.**

   Go as far as you can to make the chin rest stay on securely.

There's no need to overly tighten the chin rest. Tighten to the point where it's securely on, but not to the point where you're using too much force. Make sure you also tighten each side equally.

If you don't tighten the chin rest properly, you can get a buzzing sound on the fiddle. Make sure you tighten it as securely as you can and use cork to help keep the chin rest on the fiddle.

Try out your new chin rest and see if it feels good with various types of shoulder rests.

Holding the Fiddle

You'd think that holding a fiddle is as simple as taking your left hand and supporting it, just like you'd hold up anything else in your hand. However, you actually want to hold the fiddle with your chin and shoulder and not rely on your left hand to support it. Why? Supporting the fiddle with your left hand can

✔ Restrict what your fingers can do

✔ Promote an improper wrist

✔ Make progressing into advanced techniques (like shifting or vibrato) harder

Holding the fiddle with the chin and shoulder allows you to build proper fundamentals to do more advanced techniques. Because your hand actually has to move up and down on the fiddle in various songs, relying on your hand to hold it just doesn't work.

Applying proper fundamentals

So I can just feel how excited you are to finally learn how to actually hold the fiddle! Here I take you through the steps to do this properly:

1. **Make sure your shoulder rest is put on properly.**

   Refer to the earlier section "Putting on the shoulder rest" for instructions on how to put on the Kun, as this is the shoulder rest I use to show you how to hold the fiddle.

2. **Square your shoulders to a standard-sized music stand.**

3. **Pick up your fiddle and take a look at the side of the Kun that has the thicker-sized pad.**

4. **Place the shoulder rest side with the thicker pad directly on top of your left shoulder, making sure this part isn't too low on your collarbone.**

   If done properly, the thinner side of the pad will rest perfectly on top of your collarbone (see Figure 4-3).

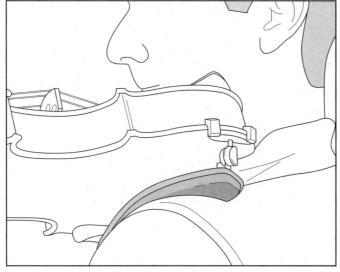

Figure by Rashell Smith

Figure 4-3: Proper placement of the Kun on top of the shoulder.

5. **Use your left hand to help support the fiddle while you're making adjustments.**

   This is just for now; you'll learn not to rely on this in the next few steps.

6. **Make sure your chin is on the chin rest.**

   It's okay for your chin to be on the right edge of the chin rest.

7. **Regarding your neck, leave a little breathing room, as the fiddle doesn't have to make direct contact with it.**

8. **Point the scroll of the fiddle toward the left side of the music stand.**

   Figure 4-4 shows you exactly how the fiddle should be pointing to your left (about 45 degrees).

9. **Verify that your fiddle is slightly tilted down toward the right but is still level to the ground.**

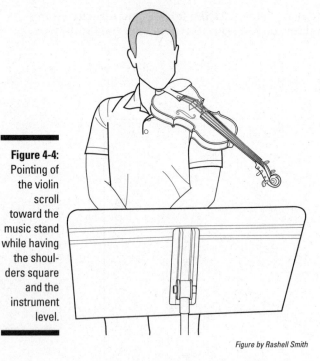

Figure 4-4:
Pointing of the violin scroll toward the music stand while having the shoulders square and the instrument level.

Figure by Rashell Smith

10. **Keep your back and head straight and pinch the fiddle between the chin rest and the shoulder rest.**

    This should allow you to hold the fiddle with no hands, as shown in Figure 4-5. Don't do this unless you know for sure you aren't going to drop it!

Figure 4-5:
Proper position of the fiddle on the shoulder without relying on holding with the left hand.

Figure by Rashell Smith

This process is uncomfortable for most beginners (especially having to hold the fiddle comfortably with no hands). You have to play around with the shoulder rest setup and your chin placement on the chin rest and practice these steps a few times before feeling comfortable. Don't allow yourself to stray from these steps, because holding the fiddle improperly can lead to bad habits that are very hard to fix later.

Developing muscles in your neck to help support the fiddle takes time. I suggest working on holding it with no hands for a few minutes each day until you get the hang of it. Try walking across the room and back a few times while holding the fiddle, but be careful not to drop it!

This process is especially important for kids because they take the longest time to develop the neck muscles to hold the fiddle properly. Many kids cheat by using their left arm to hold the fiddle instead of the proper way of relying on the chin and shoulder to hold it.

Sitting versus standing

Have you ever gone to an orchestra concert and seen all the musicians sitting in chairs? Doing this yourself is fine as long as you exercise proper fundamentals.

Youngsters should be encouraged to stand at their lessons while practicing. This promotes good posture and freer movement in the bow arm. Older folks or those with bad backs or leg problems will be more comfortable in a seated position. However, sitting in a chair can promote slouchiness, so it's important to sit with your back totally straight, your legs uncrossed, and your feet flat on the floor. Think about how you'd sit if you had a job interview and you were trying to impress your potential new boss. You wouldn't slouch back in your chair, would you? This is the same way you should sit in a chair while playing the fiddle.

The next important point you must make sure to follow is to observe all the fundamentals I talk about earlier in the chapter. It's very easy to hold the violin with your left hand, especially when you're sitting in a chair. Pay attention to these details because they're just as important whether you're standing or sitting.

Try sitting on the front of a chair if you plan to play in a sitting position. This promotes good posture and technique.

While playing the fiddle standing up, everything applies the same regarding holding the instrument properly. Many times standing up is preferable while practicing and sitting down is appropriate while playing in groups. This is just the general rule of thumb.

To play the fiddle properly, it's essential to have a music stand whether you're standing up or sitting down. When you actually start playing music, applying proper technique if your music is on the ground is difficult. You want the music stand to be face level, as this promotes keeping your instrument level.

Holding the Fiddle Bow

Did you know that most of the bad sounds that come out of the fiddle have something to do with what's going on in your bow hand? Think about a furnace in a house or an engine in a car. Wouldn't you say that it's pretty important for those systems to function properly to be able to get heat in your home or drive your car? The same goes for the bow hold — it's the engine that makes or breaks the sound that comes out of the fiddle.

In this section, I give you a detailed rundown of what you need to know about the bow hold. This is going to be like the manual to know how to work and fix your car engine!

Pay close attention to this section because it's one of the most important parts of learning the fiddle.

Placing your fingers properly

Placing your fingers correctly on the bow is the first step in getting a clean and beautiful bow stroke. Just putting fingers in random spots will make your instrument sound terrible when you start to play it. Here's how to establish the perfect bow hold:

1. **Hold the bow with your left hand on a 45-degree angle, with the stick of the bow positioned above the hair of the bow.**

2. **Bend your right-hand thumb and place the thumb tip into the groove of the bow (see Figure 4-6).**

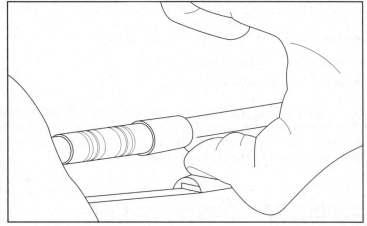

Figure 4-6:
The thumb placed into the groove.

Figure by Rashell Smith

Placing your thumb too far into the groove promotes tension against the bow. Place it on the thumb's right edge.

3. **Place the tip of your pinkie on the screw of the bow, keeping your finger slightly curved.**

   The reason why you start with the bow tilted is so that your pinkie will lie on an angle on top of the bow.

4. **Lay your fingers over the top of the bow, keeping them curved.**

See different angles of the finished product in Figure 4-7. Notice how far the index finger is on top of the bow.

Figure 4-7:
Two different angles of the finished bow hold.

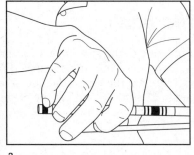

a

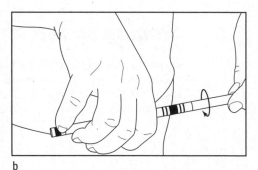

b

Figure by Rashell Smith

Here are the three points you should always remember:

- Thumb bent and the tip placed in the groove
- Pinkie curved on the top of the screw
- Fingers curved over the stick

Don't focus on putting your fingers in the perfect spot (to the millimeter) and get frustrated when your fiddle doesn't make the right sound. Putting your fingers in the right spots helps get the bow hand relaxed, but ultimately, what you're doing with the grip is what matters.

Keeping your fingers curved

One of the things you'll find yourself wanting to do is straighten your fingers out when you hold the bow, but doing so can cause bad sounds when you play the fiddle. Follow these steps to make sure you know what your fingers should look like on the bow:

1. **Put down your fiddle/bow.**
2. **Let your hand fall to your side and notice the way your hand forms naturally.**
3. **Take notice of the curve of your fingers.**

This is the natural, most relaxed position your hand can be in and the exact way you want to curve your fingers on the bow. Don't let your fingers straighten out, no matter how much you want to do it!

Staying on top of the bow

Staying on top of the bow instead of being to the side is very important in making the bow loose and relaxed. By having your fingers curved over the top of the bow (with your pinkie perched on the top), you'll be able to use your index finger properly (covered in Chapter 5) and get the cleanest sound possible. This isn't easy to do.

Holding versus gripping the bow

Something has to guide the bow back and forth so that you can make a sound on the fiddle. Your natural reaction when you start moving the bow is to grip the bow too tightly and use the wrong muscles to guide it. In Chapter 5, you learn how to apply the proper muscles to guide the bow, but for now, I set you up so that you aren't grabbing with the incorrect muscles!

REMEMBER

Each of the fingers in your hand has the ability to press up against the bow, but the only one you actually want pressing significantly and guiding the bow is the index finger. Every other finger should be relaxed as can be and not be pressing hard up against the bow.

Take a look at Figure 4-8, which shows the "banana thumb." This position gets its name because the thumb is pressing against the bow and looks like a banana in the process. This is a tendency you want to avoid.

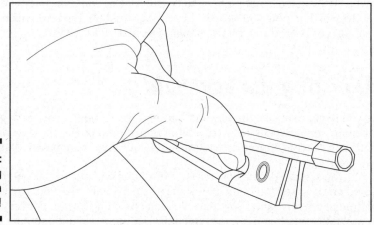

Figure 4-8:
Avoid having
a banana
thumb!

Figure by Rashell Smith

It's also very easy for your pinkie to press up against the bow. This is what I call the "pinkie stilt," and it unfortunately causes the bow not to do what it's supposed to do.

Lastly, your middle two fingers can also press up against the bow, which really can't be seen, only felt. This also causes the bow not to do what it's supposed to do.

So how do you test to see whether your bow is too tense? Grab a friend and try out the bow tension test!

1. **Grab your bow and set it on the fiddle strings.**

    Any spot will do.

2. **Adjust your bow grip and have your friend grab the bow around where your bow hand is at any random time, trying to move it in a circular motion.**

3. **Ask your friend whether there was any restriction in her trying to move the bow quickly in this circular motion.**

If there was any tension, try adjusting again.

Keep this drill in mind because it will be helpful as you get more advanced. For example, when you actually start stroking the bow, your friend can grab the bow randomly to see whether you're gripping the bow too tight. A good time to use this drill is when you learn how to cross strings, or really for any new technique that you learn. You want the bow to be loose with no restriction at all times to make a good sound.

Think about how you'd hold a baby bird in your hand. Would you grab the bird roughly as you carry it back to its home? No, you'd probably be very gentle, which is how you should think about holding the bow. This is key to your success in the short term, medium term, and long term.

Adjusting the bow hold

As you begin to stroke the bow in Chapter 5, you'll notice your bow grip changing quite often. Because it takes a bit of pressure to power the bow back and forth, it will seem appropriate to tense up your fingers to make it all happen.

When you start to do the bow stroke, your hand will move back and forth based on what section of the bow you're using. Sometimes you may be at the bottom of the bow, and sometimes you may be going toward the very end of the bow. While executing these movements, your mind will undoubtedly be thinking about other techniques, which can make you forget about the bow hold.

Here are some of the things that can happen, even if you start with a perfect bow hold:

- ✔ Your thumb begins to press against the bow and forms a banana thumb. Don't let your thumb change from the curved position.
- ✔ Your pinkie begins to straighten out. Always keep your pinkie curved!
- ✔ Your fingers start to make way to the side of the bow instead of being directly on top of the bow.

Check out Video Clip 6, which shows how some of these bad habits can happen.

Try to think about your bow grip at least once every five minutes when you practice. Don't just think about it once and then be done. Your bow grip is the number one thing that can easily change, so you want to focus on keeping it proper throughout your practicing session. Not focusing on it will lead to bad habits and ultimately bad sound.

Preventing drifting

As you play the fiddle, you'll notice your bow wanting to go different places on the strings. As you discover in the discussion in Chapter 5 about the contact point, you definitely want your bow to be in a certain spot on the strings when you play. Sometimes you'll drift away from this point though, so it's important to properly adjust back to the point where you need to be.

The tendency you'll have is to grab the bow as it starts to drift away from the spot you need to be at. This can be correct, as long as you let go of the tension in your bow hand when you start the stroke again. If you're having trouble releasing tension in your hand when making an adjustment, give yourself a few seconds to "breathe" and adjust yourself back to the right spot instead of trying to start right away. A few seconds goes a long way in helping you relax and get back to the relaxed hold that's important for your success.

If you feel yourself getting angry at all by drifting or making any bad noises as you progress into later chapters, give yourself a five-minute break. Forcing the bow to do certain things doesn't work, so the breather can help you stabilize before starting over again. You don't want to get into the habit of getting upset and angry playing the fiddle, which will make you sound worse.

Avoiding grabbing during the stroke

Many times when you play the fiddle, you'll find that as you start to put your fingers down (which you find out about in Chapter 6), you'll want to change what's going on in your bow grip. Try rubbing your stomach and rubbing your tummy at the same time. It is hard to do right?

Say that you suddenly have four notes to play that are really difficult in the left hand. You may not be thinking as much about the right-hand bow hold. It's tempting for your right hand to make similar movements as you just tried to do with your left hand.

The key to prevent this is to first follow good techniques of the left hand, which you discover in Chapter 6. The other key is to think equally about the bow hold when you play new songs. It's easy to just assume that you're always doing the bow hold right, but unfortunately, it doesn't happen that way.

Get in the habit of looking at your bow hold first before you start any song. This helps you think about the bow hold more and not just focus on the new stuff in your left hand. Make adjustments before you start a song while the bow is on the fiddle.

Chapter 5

Building a Musical Bow Stroke Sound

*I*t's one thing to play the fiddle well and another to make it sound like a horrible screeching cat (literally)! I've heard every possible bad sound a fiddle can make, and I want to help you avoid as many of them as possible.

The key to success is to think of learning the fiddle as a marathon and not a sprint. It isn't something you're going to master in a couple of months. People spend years perfecting their playing. Find enjoyment in improvement but try not to be too hard on yourself when you make mistakes. Every good fiddle player had to go through the process of mastering good technique, and they all sounded bad at times.

In this chapter, you discover the mechanics of creating a beautiful bow stroke sound, and you practice drills to build a solid foundation for playing.

Getting Familiar with Bow Stroke Mechanics

You've heard the phrase "practice makes perfect." The more you do something physically, the quicker your brain can tell your muscles to carry it out. Muscle memory doesn't care if you're doing well or poorly; it just repeats what it knows. So if you practice your bow stroke incorrectly over and over, you'll make the same mistakes over and over. Those mistakes, or bad habits, will be harder to break later. This can be discouraging and is so unnecessary.

In this section, you discover the steps of a proper bow stroke and work on drills to help with muscle memory.

The key to practicing fundamentals is to work on them one at a time. Some of the most successful new fiddlers are those who take the drills and fundamentals seriously. Don't overload your brain with too much at once. Give yourself time to think about everything and do your drills to master muscle memory.

Finding the contact point

Proper bow stroke mechanics start with understanding where to place the bow on the strings (known as the *contact point*) and what part of the bow to use to start the stroke. With the right contact point, you succeed in creating a beautiful musical sound.

Follow these steps to find the optimal contact point for your bow:

1. **Look at the bow hair and visualize splitting it into four equal parts.**

   The *bow hair* is the white part of the bow that makes contact with the strings.

2. **Put a removable sticker on the bow exactly at the point where the second equal part from where you hold it would start.**

3. **Hold your fiddle properly (refer to Chapter 4 for information about how to hold the instrument) and set the bow on the strings exactly where you placed the sticker.**

   This is generally where you always set your bow on the strings when you begin to play.

4. **Place the bow an equal distance between the fingerboard and the bridge (see Figure 5-1).**

5. **Make sure the bow is exactly parallel with the bridge.**

6. **Take the bow off the strings and practice finding the same contact point a few times (as much as you want to — don't stroke the bow quite yet!).**

   Practice your bow hold throughout this process.

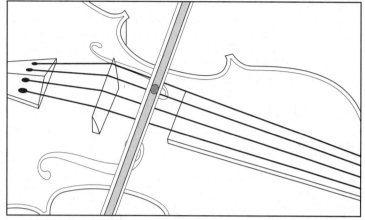

Figure 5-1:
Placement
of the bow
between the
fingerboard
and bridge.

Figure by Rashell Smith

The spot on the bow that you just found is the "golden" spot, and any divergence from it may result in an uneven tone and unsatisfactory volume.

Normally, it takes a while to build enough muscle (and visual) memory to be able to find the exact contact point without the sticker on the bow. Keep the sticker on for at least a few months and then take it off when you feel comfortable with the contact point. Don't think of the sticker as a crutch but rather as a tool to help you build proper fundamentals.

It's important to work on contact point and bow hold for at least 10 to 15 minutes initially. After that, you should work on it in the first few minutes of your practice sessions for the next four to five weeks. This is how long it normally takes to build any solid fundamental, but many beginners like to think they have enough understanding of contact point too quickly. Five weeks is nothing compared to all the years you're going to be playing the fiddle. Be patient!

Bending the wrist

Bending the wrist properly is one of the most important aspects of playing the fiddle, next to holding the bow. Most fiddle beginners have a very stiff wrist, which causes a lot of problems as they progress through more and more complicated music.

Wrist technique can be compared to writing. When you write something, you don't grab the pen in a tight fist and hope to be able to create perfect letters.

Instead, you use the tips of your fingers to get better control and precision. Using a fist grip to write is the same concept as keeping a stiff wrist, which restricts what the violin bow can do. Bending your wrist allows the bow to breathe and provides you with more precision in how you move the bow.

Start honing your wrist technique by doing what I call the *quarter drill*. Watch Video Clip 7 for a demonstration.

Moving the bow

Most likely, the very first note you play on the fiddle won't sound the way you want it to. That's totally normal, even if you have an intensive musical background. The first day you start moving the bow is one of the hardest (sounding) to get through, but don't worry — I'm here to help you every step of the way!

To start moving the bow across the strings, first watch Video Clip 8 and then follow these steps:

1. **Set the bow at the contact point and make sure you have a proper hold on the bow.**

2. **Pull the bow downward toward the end of the bow (the tip).**

3. **Push the bow back up the other way toward your sticker.**

   Keep the speed of the bow as consistent as you can. It's very easy to cut the stroke too short by going too fast or being so tense in your arm that it's hard to move. Stay relaxed!

Be sure to use your index finger to power the bow back and forth (see the later section "Using your index finger" for more on this technique). Many times, the fundamentals of using the index finger are hard to do, especially when there are other important things to consider, like bending the wrist and keeping the bow straight.

Keep these key points in mind when beginning to move the bow across the strings:

✔ The number-one bad habit of beginner fiddlers is gripping the bow too tight. Make sure that you don't change your bow hold finger pressure when you move the bow. Hold the bow as if you have a baby bird in your hand.

✔ Try getting to the very tip of the bow, even though doing so may feel uncomfortable. This is important; you get a cleaner sound when you spread things out by getting to the tip.

✔ Keep the bow speed as consistent as you can and always keep the bow moving.

Keeping the bow straight

One of the toughest things to get used to (and something that will probably feel more foreign than anything you've ever done before) is keeping your bow straight when you start moving the bow back and forth. Your arm isn't going to like the fact that it needs to extend out to be able to do this properly.

The perspective of looking down at the contact point when you begin the stroke causes some problems. You can't really see what you need to see. Find a mirror or get someone to watch you play from the side to make sure your bow is going straight across the strings, as shown in Figure 5-2.

Some new fiddlers find that they lose control of the bow when watching themselves in the mirror. I suggest video recording yourself so you can concentrate on what you're doing and then viewing how well you did it. This is also a good way of watching yourself progress.

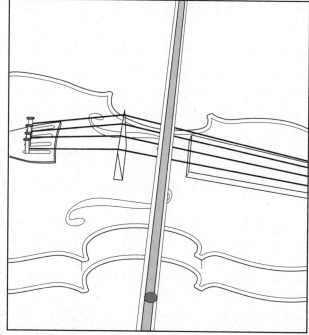

Figure 5-2:
How a straight bow should look in relation to the fiddle's strings.

Figure by Rashell Smith

Keep the angle of your fiddle at 45 degrees so that it's comfortable to get to the tip of the bow. If your arm is totally extended when you're at the tip, you'll most likely change the angle of the bow and not be straight across the strings. Watch yourself in the mirror (or video recording) to make sure you're keeping the bow straight.

If you find yourself having trouble keeping the bow straight, you can try using a *bow-right* tool — a metal clamp that clips onto the fiddle and forces beginners to keep the bow straight across the strings. Go to www.superiorviolins. com/fiddle-bow-right.html to see what a bow-right tool looks like.

With so many beginner techniques to work on, it's nice not to have to think about the bow straightness so much. Before you know it, you'll be taking the bow-right tool off as you feel more confident in how straight your bow is going.

Extending your arm

Using the small muscles in your arm is important when you play. Because you use your shoulders and big muscles for a lot of things, your instinct is to use them to extend your arm too. Unfortunately, doing so causes irritating sounds like bow squeaks (a most unpleasant sound!), bow bouncing, and other problems.

The following steps show you how to use your arm properly when bowing back and forth.

1. **Put your bow at the contact point.**

2. **Place your elbow at the exact height of the fiddle and place your bow on the D string.**

   I go into more detail about the exact placement of the elbow for other strings later in this chapter.

3. **Extend your entire arm and move the bow about 1 inch from the contact point.**

   This is the only time you should move your entire arm in the bow stroke. After this you'll keep your elbow and arm in the same position for the rest of the bow stroke.

4. **Go all the way to the tip of the bow, but don't use any of your upper arm to help extend your arm out.**

   You can watch your elbow to make sure it stays in the same place. There should be no shoulder or up-and-down elbow movement in this step — only forearm movement.

5. **As you start to go back in the other direction from the tip of the bow, bend your wrist as you did earlier in this chapter.**

   As you bend your wrist, you'll be tempted to move your upper arm and shoulder as well (just like I told you not to do in Step 4). Don't do this until you reach 1 inch from the contact point.

6. **Use your elbow and upper arm to get back to the contact point.**

   To do another bow stroke, repeat from Step 3.

If you do Steps 4 and 5 incorrectly in this drill, you'll have done what I call the *gradual arm extension,* which means extending and moving the arm at the same time. This promotes using the proper muscles instead of big muscles, causing bow bounce and crooked bow movement. It's important not to move your shoulder and upper arm at all after you get past the 1-inch point. Coming back the other way, don't bend your wrist and move your arm at the same time. Remember, it's all about the small muscles, so be very deliberate in doing all the preceding steps. I know this feels weird, but you'll get the hang of it with enough practice.

You should do a few drills, such as those in Video Clip 9, to really make sure you're doing the arm extension properly.

Your first option is a drill called the *wall practice.* Just follow these steps:

1. **Put your bow at the contact point.**

2. **Put your elbow up against a wall at instrument height.**

3. **Keep your fiddle still and practice moving the bow back and forth.**

   Don't move your elbow from this position. This helps you not to use your upper arm and shoulder when playing.

Another good drill for proper arm extension is called the *armchair drill.* Here's how to do it:

1. **Put your bow at the contact point.**

2. **Find an armchair or hard surface that you can put your elbow up against.**

3. **Keep your elbow in place and practice going all the way to the tip of the bow and back.**

   This drill helps you not to rely on your upper arm and shoulder to move the bow.

You should bow by moving your arm 1 inch when you're going away from the contact point and 1 inch coming back to the contact point. Technically, the wrist drill doesn't have you moving your arm in the stroke, but the arm extension drills do have you moving it 1 inch. The other drills are still very helpful to understand how you shouldn't rely on your shoulder and upper arm to bow.

Guiding the Bow

If I told you to grab a big heavy box and take it across the room, you'd use all the muscles you have to pick it up and move it. You'd give it everything you've got! Your tendency is to use your biggest muscles not just when lifting a box but also when doing a lot of things in life. Unfortunately, this is the exact opposite of what you want to do when playing the fiddle. Unless you want to create music that sounds more like howling dogs or screeching cats, you need to guide the bow properly!

The key to guiding the bow is managing bow tension — not by using your big muscles but by using your index finger. What makes this process so hard is that you don't feel like you're using the proper muscles instead of big muscles at all — it feels more like you may drop your bow. But feeling like you're going to drop the bow is the relaxed and light hold you're looking for. I know that sounds odd, and it's tough to do, but it'll help you a lot as you endure this process for the next few days. Hang in there and don't worry. I go over all the helpful tricks that have worked for me in showing beginners how to guide the bow.

Everyone struggles through this at first, but not forever! Give it some time and you'll start making beautiful fiddle music before you know it.

Avoiding tension

The key to getting a nice musical sound is managing bow tension. Understanding this goes a long way in efficiently advancing on the fiddle. Not understanding this typically leads to a lot of frustration, with beginners wondering why they aren't getting a decent musical sound.

Keep these things that could be causing bow tension and poor sound in mind when you're starting out with bow strokes:

- ✔ Avoid a tense bow grip. This includes having too much pressure against the bow with your thumb or fingers.
- ✔ Avoid a stiff wrist. This normally comes from not bending the wrist as you move the bow toward the frog from the tip of the bow.

✔ Make sure you're extending your arm properly.

✔ Work on keeping your shoulders from getting tense.

At any given point in the bow stroke, your movement should be as loose as possible (flexible). A flexible bow allows the strings to respond properly, which is how you get a good sound.

Loose movement refers to the bow's tension, not the looseness of the bow hair. Although you may be tempted to change your bow hair a lot to manage bow tension, this really has little to do with it. Refer to Chapter 3 to know exactly how tight to have your bow.

Here's a way to test whether your bowing is tense or flexible: Have a friend randomly grab your bow some time during your bow stroke — seriously. If it's hard for your friend to grab the bow and twist it from side to side, then your bow is too tense. You'll notice that the hardest place to keep the bow flexible is when you start going toward the tip of the bow.

Preventing bow squeaks, bouncing, and wispiness

I can guarantee that you're going to have some work to do in the first five weeks of learning the fiddle. Because you have so many things to remember and work on, you're bound to have some issues with technique. The key is working through these things and not getting too frustrated. Everyone struggles in the first five weeks.

The most common problems you'll have to deal with are bow squeaks, bow bouncing, and wispiness. The following list walks you through what each of these are so you can identify what you may be hearing and fix it.

You can also watch Video Clip 10 to get a clear idea of how to fix these mistakes.

✔ **Bow squeaks:** The dreaded bow squeak! This is when the violin makes a heavy, unwanted sound. It can be a crunchy or scratchy sound or an imperfection in the tone, and sometimes it can sound like fingernails on a chalk board. Your friends and family will *not* want to listen to this, and neither will you.

How to fix it: The bow squeak has everything to do with bow tension (not hair tension), which is covered in the preceding section. It can also be caused by the speed of the bow. Try relaxing your grip more and make sure you have a nice loose grip at the tip of the bow. You can also try speeding up the bow and making sure you're not too close to the bridge — both can cause bow squeaks.

✔ **Bow bouncing:** This is when you're going down the bow and, all of a sudden, the bow decides to jump up slightly and ricochet against the strings. This causes a jerky sound and can be very annoying.

How to fix it: While bow squeaks are typically caused by tension in the hand and fingers, bouncing is caused by having a tense arm and using your arm muscles. Try relaxing your shoulder and make sure you're extending properly (covered previously in this chapter). Later in this chapter, you find out how to use your index finger to prevent the bow bounce.

✔ **Bow wispiness:** So, you can't seem to get enough contact with the strings, and instead of getting a full sound, you're getting a very light, airy sound. This is what I call bow *wispiness*.

How to fix it: Bow wispiness is caused by the opposite things that cause bow squeaks and bow bouncing. You're either moving the bow too fast back and forth or not pressing down hard enough with the index finger. It's also possible that your bow doesn't have enough rosin on it.

Another cause of bow wispiness is playing over the fingerboard, or too close to the bridge. Refer to the beginning of this chapter to further understand the contact point, where your bow should be when playing across the strings.

Every beginner deals with these issues. Even if you practice a lot in the first few months, you'll still have to work through them, but keep them in perspective.

Using your index finger

Making use of your bow hand index finger (usually just called *index*) is one of the most useful concepts to master — and the hardest. When you're *transitioning,* or changing directions with the bow, you only use your index finger. The actual transition should have nothing to do with the other fingers or muscles. Using your index finger on your bow hand is what lets you play fast and efficiently. If you use your big muscles to guide the bow instead of your index finger (like most people do), you'll have a hard time playing songs like "The Devil Went Down to Georgia" (by the Charlie Daniels Band) fast and accurately. You'll also have trouble preventing squeaking and scratching sounds as songs get more difficult. Trust me, you want to master this as soon as possible!

If you think about it, something has to help power the bow from point A to point B. Something also has to help power the transition when you run out of bow and have to go back in the other direction. This concept is similar to needing an engine to drive a car. What helps the car get from point A to B? Without an engine your car won't move even an inch — unless you decide you want to push!

So, would you rather have a 50 horsepower (HP) engine or a 500HP engine? My guess is you'd rather have the 500HP engine to accelerate the car at a much faster rate! But here's where the car engine analogy doesn't quite work — you need the 50HP engine for fiddle playing, and that's your index finger. A 500HP engine (the big muscles) can cause many problems that will restrict your ability. This is going to really challenge your way of thinking (and moving) because every natural instinct will tell you to use your big muscles.

You may think that the most comfortable way to transition the bow is by using your shoulder, upper arm, or forearm. You may think any of these will do, but that isn't the case. Using anything but your index finger will restrict you now (and definitely later) from getting the type of transition that will sound as smooth as butter. It all comes down to using your index finger instead of your big muscles.

Using your index finger is like nothing you've ever done before and will feel very unnatural at first. Give it some time and trust me on how important it is. Although it may not be noticeable to the naked eye, the motion of the index finger is similar to a wide U shape. This motion is a lot easier to recognize when your finger isn't actually on the bow, as shown in Figure 5-3. What you won't see when your finger is on the bow is that it's pressing down into the stick and adding weight onto the strings (for louder sound). This pressing down action applies to both up and down bows.

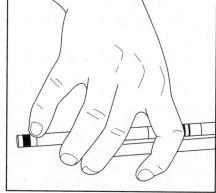 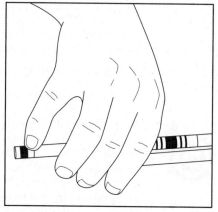

Figure 5-3:
The motion of the index finger on and off the bow.

Figure by Rashell Smith

You should have a relaxed bow hold while you're using your index finger. A common tendency is to tense up multiple muscles rather than just the index finger.

Feeling confused about the index finger? Watch Video Clip 11, which explains in detail what's happening with the index finger during the bow stroke.

Even if you understand the importance of the index finger, it takes more than that to master the ability. It can take weeks or even months to start feeling and hearing a difference in sound. Practice, practice, practice and you'll be glad you put in the time with this concept. Nothing replaces repetition, so don't underestimate the drills.

Doing the index drill

After you understand what the index finger should be doing, you need to work on muscle memory. Do so by doing the index drill (see Video Clip 12 for a demonstration):

1. **Set your bow at the contact point of the strings.**

2. **With a relaxed and proper bow hold, press your index finger down into the stick three times.**

   Don't change anything with your bow hold as you press down. Make sure that you aren't moving the bow hairs at all while doing this but instead that you're bringing the stick down into the hairs. Don't be afraid to flex the stick down into the bow; it's made to withstand the pressure.

3. **Pick up your *back fingers* (middle finger, ring finger, and pinkie) after (you do this after you press down three times).**

   Do this three times and remember that the violin is helping you hold the bow up. This can help separate what the index finger and back fingers should be doing. They don't work together at all! Don't rely on these fingers at all to press down into the bow.

4. **Repeat from Step 2 in the middle of the bow and at the tip of the bow.**

   I suggest rotating this process for at least a few minutes.

Watch yourself do the index drill in the mirror and make sure you see no muscles moving in your upper arm as you're pressing. If you notice any muscle movement (there should be none at all), try simplifying by taking the bow out of your hands. If I told you to move your index finger quickly up and down, this doesn't require your arm to go up and down as well, does it? Now try the drill again and try not to use your upper arm or back fingers to press down. Use just the index and nothing else.

Focusing on your thumb

Technically you don't need your back three fingers at all when you play the fiddle. The only purpose they really serve is to help you with the feel of the stroke. As you become more proficient, you'll learn that the pinkie is very important for balance, especially as you play closer to the frog, and also in the execution of some dynamic effects. But as far as pressing, guiding, and moving the bow, you shouldn't use your back fingers at all (think of them as always sleeping). The most important two fingers that you should use to do the index drill are your index finger (applies pressure) and your thumb (absorbs the pressure of the index).

Try picking up a sponge or small object with just your index finger and thumb. If I told you to squeeze the sponge, you wouldn't have to use your back fingers to do that, right? It isn't such a strong and large object that it requires every muscle you have to press into it. The same concept applies to putting pressure down into the bow with the index drill and bowing in general (the bow only weighs around 60 grams). You don't have to use all your fingers to apply pressure to an object. The reason why you don't want to use all your fingers to apply pressure to the fiddle bow is because doing so can cause the bow to make bad sounds (tension).

So what exactly should your thumb be doing during the index drill and with bowing in general? Think again about lifting the sponge. The thumb acts as a base to carry the sponge to make sure it doesn't fall as you apply pressure with your index. This is the same concept as holding the bow. If your thumb isn't at all on the bow, the bow will fall over as you apply index pressure. So basically, your thumb is holding the bow up for you as you apply pressure down with your index. Just remember not to apply side-to-side pressure against the bow with your thumb because doing so causes bow tension. Your thumb should be *barely* on the bow and is only there to hold the bow up.

Focusing on your pinkie

An important part of playing the fiddle is having your pinkie curved, which helps create a flexible movement of the bow. You can easily overlook this with so many other things going on, but I highly encourage you to do this properly right off the bat, as it can be hard to fix later on.

Here are some things that can happen if your pinkie isn't properly curved:

- You may cause tension in the bow, which will lead to bad sound and the inability to play fast.

- You'll rely on your pinkie instead of your index finger to guide the bow. Although you won't notice the difference at first (using the index or pinkie to guide the bow), you'll find it difficult to create a clean sound in harder songs later on down the road.

✔ You'll struggle to play at the frog down the road, which will restrict your ability to use the entire bow.

Throughout this chapter, I show you how to avoid using big muscles in the bow stroke so that you can properly use your index finger. Normally, when you finally start to do this properly, your pinkie or thumb is always next in line to be improperly used to guide the bow. Don't let this happen to you, as you need to keep your thumb and pinkie curved while using your index finger. It's not easy to do at first!

I have a great drill that helps with pinkie flexibility. I call it the pinkie drill! Check it out in Video Clip 13.

Anticipating to create clear musical sounds

When you think of changing directions with the bow (I refer to this earlier as *transitioning*), think about playing with a yo-yo. How do the fiddle bow and yo-yo motion compare? A big part of getting the yo-yo to come back into your hand is anticipation — preparing for the ball to come back up. If you just throw the ball down and don't anticipate it coming back, you won't have much luck getting the ball to roll nicely back up the string. Transitioning the bow has a lot to do with anticipation as well — getting ready to move the bow in the opposite direction. If you only think about going one direction, you'll have a tough time moving the bow smoothly (this is key!) in the other direction. See Figure 5-4 to understand the thought process relating to anticipation in the bow stroke.

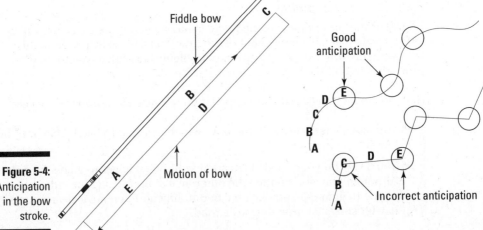

Figure 5-4: Anticipation in the bow stroke.

Figure by Rashell Smith

So, which muscles are used primarily to transition the bow and anticipate the bow change? The small muscles. If you remember from the preceding section, your index finger has a lot to do with transitioning the bow. The other important part of transitioning is the wrist. Just like you'd use your wrist to guide the yo-yo back and forth, you use your wrist to help guide and anticipate the bow stroke.

Flexibility in your wrist is important when transitioning the bow. If you have a stiff wrist, it won't work at all when moving the bow back and forth. Recall earlier that I said having a stiff wrist is like grabbing a pen with your fist and trying to write accurate letters. It doesn't work!

Are you wondering how you can practice all this with everything else going on? The key to building any solid fundamental, including using the wrist to transition, is to simplify the technique with drills. The drill that I'd like you to work on for at least five minutes a day for the next four to six weeks is called the *transition drill.* You'll start to see significant improvement after a couple of weeks:

1. **Set the right side of your wrist against a hard surface, preferably a door frame (a wall doesn't work as well with this drill).**

   Make sure you have enough pressure against the frame so that you can't move your forearm at all. You should be able to freely move your wrist. You can also have someone grab your forearm right below your wrist to restrict the forearm from moving.

   Normally, to move the bow the entire length from sticker to tip, you have to extend with your forearm. In this drill, though, you shouldn't move your forearm at all, so you'll only be able to move the bow so far. If your forearm is moving at all, it means you're using the big muscles to transition instead of the small muscles. Remember, you're working on the transition, which is done by the wrist and the index finger only. No forearm needed — but trust me, it will want to move!

2. **Move your wrist in a large circular motion for about a minute.**

   This helps you loosen up for the drill. Make sure there's no forearm movement.

3. **Put your bow at the contact point on the strings.**

   Try moving the bow (*throwing it* is another way I describe it) a few inches back and forth, using your wrist and index finger.

   If you can only move a few centimeters, that's okay. The farther you can move without using anything but your wrist and index finger, the more flexible you are in your wrist.

It's a lot easier to move the wrist and stay relaxed with no bow in your hand. Do you notice that things tend to tense up when you set the bow in your hand? Don't let this happen. Your goal is to ultimately be so relaxed that it's like there isn't a bow in your hand at all.

4. **Go back and forth on any string, focusing on transitioning the bow with your wrist and index finger.**

   Think *small* muscles and stay as relaxed as possible.

Watch Video Clip 14 to make sure you're doing this drill properly.

Don't worry about the type of sound you create in this drill. It's not a drill for creating good tone but for setting you up for success later on with your bow stroke. The more you do this drill, the more muscle memory you'll create, and eventually, it will translate into your actual bow stroke.

Make sure you keep the proper bow hold in this drill. You'll notice that it's very easy to try to stiffen your thumb and pinkie to help in the transition. It's better to go less distance and do it correctly than to go farther and do the drill incorrectly.

Now that you've worked on the transition drill, you're that much closer to using the proper muscles when moving and transitioning the bow. The harder your pieces of music get, the harder it is to continue to do proper technique when it comes to moving and transitioning the bow (as well as most fundamentals). Always take time to work on drills because they should be an ongoing practice.

Go on YouTube and browse fiddle music videos. Closely watch the hand/wrist technique that the fiddle player uses. Do you notice a little flick of the index finger and a fluid moving wrist while the person plays? If you don't see what I'm talking about, search for one of my favorite fiddle players in the world, Mark O'Connor. He has tons of videos of him playing, and he has almost perfect wrist and index technique. Everyone needs to work on this, and as you can see from how good Mark O'Connor is, it's well worth the time to spend to master it.

Playing Strings D and A

When you're able to move and transition the bow correctly, the next step is to try playing on different strings. For the first few weeks, work only with the middle two strings, D and A, so that you don't make things too complicated yet. The fiddle strings from thickest to thinnest are G, D, A, and E, as shown in Figure 5-5. As you look at the strings from playing position, the D is the second string from the left, and the A is the next one over to the right.

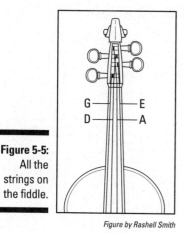

Figure 5-5:
All the strings on the fiddle.

Figure by Rashell Smith

Crossing strings

Because the fiddle has multiple strings, you need to understand how to get the bow from one string to the next properly (and smoothly). What most people do when *crossing strings* (moving the bow to a different string) is use their big muscles (again!) instead of keeping the arm muscles relaxed.

Here's how to cross strings properly:

1. **Set your bow at the contact point of the strings and position your elbow with the height of your instrument.**

   This is what I call *D string elbow position,* as shown in Figure 5-6.

2. **Stay on the D string first and practice moving the bow back and forth to create a sound on it, making sure the height of your elbow stays put.**

   When you start moving the bow, the elbow only moves 1 inch when coming to and from the frog, as I show you previously (I'm referring to the height here). The only time the height of your elbow should change is when you actually switch strings, which you don't do until the next step.

3. **Now move your *bow plane* (angle at which the bow is at in comparison to the strings) over to the A string by moving your entire arm downward.**

   Use your index finger to help keep the bow hair in the same spot when you move to the A. Your A string elbow position should be in between where your D string elbow was and where your elbow would be if it were at your side. See Figure 5-6 for the height of the A string elbow. Also notice the height of the elbow on G in Figure 5-6 and the E string in Figure 5-6 for future reference.

E string elbow (lowest)   A string elbow (higher)

D string elbow (higher)   G string elbow (highest)

Figure 5-6:
All elbow
positions.

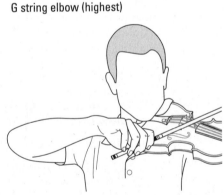

Figure by Rashell Smith

4. **Practice moving your entire arm up and down to move the bow plane from D string to A string, as shown in Figure 5-7.**

   Think mostly about moving your elbow to the proper position when doing this step. Don't change the bend of your wrist at all to move the bow plane.

5. **Move the bow back and forth four times on the D string.**

   Each one of these movements from contact point to the tip is called a *bow stroke*. Think a lot about previous fundamentals and try not to hit any string but the D.

6. **Now *quickly* transition the bow plane to the A string using your entire arm.**

    Your elbow should have moved downward to where I mentioned earlier.

7. **Do four bow strokes on the A string, thinking about moving the bow with bow fundamentals in mind.**

8. **Move the bow plane back to where it was for D. Repeat from Step 6.**

Notice in Figure 5-7 the incorrect way to do this drill, which is using your wrist instead of your entire arm as a system to change strings. Doing so causes more inaccurate string changes, so you definitely want to make sure your elbow is moving to change strings and not your wrist at this point.

In the future, there will be times when moving your wrist slightly to change strings is helpful, but I don't recommend it at first. You want to first establish a solid foundation of switching strings with your arm, and later you can get help with your wrist in fast passages. For now, just make sure you're changing crossing strings with your elbow and not your wrist.

Figure 5-7:
Moving the
arm as a
system to
change the
bow plane.

Figure by Rashell Smith

Here are some things to look out for when changing strings:

✔ Make sure that your instrument is level to the ground and that you're holding it properly.

✔ Keep the bow away from the fingerboard because it's harder to stay on only one string the closer you are to the fingerboard.

✔ Don't dip your elbow when you're bowing on the D or A string. Only change the height when you change strings.

- ✔ When crossing to the D or A string, don't have a tense arm. Keep your upper bicep relaxed, especially when you start the stroke.

- ✔ Don't use just your wrist to move the bow plane up and down. This is the one time where using your arm is necessary.

- ✔ Don't change your bow grip when moving the bow plane up and down. Everything is guided by the arm system, and you shouldn't be forcing it by pressure in your hand.

- ✔ Don't cut off the bow stroke short. Make sure you get to the tip with each bow stroke and try to follow as many of the proper moving and transitioning techniques as you can.

- ✔ Avoid crossing slowly. You can create a bad sound by being in between strings too long.

Make sure you understand that changing strings, moving the bow, and transitioning the bow all require different techniques. When you find the proper bow plane by changing strings, it's all about moving the bow and then transitioning the bow.

Although you use your entire arm in the crossover, that doesn't mean that your muscles should be tense while changing positions. Think of it like this: If I told you to raise your hand up, you wouldn't flex your muscle as hard as you could to help you achieve that movement, right? The same concept applies to crossing strings.

There's no advantage to going slow through this process. You want to get out of that in-between elbow position as quickly as possible or the fiddle will sound bad when crossing from one string to the next. It works much better to move as quickly as possible, while not tensing up your arm, of course. You don't want your arm to be tense when you move the bow from one string to the next.

Avoiding hitting multiple strings

Although you'll eventually work on the technique of hitting two strings at once, doing this as a beginner is most likely nothing but an accident. It will happen more often than you want it to. You'll start moving the bow and you'll have every technique perfectly in place except one — keeping the bow in the right plane. As I show you previously, the bow plane must be at a certain point to be able to play on either the D or A string. You may notice that some of the bow stroke — the D string, for example — sounds fine, but then toward the tip, you start to get an unpleasant sound. For some reason you've hit another string — in this case either the G or the A. Why is this happening?

Here's the ultimate way to test out your bow plane:

1. **Find a mirror and face yourself directly in front of it with your fiddle.**

2. **Put your bow at the contact point and start moving the bow on the D or A string.**

3. **Make sure you get to the tip of the bow.**

   Do you notice that as you start to approach the tip, your bow starts to change its plane? In other words, do you notice the bow curving as you get more toward the tip or does it always point like a straight arrow in the same direction? If it's not quite pointing like a straight arrow, don't worry — you'll get there with time and practice.

It's very common to change the bow plane toward the tip, for reasons I've already mentioned. As the bow begins to move away from you, your instinct is to grab it harder for fear of losing it. If you're doing this (maybe the pesky thumb is causing it), it's very easy for the bow to slightly change planes (it only takes a little bit), which causes the bow to hit other strings as you go toward the tip.

Another cause of an improper bow plane is not extending the arm correctly. As I show you previously, it takes forearm extension to move the bow toward the tip. If you aren't doing this properly, it's too easy for the bow to not only go crooked but also change the bow plane, which causes you to hit other strings.

Another thing to check for in the mirror is how much you're bending your wrist when moving the bow from the tip up toward the frog. If you're keeping your wrist stiff, your arm is controlling the bow too much, causing the bow to change planes as well.

As you can see, bad technique can pile up into a big old mess. If you pick and choose which techniques you want to work on, you'll find that many songs and techniques you want to play are very difficult (compared to someone who takes all the techniques more seriously). For example, if you skipped to just wanting to know how to avoid crossing strings and haven't been practicing moving the bow or transitioning the bow properly, you'll find keeping the bow plane straight very tough. My suggestion is that you do whatever you can to really grasp the fundamentals. Without understanding and working on fundamentals, you'll have a pile of bad habits and, ultimately, bad sound. Sorry to bring you this bad news, but if you're relatively new to the fiddle, it should warn you to start changing some of your habits!

Rocking bow drill

One of the most important things associated with crossing strings is being relaxed with your arm as you move up and down (you know, like a chicken!).

Having a tense and improper movement of the arm can really cause bad sounds and can really restrict your ability to play fiddle. You'll come across lots of fiddle songs that require speedy crossovers, and without doing this technique properly, you'll be left in the dust. To help with keeping a relaxed and efficient crossover arm, here I show you a drill that has worked for many other players: the rocking bow drill.

1. **Set your bow at the contact point of the strings.**

2. **Form a proper bow hold.**

   Don't skip over this step, as the bow hold is very important in this drill.

3. **Without ever bending your wrist, move your arm as a system from the G string elbow position down to the E string elbow position.**

   Try not to make any sound as the bow "rocks" in place from string to string. Take no more than one second to get your elbow from the G to the E string. Don't cheat by going only part of the way!

4. **Pick up your bow and move it to the middle, between the contact point and the tip.**

   Do the same rocking bow motion up and down and try not to make a sound.

5. **Now try doing the same rocking motion at the tip of the bow.**

   You'll find this is the hardest place to keep the bow relaxed and avoid any sort of noise.

The rocking bow drill is great because it helps you manage bow tension. If you remember what I show you earlier in the "Crossing strings" section, managing bow tension is what's important to get a good crossover sound. Eventually, you should feel comfortable moving your entire arm up and down and not get much, if any, surface noise when crossing.

Also, how you use your index finger during the rocking bow drill is very important. You need to find the right balance of pressure not just during this drill but similarly when you're crossing strings playing the fiddle. If you press too hard, you'll find it more difficult to get the clean crossover sound. If you don't press enough, you'll glide across the strings and not be able to stay in the same fixed position. Practice using your index finger and experimenting with various pressures as you go up and down in the drill. Doing so goes a long way in how you transition and cross strings while playing.

The reason why the rocking bow drill is so hard to do at the tip of the bow is because your hand is the farthest away from your body. With this in mind, really try hard to work on staying relaxed at the tip of the bow because this is the point where you'll have the most trouble with avoiding bow tension. I've never seen anybody have an easier time at the tip of the bow than at the contact point.

It's very easy to cheat in this drill by using your wrist to help rock the bow across the strings. Crossing strings at the beginner level has nothing to do with moving the wrist at all but instead is a complete system movement of the arm, forearm, wrist, and hand. Think of it like this: If I froze your entire arm except for your shoulder, you wouldn't be able to extend your forearm or move your wrist. As you go up and down in the drill, act like everything but your shoulder is frozen to help you move everything together as a system.

Another way to cheat is by not moving your arm system all the way down to the E string elbow position. Your elbow position should be right at your side, so if you're going down and there's a space between your side and your elbow, you're not doing the drill properly. If you find trouble doing that, most likely you have some tension somewhere — potentially in your upper arm, forearm, or fingers. Stay relaxed!

So what are some things that may be causing you to make a sound while doing the rocking bow drill? Check out some of the possibilities:

- Your upper arm is flexed at some point in the rocking motion. Think of raising your hand up and down. Do you need to have your muscle flexed to do this?

- You're changing pressure in your bow hold. It's very easy to use the thumb and/or pinkie to help in crossing the bow.

- You're moving so slow that tension is very hard to manage. Try not taking more than a second to get all the way from the G string elbow position to the E string elbow position in the drill. You should literally look like a bird trying to fly!

Practicing the Drills

The key to establishing a great musical sound and putting yourself on the path to success has everything to do with building proper technique. I've been playing fiddle since I was a very young boy, and it's all second nature to me now. But if I were to switch hands and play the fiddle, with the fiddle bow in my left hand instead of my right, I'd struggle just like you're struggling right now (I wouldn't want you to hear how it sounds). So why is that exactly? The reason is muscle memory. Studying and understanding everything about techniques only gets you so far because you still have to put them into practice. The best way to do this is simply by working on each of them individually in your practice sessions.

I suggest you work on drills for a third of your practice session. That means that if you spend the next 30 minutes practicing, work on your drills for 10 minutes. I've created a schedule based on how long you should be doing the drills I go over in this chapter. After five weeks, you may want to replace some of the drills with others; it normally takes this long to build solid muscle memory.

- ✔ **Contact point:** Practice finding the contact point along with working on your bow hold. Do this drill for one minute.

- ✔ **Quarter drill:** Practice moving your wrist properly while keeping the coin on your hand. Do this drill for one minute.

- ✔ **Mirror practice:** Play your fiddle while watching yourself in the mirror. Focus on keeping your bow straight and getting to the tip. Do this drill for three minutes.

- ✔ **Index drill:** Press down into the stick in different parts of the bow. Do this drill for two minutes.

- ✔ **Wall practice:** Practice moving the bow while up against the wall. Do this drill for two minutes.

- ✔ **Rocking bow drill:** Practice moving the bow up and down without making any sound. Do this drill for one minute.

The key to a great practice session starts with understanding quality over quantity practice. If you just pick up your fiddle and don't really think about what you're doing and working on, the practice won't be very effective. Don't think so much about the amount of time you're practicing; instead, think about the quality of time you're putting in. Just 15 minutes a day with drills is enough to build great technique within a few weeks.

Chapter 6

Working with the Left Hand

*H*ave you seen all those little ridges on the fingerboard of a guitar? Those ridges are called *frets,* and they make finding exact pitches on a guitar much easier than doing so on the fiddle. If you put your finger on the string between any two frets on a guitar and pluck that string, the sound you get is the note you're looking for. Not so for the fiddle. It has no frets, so placing your finger on a string feels to the novice like flying blind.

So, how do you know exactly where to find a certain note on the fiddle? The answer is in understanding and practicing proper technique. In this chapter, you go through the steps it takes to build enough technique to know exactly where your finger has to go to play certain notes. Trust me though — it isn't easy. You'll have to work hard by using the tools I recommend to you, and you'll need to practice, practice, practice!

Focusing on the Thumb and Wrist

When you play the fiddle, it's important to understand left-thumb position and the position of your wrist. Proper thumb and wrist position sets you up to put your fingers in the proper spots and avoids restricting you down the road, when I show you how to do vibrato and shifting.

As I discuss in Chapter 5, having a relaxed right hand is very important to avoid bow tension. Being relaxed with your left hand is also important, so make sure you go through the next few sections with that in mind.

Figuring out where to place your thumb

Establishing good fundamentals to be able to find the correct notes on the fiddle starts with the thumb. For many activities, placing your fingers close to where they should be is enough. For example, you can still write on a piece of paper correctly whether your thumb is a little bit higher or lower. This isn't the case when playing the fiddle. Your fingers (including the thumb) need to be in exactly the right spots.

There's a lot more leniency in how you can hold the bow compared to how and where you should place your fingers. Try to be as precise as you can by following everything that I suggest very closely.

Follow these steps to know exactly where your thumb should go on the fiddle:

1. **Hold your instrument under your chin properly with no hands.**

2. **Place your thumb at the neck, about an inch above the nut.**

   The *nut* is the slightly elevated ridge at the very end of the fingerboard, where the string actually touches the fingerboard.

3. **Point your thumb upward.**

4. **Place the top of your thumb about even with the height of the fingerboard.**

   There are different schools of thought on the height of the thumb on the fingerboard. The biggest thing is being consistent with whatever height you choose from the beginning, as this leads to better note finding and other techniques I cover in Chapter 15. In any case, your thumb should never grip the neck; the neck should simply rest on your thumb.

5. **Place a sticker in this spot so that you know where it is in the future (see Figure 6-1).**

   Small rounded stickers work well. You can find finger-placement stickers made just for this purpose online or at your local violin shop.

Keeping your wrist straight

As you can see, Figure 6-1 shows the wrist perfectly straight. This is how you should always keep your wrist because you can't accomplish many fiddle techniques with a collapsed wrist. This is very important!

If you have a problem keeping your wrist straight, you're probably relying too much on the left hand/arm to hold up the fiddle. Keeping your wrist straight begins with holding the fiddle properly with your chin and shoulder.

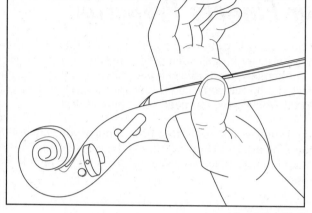

Figure by Rashell Smith

As I show you in Chapter 4, it's important to hold the fiddle without relying on your left hand. You should hold the fiddle 85 percent with your chin and shoulder and 15 percent with your left hand keeping the fiddle level (known as the *85-15 rule*). This may not feel comfortable initially, but you'll get used to it. Try the following to see exactly how much help you need from your left hand:

1. **Set up your shoulder rest and hold the fiddle with no hands (refer to Chapter 4 for details).**

2. **Place your thumb in the right spot.**

3. **Lightly pinch the other side of the fiddle neck with the inside of your left hand.**

   Your index finger should touch the side of the fiddle at the knuckle adjoining the palm, and your fingers should be curved up and over the fingerboard. The exact spot is shown later in the chapter.

4. **Twist your left hand so that the right side of your hand is 1 inch from your neck.**

   Don't force this movement with your arm, as it should just entail movement of your hand.

5. **Slide your hand up and down the fingerboard.**

   Are you able to do this without your neck constricting or tightening up? If not, don't grab the neck so tightly.

If you found yourself having to loosen up to be able to move fluidly, this is the adjustment you'll need to make each time you play the fiddle. Eventually, you'll need to move your hand up and down to do other techniques. This is a good test to show you how important it is to hold the fiddle loosely with your left hand.

Placing Your Fingers Properly

Think about how many keys/notes a piano has — 88 total. Do you think the fiddle has more or fewer notes? Most people would say a piano is able to play more notes, but actually, the fiddle can play more — each string has over 30 notes! This fact should tell you that putting your fingers in the right spot is pretty important. You're going to need some help at first.

In this section, I show you step by step how to place your fingers down properly on the fingerboard. I start by explaining the role of each finger — soon you'll understand how to place your fingers down on the middle two strings with no problem!

Understanding finger numbers

For finger numbering, each one of your fingers on the left hand, except for your thumb, represents a number. No fingers down on the fingerboard (a position known as *open*) also represents a number. The numbering goes as follows:

> No fingers: This is considered value 0, or open.
>
> The index finger: This is considered your first finger, or value 1.
>
> The middle finger: This is considered your second finger, or value 2.
>
> The ring finger: This is considered your third finger, or value 3.
>
> The pinkie: This is considered your fourth finger, or value 4.

I refer to finger numbers often, so you need to know exactly what finger is your first finger, your second finger, and so on without even having to think about it. This will go a long way toward helping you to read music in Chapter 7 as well.

Fingering progression

For the first couple of weeks, it's important that you master nothing else but notes on the D and A strings — the middle two strings. Because I'm not showing you exactly how to read music yet, I want to explain each of the notes on these two strings using what's called *finger notation*. As you can see in Table 6-1, finger notation shows which finger to put down on the fiddle by the string and finger being used.

For now, the second finger notes are sharp notes (designated by ♯), which basically means they're a higher pitch than the standard letter note. The reason why I'm showing you the higher-pitched second finger notes first is because they work well in learning basic songs.

Don't worry about the pinkie finger for now; you'll find out how to use this finger later.

Listen to Audio Track 5 to hear what the basic note pitches should sound like.

Table 6-1	**Finger Notation for the D and A Strings**	
Note	*Finger Placement*	*Pitch*
D0	No fingers down on the D string	D
D1	First finger down on the D string	E
D2	Second finger down on the D string	F♯
D3	Third finger down on the D string	G
A0	No fingers down on the A string	A
A1	First finger down on the A string	B
A2	Second finger down on the A string	C♯
A3	Third finger down on the A string	D

Take a look at where each of these notes falls on the fiddle in Figure 6-2.

Figure 6-2:
The fingerboard showing where the basic notes are located in the key of D.

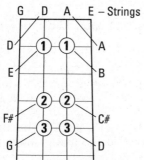

Figure by Rashell Smith

When you're done with note D3, the next note you play in the progression is A0. This change from one note to the next means you have to cross over to the next higher string to play the next note in the progression. When you start using the bow, this switch from one note to the next is called a *bow crossover* (string crossing).

Putting on stickers

Before you actually start making contact with the fingerboard to make different notes, you need to put down a set of stickers so you know exactly where your fingers will be going. Don't rush through this process; the closer the stickers are to the correct spots, the more in tune you'll be.

1. **Get a set of round stickers or finger tape.**

   Either of these can represent where to put fingers down on the fiddle.

2. **Tune the D string as precisely as possible (see Chapter 3 if you need help tuning).**

3. **Take your 1st finger and put pressure down on the D string in the same spot vertically as your thumb sticker.**

4. **Pick the string with your finger to get a sound.**

5. **Adjust the finger until your tuner reads "E."**

   Try to get as close as you can to exact pitch.

6. **Keep your finger in the perfect "E" spot and peel your sticker with the other hand.**

7. **Now for the tricky part: Slide the sticker as close as you can to the spot where your finger is.**

8. **Check again to make sure your D is in tune.**

9. **Put your finger directly over where you placed the sticker and match perfect "E" on the tuner.**

10. **If your finger is covering the sticker perfectly, you're done with that note.**

    If you find that you aren't quite in the right spot, adjust the sticker accordingly.

11. **Do the same thing with F♯ and G.**

    Remember that the tuner should read "F♯" — not just "F" — for you to place the sticker properly.

You may have to clean off the gunk from the sticker if you adjust too many times. You may also want to try a new sticker after a few attempts to make sure it sticks well enough.

Although you won't be working with the 4th finger for a while, you can still place the sticker on the fingerboard where it should go. On the D string, your 4th finger will be an A pitch (yes, the same pitch as your open string next door). You can follow the preceding steps to place the 4th finger sticker, which will be about the same distance as your 1st finger is from your 2nd finger.

Don't feel like you're cheating by using stickers. Because the fiddle is fretless, you need to know exactly where to place your fingers to sound your best. I agree that the stickers shouldn't be on your fiddle forever, but you really do need them now. Give yourself a timeline of about 6 to 12 months and stick to it before you take off the stickers.

Now that you have your stickers in the right spot, it's important to note what they represent. Because all the first finger notes across the fiddle are parallel to one another, you don't need to put stickers on every string. Using the finger tape does represent this clearer than the round stickers, but either one works.

Check to see how your first finger sticker lines up with your thumb sticker. The first finger and thumb should be parallel. If they're off slightly, adjust your thumb sticker.

Keeping Your Knuckles Up

Before I show you how to put fingers down on the fingerboard, I want to show you a very important fundamental called *keeping your knuckles up*. This is one of the two most important fundamentals to get right the first time because it can lead to either great fiddle playing or struggles to find the correct notes.

Keeping your knuckles up means you have to have your hand high enough to be able to find every note on the fiddle without having to reach with your hand. Your hand should stay still as your fingers move.

When you start to put your fingers down on the D and A strings, you may find it easy to reach notes with your fingers. Don't lower your knuckles because of this, though; eventually, you'll have to play notes way over on the G string and then jump to the E string. You want to get your knuckles really high early on, so you can reach notes efficiently in the future.

The following steps show how to achieve the perfect hand position. Refer to Video Clip 15 to make sure you're doing this properly.

1. **Put on your shoulder rest and hold the fiddle without using your hands.**

2. **Place your thumb in the correct position.**

   Make sure your wrist is straight (don't let it collapse in).

3. **Make contact on the fingerboard.**

   Make sure you don't let your thumb lift up along with your hand. You want the right side of your left hand to lift up slightly more than the left side.

4. **Turn your hand inward while keeping everything else in the same spot.**

   This turn should make the far right side of your hand about 1 inch from the neck.

5. **Curl your fingers without changing your hand position.**

   It's all in the fingers!

The reason why I emphasize the knuckles up so much is because it'll seem a lot easier to you to dip your hand low and have flat fingers. This won't make a big difference at first, but later it will make a huge difference in your playing speed and the accuracy of your finger placement. So you may as well do it correctly from the beginning!

It's very easy to force your hand higher instead of your knuckles. That means you'd be painfully twisting your arm to create that extra height. This is very uncomfortable and not the way you should be doing it. Relax your hand and refer to the 85-15 rule in the earlier section "Keeping your wrist straight." If you're not relying on holding the neck with your hand, you should be able to raise it slightly without forcing your arm muscles into action. If you're having trouble with this, see the later section "Being Relaxed."

Keeping your knuckles up is one of the hardest fundamentals to get used to at first, but within a few weeks, it will feel a lot more comfortable. After you get used to it, you won't have to think about it as much in the near future. However, if you do it the wrong way from the beginning, it'll be very hard to change. Trust me; this is one of the most important things to do properly on the fiddle from the beginning.

Before getting into actual placement of fingers, practice this technique for the next few days. Really get a feel for how your hand should form onto the neck of the fiddle. You want to have this fundamental down because it's too easy to forget. Write a big note that says "KEEP YOUR KNUCKLES UP!" and put it on your violin case.

Contacting the Fingerboard Properly

Placing fingers properly on the fingerboard is all about proper contact. It doesn't take pressing down hard, which is a bad habit to get into. You also don't want to press down so lightly that you don't get the proper sound. Pressing perfectly requires that you understand exactly how you should place your finger on the string.

Follow these steps to go through the process of plucking your first note on the fiddle:

1. **Hold the fiddle properly with your chin and shoulder and put your left hand into proper position.**

2. **Make sure your knuckles are up high.**

3. **Place your 3rd finger on the D string with the very tip of the finger.**

    You want to use the part of the skin that's right next to the nail. Don't use your nail, but the closer you can be to it the better. Keeping fingernails short really helps to do this properly. Sorry, ladies!

     Slamming down your fingers too hard on the fingerboard can cause an unnecessary slapping noise. Try to avoid this by keeping your fingers close to the fingerboard and placing them down nicely. You want to place down your fingers quickly but avoid this slapping noise.

4. **Take your right hand and get into plucking position.**

    This means putting your thumb on the corner of the fingerboard and using your right index finger to grab the string (see Figure 6-3).

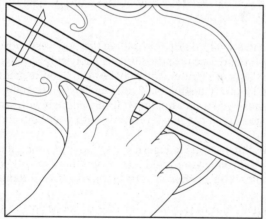

Figure 6-3:
Proper
plucking
setup.

Figure by Rashell Smith

5. **While keeping your finger down on the string with your left hand, pick the string with your right.**

    Don't be afraid to pluck the string semi-hard, so that it produces a loud enough sound.

If you notice a dead noise that doesn't ring out, you need to put more pressure down on the fingerboard. If you notice a nice ringing sound, try lightening up on the fingerboard and see whether you still get the ringing sound from before. You want to press down just enough so you get this ringing sound, but not harder than you have to.

Listen to Audio Track 6 to hear the sound you should make when your finger creates proper contact with the fingerboard. Part one is an example of not pressing hard enough, and part two is an example of pressing just right.

Practice this with other notes until you feel comfortable with the contact. Notice the indent on your finger. If you find the indent on the fat part of your finger, you need to press down more on the tip of your finger. Remember to keep your knuckles up during this process.

Being Relaxed

Have you ever lifted weights? Think about how hard you have to grip to hold various weights. Do you squeeze hard when you shake hands? Do you lift heavy boxes often? If you can relate to any of these things, this section is going to be especially important.

Just like I talk about the baby-bird grip for holding the bow very loose, the same thing is true for the left hand. Because the fiddle is likely still a foreign object to you, it's too easy to squeeze tighter. You may be afraid you're going to drop the thing you just paid a pretty penny for. If you feel like you're going to drop the fiddle, it isn't because you aren't holding it firmly enough with your left hand — it's because you aren't holding it properly with your chin and shoulder.

Take a look at the two illustrations in Figure 6-4. If you find yourself looking like Figure 6-4a, you may be forcing your hand into proper hand position, which is incorrect. There shouldn't be any flex in your bicep to get your hand up.

If you're sore after a half hour of playing, there's too much tension somewhere. If I asked you to stand and hold your hand up without your fiddle (on and off) for 30 minutes, my guess is you wouldn't be sore in the morning. Being sore at any time (even if you're an older player) is a sure sign that you aren't doing something quite right.

Continue to go through the setup drills carefully over the next few days until you feel you're applying the least amount of tension possible to the instrument. You don't want this tension to be around when you start advancing on the instrument!

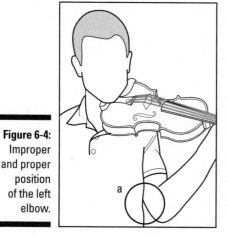

a   b

Figure by Rashell Smith

Figure 6-4:
Improper
and proper
position
of the left
elbow.

Building Solid Finger Angles

As you know, bowling is a sport in which you throw a ball down a lane to try to knock ten pins down. If you've ever done this before, you know that you start a little bit behind a certain line and then run up (forward) as close as you can to the line and throw the ball. But what if I said you had to bowl differently from this?

What if I turned you 45 degrees to the left? Now, instead of facing the pins directly, your shoulders are facing the corner of the bowling alley. You can still see the pins fine, but you have to keep your shoulders pointed at the corner of the bowling alley as you run up to throw the ball. This would be pretty awkward, wouldn't it?

This bowling analogy shows that lining up your shoulders properly is important, and similarly important is the way your fingers are angled on the fiddle. If they aren't in the right position, playing would be like trying to bowl with your shoulders pointing in the wrong direction. You wouldn't knock over as many pins, now would you?

Check out Video Clip 16 to see what your finger angles should look like and how to do the following steps:

1. **Place your fingers perpendicular to the fingerboard and press down with your 2nd finger on any string.**

2. **Take your 3rd finger and try to stretch as far as you can toward you while keeping your 2nd finger in the perpendicular position.**

   It's pretty hard to reach far, isn't it? Figure 6-5 shows how this would look.

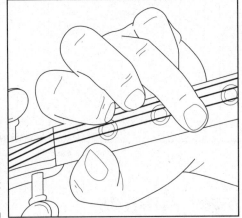

Figure 6-5:
The finger
placement
drill.

Figure by Rashell Smith

3. **Now make an adjustment to point all your fingers at your left shoulder. Place your 2nd finger down (pointing at your left shoulder) and see how far your 3rd finger can stretch.**

   A lot farther, right? This is the proper way to angle your fingers.

In summary, you have to keep your fingers angled back. Although reaching with your hand to find notes may seem more logical, you want your fingers angled back properly so that you can locate notes easier.

Practice seeing how still you can keep your hand while finding notes on any of the strings. Although you haven't learned all the notes yet, you can still practice not moving anything but your fingers. If you start off with your knuckles properly up and your fingers perfectly angled back, you'll be able to find every note without having to adjust your hand.

Having big hands helps in both keeping your knuckles up and your fingers angled back because you have more leeway in how high and how far back you have to be. The smaller your hands are, the more important it is for you to do this process correctly.

Now that you understand proper fundamentals for your left hand, keep in mind to check your hand position often. As you start to focus on other things, your hand will want to change positions, and without being aware of it, you can easily slip into a bad habit. The good news is that it takes about four weeks to build a bad habit. If you're putting these drills into your rotation, you'll be fine. The worst thing you can do, though, is to feel overconfident after a few good attempts and then slip into doing it the wrong way. This is very common; don't let it happen to you!

Working with D and A String Notes

Earlier in this chapter, I discuss the notes on the D and A strings, but you haven't yet put them into action. If you remember from the notation, notes are identified by the string and the finger number (see the earlier section "Fingering progression" to brush up).

Now it's time to put a few progressions into action! Here's how to set up to pluck a progression:

1. **Hold the instrument properly with your chin and shoulder.**

2. **Place your left-hand thumb in the correct position.**

3. **Put your hand high in relation to your neck so that you're playing notes with your knuckles up.**

4. **Twist your left hand so that the right side of your hand is 1 inch from your neck.**

5. **Put your right-hand thumb on the corner of the fingerboard.**

6. **Get ready to grab the string with your right index finger and to pluck some basic notes on the D and A strings.**

Because I haven't shown you how to read music yet (see Chapter 7), I list the following progressions in notation form. The letter signifies the string I want you to play, and the number refers to the finger number (see the earlier "Understanding finger numbers" section if you need a refresher on finger numbers).

Progression #1

D0 D0 D1 D1 D2 D2 D3 D3 A0 A0 A1 A1 A2 A2 A3 A3

Progression #2

A3 A3 A2 A2 A1 A1 A0 A0 D3 D3 D2 D2 D1 D1 D0 D0

Now listen to Audio Track 7 to hear what these two progressions should sound like.

As you can see, these progressions cover all the notes I discuss previously in this chapter. Playing these progressions together is what's called the *D major scale.* Congrats on playing your first scale!

I show you how to understand counting and rhythm in Chapter 8, but for now I suggest trying to pluck the notes along with me on the audio track. Avoid plucking any one note faster or slower than another note. Because playing with no fingers down on A/D isn't that hard, your tendency may be to rush and play notes faster than the timing suggests. Practice plucking on your own, and when you feel comfortable, follow me on the audio track.

Tucking the half step close

The distance between the notes that you're required to play (the 1st finger E and 2nd finger F#) is called a *whole step.* Notice how wide the space between your fingers is. The more you play these notes, the more you'll feel comfortable knowing how wide a whole step is, and eventually, you won't need your stickers.

The space between your 2nd finger F# and 3rd finger G is called a *half step.* You place your fingers right next to each other, a closeness that is often not pointed out. Here's an exercise to help you understand how close your fingers should be:

1. **Make sure your D string is in tune.**

2. **Hold your fiddle on your chin and shoulder.**

3. **Place your knuckles high with your fingers angled back, like I explain earlier in this chapter.**

4. **Place your 2nd finger down on the D string and match this pitch with the tuner; it should read "F#."**

5. **Leave your F# down and find the G with your 3rd finger using your tuner.**

6. **If you have big fingers, you'll notice your fingers are almost on top of each other; if you have smaller hands, you should notice a slight space.**

This spacing is very important to feel moving forward. Whenever you play in the key of D (this is the key I've been showing you), you should keep your 2nd and 3rd fingers very close together as you lift them up and place them back down.

Figure 6-6 shows where your 3rd finger should be as you're placing your 2nd finger down.

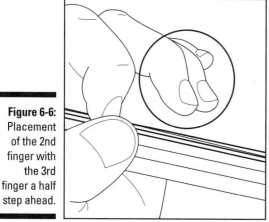

Figure 6-6:
Placement
of the 2nd
finger with
the 3rd
finger a half
step ahead.

Figure by Rashell Smith

Plucking to "Mary Had a Little Lamb"

An easy song that you can play on the fiddle that requires playing only on the D string is "Mary Had a Little Lamb."

The "R" you see in the notation shows spots where you do nothing in the music. This is called a *rest,* and I talk about rests in Chapter 7. For now, just know that these are spots where you don't play anything for the same length of time as you would play any of the notes.

"Mary Had a Little Lamb"

D2 D1 D0 D1 D2 D2 D2 R D1 D1 D1 R D2 D2 D2 R

D2 D1 D0 D1 D2 D2 D2 D2 D1 D1 D2 D1 D0 R R R

Follow Audio Track 8 to get a good feel (again) for playing the piece properly in rhythm.

You can always use your tuner to make sure you're putting your fingers in the right spots. Don't get overly technical with this though, as it's impossible to hit every note perfectly. Try to get within the range of 15 degrees, but keep in mind that this is difficult for the beginner. Obviously, the closer you are to the correct note the better, but remember that you're dealing with a fretless instrument.

Ninety-five percent of the people who go through this process are tempted to try to use the bow. If you really want to become a great fiddle player, take at least a week or two and master the fundamentals before attempting to play these progressions with the bow.

Part III
Unlocking the Keys to Reading Music

Counting	Option 1 (best)	Option 2	Option 3
	1 1 2	2 2 4	4 4 8
	1 2	2 4	4 8
	1 3	2 6	4 12
	1 4	2 8	4 16
	2 2	4 4	8 8

web extras

Head to www.dummies.com/extras/fiddle for a free article that defines some well-known musical symbols outside of the ones included in this book. These musical symbols are what I would consider "musical road signs" because they tell you how many times to repeat a song, and where you can jump to extend a song or make it shorter.

In this part . . .

- ✔ Discover details about the different types of musical symbols and how to read music on the lines.

- ✔ Understand how to count and keep rhythm.

- ✔ Pick up your fiddle and apply your musical knowledge to some basic tunes.

- ✔ Expand your skills with some trickier fiddling and more complex fiddle tunes.

Chapter 7

Understanding How to Read Music

Remember the first time you learned how to ride a bike or drive a car? Or even before that, do you remember learning how to read and write? These are skills that, once learned, you can apply almost universally in your life without even thinking about it. There's always room for improvement in any skill you learn, but you carry the basics with you for the rest of your life.

Learning to read music, although daunting for many people at first, really isn't that difficult after you learn the fundamentals. When you grasp the basics, you'll be able to read the thousands of fiddle tunes just waiting for you out there.

In this chapter, you discover the basics of reading music, which you can then carry over to many other instruments. Of course, the focus is on the fiddle, which will allow you to start playing tunes. Eventually, you'll be fiddling songs you thought you'd never be able to play!

Reading Music Basics

The goal of reading music is to understand what each symbol means and then to translate it to what to do on your fiddle. This section focuses on understanding the basic quarter note, notes on the music staff, intervals, measures, and musical symbols.

Take this section as slowly as you need to, as you shouldn't try to digest it in one day. If you've never read music before, I recommend taking it as slowly as possible and referring back to it as needed. Don't let the chapter hold you back from progressing forward, as you can always look back when there's something you don't understand in a musical piece.

Getting acquainted with the quarter note

Learning how to read music begins with understanding the basic quarter note: ♩. This is the most common note you'll see in music, representing one bow stroke or one beat. As you can see, the quarter note is symbolized by a black oval attached to a black stem. As you look at different types of notes, you'll see changes in both the stem and the oval that represent changes in the note's rhythm/speed. Chapter 8 covers other types of notes, but in this chapter, you only work with the quarter note.

You may see a note stem pointing up or down. This doesn't have any effect on the rhythm or pitch. You'll see the stem pointing down when the note is higher (to fit better on the lines) and pointing up when the note is lower on the lines. Bottom line: Don't worry about whether the stem is pointing up or down.

Minding the music staff

Figure 7-1 shows the *music staff* — the lines that music notes are placed on. Notice that the staff has five lines, and letters are assigned to each of the lines.

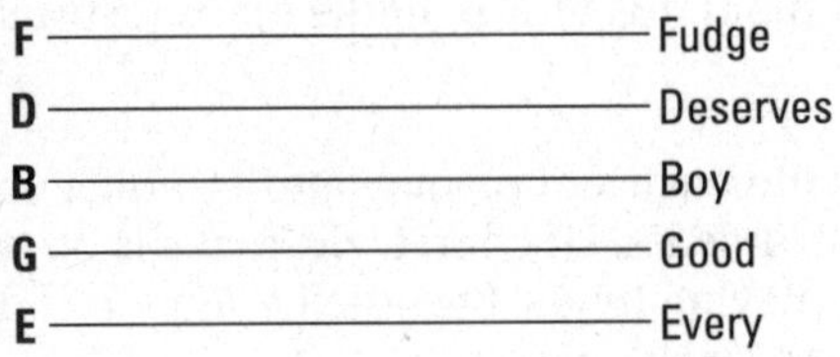

Figure 7-1:
The music
staff with
letters on
each line.

F ———————————— Fudge
D ———————————— Deserves
B ———————————— Boy
G ———————————— Good
E ———————————— Every

Figure by Rashell Smith

An easy way to remember the letters associated with each line (E-G-B-D-F) is to memorize the phrase *every good boy deserves fudge*. Every beginning letter of this phrase represents the notes associated with each line, beginning with the bottom line.

In between each of the lines are blank spaces, which are also used for musical notes. As you can see in Figure 7-2, the four spaces conveniently spell the word *face* for the notes associated with them (F, A, C, and E). Pretty easy, right?

Figure 7-2:
The music
staff with
letters on
each space.

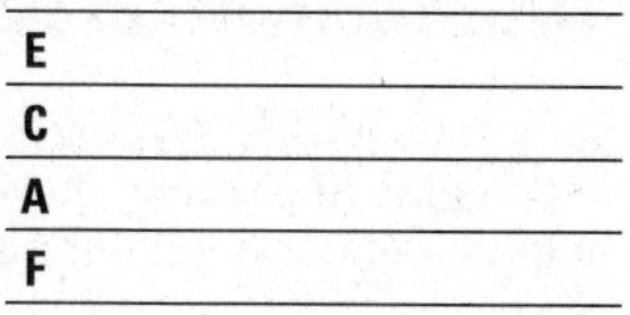

E

C

A

F

Figure by Rashell Smith

There are more notes associated with the music staff than just the ones in Figures 7-1 and 7-2. For example, if there's a note directly below the staff, it's a D, and if it's above the staff, it's a G. Figure 7-3 shows a range of musical notes that go from D to G, with both the letter form associated with each spot on the lines and spaces and the notation form that I cover in Chapter 6. Remember that the notation refers to the note you're playing, the string (G, D, A, or E) you're on, and the finger (0, 1, 2, or 3) you're using. If you need a refresher on finger numbers, see Chapter 6.

Figure 7-3:
Range of
musical
notes in
letter and
notation
form.

D   E   F   G   A   B   C   D   E   F   G

D0   D1   D2   D3   A0   A1   A2   A3   E0   E1   E2

Figure by Michael Sanchez

Counting the alphabet (A-B-C-D-E-F-G) is similar to reading notes on the music staff. Do you see how the letters on the right side of the diagram go up, just like you'd say them in sequence in the alphabet?

Notice that after you reach G in the first line of Figure 7-3, the letters start over again with A. This is the way music works; there's no note H, so after G, the notes start over again with A.

It's helpful to know both the letter of each note and the notation. I highly recommend creating flash cards of these notes that include the position of the note on the staff on the front of the card and the letter and notation on the back. You should know these so well that eventually you won't even have to think about it.

Jumping around with musical intervals

Having a complete understanding of what letter (A, B, C, D) corresponds with each spot on the lines is great, but it can be confusing when you begin jumping from note to note. In this section, I help you understand jumping from note to note in music.

Because you need to be able to read music quickly to play fiddle tunes at the speed they're supposed to be played, understanding how notes relate to one another is helpful. Understanding *musical intervals,* the distance notes are from one another, is a quick way to work up speed without necessarily relying on the letter or notation of the note.

Figure 7-4 shows two music notes: one on a space and one on the line above it. This is called a *musical 2nd.* These notes represent different fingers you'd put down on the fiddle.

Figure 7-4:
Musical
interval 2nd.

Figure by Michael Sanchez

The first note you see in Figure 7-4 is an F (D2), followed by a G (D3). What you see in the parentheses is referring to the string and finger you use. So F (D2) means that the first note is known as the letter F, and in notation form, you play it on the D string with your 2nd finger (middle finger) placed down. In the second example, G (D3) means that the note is known as a G, and you play it with your 3rd finger (ring finger) on the D string. Do you see how if you go from F (D2) to G (D3), you're basically moving up one letter/finger?

If you didn't know that the second note was a G, you could think of it this way instead, which is what I call *thinking in intervals:*

Music note   F + 1 = G

In other words, if you're on the letter F and you go up one spot on the music staff, you'll be at G, which is F+one space. G follows F in the alphabet, right?

String & finger number   D2 + 1 = D3

Here you're on the D string with your 2nd finger down, moving up one notch on the musical staff with your 3rd finger. You don't have to know that it's a G, only that you go up one letter.

Got it? Instead of having to know the note is a G, you can just tell your brain to put one more finger down, which would be a 3rd finger. This approach works well for some people who may struggle to get the hang of reading music.

Figure 7-5 helps you understand the musical 3rd.

Figure 7-5: Various musical 3rds.

D(D0)   F(D2)   G(D3)   E(D1)   G(D3)   B(A1)

Figure by Michael Sanchez

Look at the first two notes on the staff in Figure 7-5 and notice how they go from a space to the space directly above. Anytime you see this happen (also line to a line), the notes represent the interval of a 3rd. Do you notice that the note goes up two letters?

Here are a couple of examples. I know this can be confusing because I'm mixing finger notations and music notes, but hang in there!

Music note   D + 2 = F

Or

String & finger number   D0 + 2 = D2

If you're on the letter D (D0) and a note you encounter is a space above (a 3rd), you're going up two notes. This would mean the note is D + 2 (F) or D0 + 2 (D2).

If this still doesn't make sense, think about the musical alphabet (A, B, C, D, E, F, G). Look at the letter D. If I asked you to go over two places to the right, wouldn't you say the letter F?

Take a look at the second set of notes in Figure 7-5 and notice that instead of going up two spots, you're going down two spots. The first note in this example is G (D3), and you want to figure out what the second note is. Because it's going down two spots, the same rule would apply as in the earlier example, only the opposite:

Music note   G – 2 = E

String & finger number   D3 – 2 = D1

If you're on the letter G (D3) and the next note is on a line down (a 3rd), you can think of it as G – 2 = E, or D3 – 2 = D1. Again, you don't need to know that the note is E/D1 because you can rely on looking at it in interval 3rds.

Look at where the open strings (no finger numbers) are on the staff. You can use these spaces as markers and then count up and down from them. So, one notch up from D (D0) is D1, followed by D2 and then D3.

It's important to understand both the letter (A, B, C, D) and the notation of the notes (A0, A1, A2, A3). The letter will help you when I begin to discuss *key signatures* — how notes are changed into sharps (♯) and flats (♭) — and the notation is helpful in understanding what finger to put down and on what string. I usually think in musical notation when I play music because I think it's easier to do intervals when you're dealing with a number and not a letter (D3 – 2 = D1).

Take a look at the last set of notes in Figure 7-7. This is a little trickier, as you must jump from the D string to the A string and start the musical alphabet over. The first note is G (D3), and the second note, going up two spots, is B. Here's the musical math:

Music note   G + 2 = B (the first one is A because the alphabet starts over, followed by B)

String & finger number   D3 + 2 = A1

Here, you're on the letter G (D3), and you see that a note is two spots above (line to line), so you jump a string from 3rd finger to 1st finger. Going up two notches from 3rd finger takes you back to 1st finger. You also jump from letter G to letter B because the musical alphabet starts over again after the letter G.

Jumping farther with ledger lines

Because intervals can jump higher or lower than a 2nd or 3rd, it's necessary to understand the exact placement of notes. Fiddle notes can jump higher than you'd want to know, and if they go farther than a 3rd, counting in intervals is really not effective.

To understand how far jumping can really go, I want to extend your knowledge to all the notes in *first position*. These are all the notes you can play without shifting your hand up the fingerboard, as shown in Figure 7-6. To go as high and low as possible, you need to understand *ledger lines* — lines extended above or below the staff that enable the composer to notate a higher/lower range of musical notes.

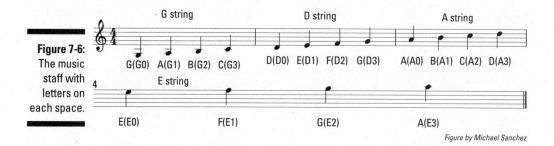

Figure 7-6: The music staff with letters on each space.

Figure by Michael Sanchez

The ledger lines you see in Figure 7-6 give you a larger range of notes you can play on the fiddle. The notes you see at the bottom, below the music staff, are notes you'd play on the low-pitch string (G string). If you look above the music staff, you see an extra note you can play on the E string. I show you how to play some higher notes that aren't listed in Figure 7-6 in Chapter 15.

Adding musical symbols

The English language has many different symbols that represent different things. For example, a period indicates the end of a sentence, and a comma represents a break in a sentence. Similarly, music has many symbols that mean different things.

Take a look at the musical line in Figure 7-7.

Figure 7-7: Musical line with basic musical symbols.

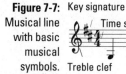

Figure by Michael Sanchez

Do you see the unique-looking symbol all the way to the left on the musical staff? This is called the *treble clef.* There are actually three types of clefs in music: treble, alto, and bass clef. The fiddle always uses the treble clef, and all the notes I've shown you so far are associated with this clef.

If you see a clef other than a treble clef, the music isn't designed for the fiddle. The viola, for example, uses the alto clef, and many lower-register instruments use the bass clef. In piano, the right hand is represented by the treble clef, while the left hand is represented by the bass clef. This means you can play the top line of piano music on the fiddle (the treble clef line), but not the bottom (unless you can convert it in your head, which is highly unlikely!).

Also in Figure 7-7, notice the pound signs located to the right of the treble clef. This is the *key signature,* which tells you the key of the tune and also indicates what notes in the tune should be played sharp or flat, which you'll read more about later in this chapter. The ♯ symbols relate to sharps, while the ♭ symbols relate to flats. The ♯ and ♭ symbols in the key signature refer to specific notes that are sharp/flat and are placed on the specific line/space that corresponds to the letter.

Do you see the vertical lines on the staff in Figure 7-7? These are called *barlines* and are used to separate music into *measures.* A measure consists of the notes located between a pair of barlines. Figure 7-7 has four musical measures.

Another important musical indicator you see in Figure 7-7 is the *time signature* — numbers on the staff that are used to tell how many musical beats there are in each measure. I go over the details of what these numbers mean in Chapter 8.

Identifying All the Possible Fiddle Notes

I hate to be the bearer of bad news, but there are a lot more notes on the fiddle that are in between the notes I showed you earlier in the chapter! When you see a piano or keyboard, do you notice that it has white *and* black keys? The white keys on the piano represent the main musical notes (A, B, C, D, E, F, and G), while the black keys are in-between notes.

Make sure that you understand the basics of all the notes on the musical staff before going on to the next part of the chapter. If you don't feel comfortable with notes yet, I highly recommend you create flash cards and study them for a while.

Understanding sharp key signature

In music, a note can be *sharp,* which means it sounds a half pitch (half step) above the original note. The sharped note is represented by a simple ♯ symbol placed to the right of the note.

This type of note can also be represented in the musical staff by the key signature. The key signature indicates which notes in a tune are either higher (sharp) or lower (flat) than they normally are.

If there was no such thing as a key signature in music, the notes in Figure 7-8 would be the notes you'd play on the fiddle. As you start to learn different key signatures, the finger placements shown in Figure 7-8 will vary from one key signature to the next.

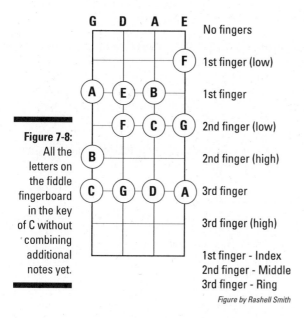

Figure 7-8: All the letters on the fiddle fingerboard in the key of C without combining additional notes yet.

Figure by Rashell Smith

The key signature is always located to the right of the treble clef symbol and contains different symbols that tell you when to change the way you play a note. You'll see either ♯ symbols, ♭ symbols, or no symbols.

If there's no key signature, the tune is in the natural state of musical notes, or the key of *C natural*.

The notes associated with the key of C are A, B, C, D, E, F, and G.

- The A is a space away from the B (this is considered a *whole step*).
- The B is right next to the C (this is considered a *half step,* and your 1st and 2nd fingers should touch each other).
- The C is a whole step away from the D.

✔ The D is a whole step away from the E.

✔ The E is a half step away from the F.

✔ The F is a whole step away from the G.

✔ The G is a whole step away from the A.

In C major, all the 1st-finger positions are similar, except on the E string. Do you see how the 1st-finger position on the E is lower than the rest? The spots that you see on the G, D, and A are what I call *normal 1 positions*. The spot where you see the F note is what I call *low 1 position*.

Notice that all the 2nd-finger positions on the D, A, and E are in the same position, but the 2nd finger on the G is in a different position. I refer to the 2nd fingers on D, A, and E in this key as *low 2* and the one on the G string as *high 2*. Low 2 and normal 1 positions are touching, while high 2 and normal 3rd finger are touching. All the 3rd fingers are in the normal 3rd-finger position all the way across.

Take a look at Figure 7-9 to see how it looks to play your fingers together as a half step and away from each other as a whole step.

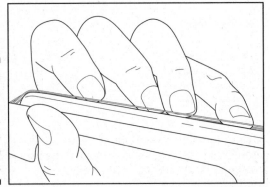

Figure 7-9:
Half-step formation and whole-step formation on the fiddle.

Figure by Rashell Smith

When you're playing in a certain key, you should constantly think about where your half steps are because they're the easiest to miss. For instance, in the key of C, you're always trying to be aware of the half steps B to C and E to F. This is where you have to be very conscious of your fingers being close together to allow you to play in tune. Do you see where this all applies in Figure 7-8?

Now if you add a ♯ to the key signature, that raises one note in the musical set A-B-C-D-E-F-G. The change would bring the F a half step higher, to an F♯. So now, the musical set of notes would be A-B-C-D-E-F♯-G. This would change the key from C major to G major. Take a look at Figure 7-10, which looks similar to C major except that all the F's are now F♯'s.

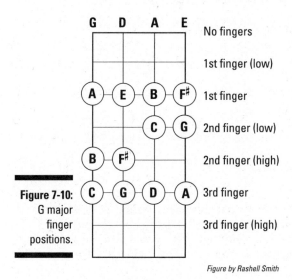

Figure 7-10: G major finger positions.

Figure by Rashell Smith

The difference between C and G major is only one note, which is F♯. In C major, the note is just F, while in G major, the note is F♯. This one difference makes certain songs sound a lot different and is very important to understand. The half steps in G major, which you can see in Figure 7-10, are between B and C (just like in C major) and between F♯ and G.

TIP

The first thing you should do when you look at a fiddle piece is check the key signature. Understanding the differences among key signatures helps you know exactly where to put your fingers down on the fiddle.

Now if you add another sharp to the key signature, you'd have two sharps, which would be considered the key of D major. This is a very common key signature, and it means that you should play F♯ and C♯. Take a look at the D major finger positions in Figure 7-11.

Look at how things relate to one another in Figure 7-11. For example, F♯ and G are half steps on the D string, and C♯ and D are half steps on the A string. This means that you play the notes very close in pitch, and your fingers should be close together on the fingerboard.

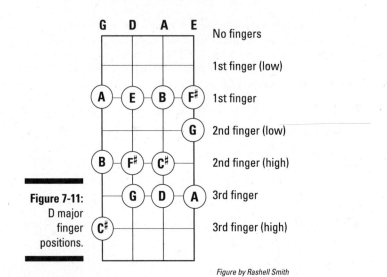

Figure 7-11: D major finger positions.

Figure by Rashell Smith

When you look at the key signature, you'll always be dealing with the same order of sharps (and eventually flats, which you'll learn about soon). For example, if you see two sharps in the key signature, you'll never deal with anything but F♯ and C♯. Everything goes in order and never changes! The order of sharps is F, C, G, D, and A.

Adding another sharp to the mix would put you in A major. This means that you have to play F♯, C♯, and G♯ notes. Take a look at Figure 7-12, which shows all the A major finger positions.

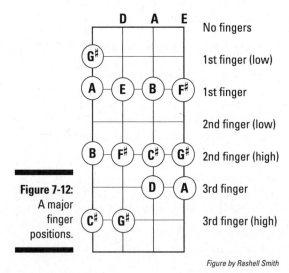

Figure 7-12: A major finger positions.

Figure by Rashell Smith

Do you see how many notes are sharp in this key signature?

With A major, it's important to make sure your 3rd-finger positions are high on the G and D string. You can easily miss this, but it makes the song sound more in tune. When you learn to put your 4th finger (pinkie) down, your high 3 on the G and D should be touching your pinkie.

If you don't understand what I mean by the high 3, look at the G major finger placements in Figure 7-10, where the 3rd finger is on the G and D string. Compare this to the location of the 3rd finger in A major. Do you notice how the 3rd finger on the G and D strings is in a higher position? This is what you call a high 3rd finger, and it happens on the G and D string in the key of A.

Here are the most common sharp notes used in music, along with the standard notes. Remember, notes start over again after the last letter in the sequence:

A, A♯, B, C, C♯, D, D♯, E, F, F♯, G, G♯

Earlier in this chapter, I cover the F♯, C♯, and G♯. If you add another sharp, it would be D♯ (key of E), and if you add one more, it would be A♯ (key of B). I'd say that 99 percent of all fiddle tunes are covered by these five sharps; adding in a sixth or seventh is rare and more common in classical music.

If you were to play each one of the notes in the preceding list, they'd sound the same as playing every note on the piano. This would include all the white and black keys, and it's called the *chromatic scale*.

Going down: Flats

As you know from the preceding section, sharps raise any musical note by a half step. The opposite of the sharp is the *flat*, which lowers any musical note by a half step. A flat is indicated by the symbol ♭ next to the note. Here are the most common flats in music:

A♭, B♭, D♭, E♭, G♭

As you can see, again you're skipping two notes — C♭ and F♭. This is similar in concept to what I talk about in the sharp section. Note that C♭ would actually be considered a B, and F♭ would be considered an E. Here are all the possible notes in music in flat mode:

A♭, A, B♭, B, C, D♭, D, E♭, E, F, G♭, G

In the section on sharps, I discuss half steps and whole steps. Here's how they apply to flats:

A to B♭: Half step

B to C: Half step

D to E♭: Half step

A to B: Whole step

D♭ to E♭: Whole step

All the half steps mean your fingers should be touching on the fiddle, while all the whole steps mean they'll be a space apart.

So how do you know whether you should be thinking of notes in sharps or flats? The answer depends on the key signature you're dealing with. Remember, the key signature is located right next to the treble clef symbol, and it tells you whether the song you're playing should be played in flats or sharps.

Figure 7-13 shows two different fingerboards with musical notes on the fiddle. The first one is full of sharps, and the second is full of flats.

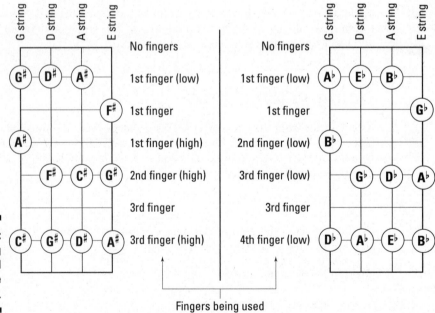

Figure 7-13: Comparing sharps and flats on the fingerboard.

Figure by Rashell Smith

Notice how the letters A through G are exactly the same on both the left and right diagrams. It doesn't matter what notes you're dealing with; these always remain the same whether you're dealing with flats or sharps.

You'll see that the flat on the left diagram has a different name than the flat on the right diagram. For example, take a look at any spot that has the note F♯ on the left diagram. Do you notice it has the name G♭ on the right? Next, notice that all the spots that say A♯ on the left are named B♭ on the right. Here are all the sharp notes with their corresponding flats:

A♯ B♭

C♯ D♭

D♯ E♭

F♯ G♭

G♯ A♭

A flat in the key signature tells you that you should be thinking of the notes in flat mode and not in sharp mode. A sharp in the key signature tells you that you should be thinking of the notes as sharps and not flats.

Understanding flat key signature

Sometimes when you read fiddle music you encounter one or more flats in the key signature. This means that some of the notes you'd normally play a certain way are lowered in pitch. This opens up your range to some unique keys you can play in, including F major (one flat in the key), B♭ major (two flats in the key), and E♭ major (three flats in the key).

When you see at least one flat, you can always assume that nothing is sharp. You'll never see both flats and sharps in the key signature.

The order that you'll always see flats in is B, E, A, and D. Yes, that spells a word! So if you see three flats in the key signature, it refers to B♭, E♭, and A♭.

If you see a B♭ note, you don't play it in the B finger position. Instead, you play it a half step lower than where you play the normal B note. This goes for any B♭ position on the fiddle, including one on the G string (low 2 on G), one on the A string (low 1 on A), and one on the E string (low 4 on E). These three spots each represent a B♭ note and are a half step lower than normal B.

Take a look at C major in Figure 7-8 earlier in the chapter. This figure shows where all the natural notes are played on the fiddle and how things look before you add any flats into the key signature. Also, check out the previous sections on key signatures and half steps/whole steps, which I refer to often in this section.

When you see one flat in the key signature, it always changes the letter B from B natural to B♭. This affects three different notes compared to playing in C major on the fiddle. Figure 7-14 shows the finger spots for the key of F (one flat in the key signature).

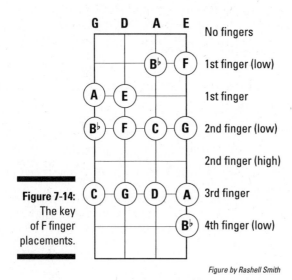

Figure 7-14: The key of F finger placements.

Figure by Rashell Smith

Now the B's are located in a different spot than the natural position of notes in C. All the B's are B♭ because of the key signature, which means that all the A's and B♭'s will touch.

Here are some other things to note:

✔ The 2nd finger on the G string is located a half step away from the 1st finger (A).

✔ The 1st finger on the A string is in the low position, which is a half step away from the open A.

✔ The 4th finger on the E string is now next to the normal 3rd finger on the E string.

You need to be aware of a couple of things when you start playing in this key signature. It's very easy to dip your hand back and move your wrist to find some of these notes, which will pull your hand out of position. This won't happen in sharp keys, but make sure you're especially aware of it in flat keys. Figure 7-15 shows the correct way to play any low 1 position on the fiddle.

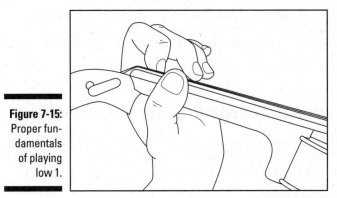

Figure 7-15:
Proper fundamentals
of playing
low 1.

Figure by Rashell Smith

I call this finger position with your 1st finger the "finger squeeze." It allows your hand to stay in the same position so that you don't have to make the unnecessary movements to find notes after the low 1. Doing this properly helps you play fast on the fiddle and play more in tune.

Adding another flat to the key signature would put you in the key of B♭. It's important that you realize that the key is B♭ and not B, as B major has five sharps! Figure 7-16 shows the finger spots for the key of B♭.

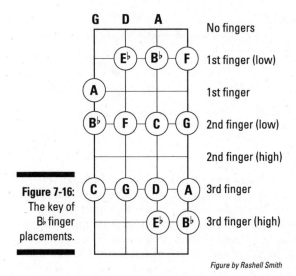

Figure 7-16:
The key of
B♭ finger
placements.

Figure by Rashell Smith

When you see two flats in the key signature, the second flat is E♭. This means that all the regular E note positions on the fiddle are now a half step lower than normal. Now the finger squeeze is applied to the 1st finger on the D string.

You'll never see sharps and flats combined in one key signature. It's possible to see a key change in the middle of a song, where the key signature may change from one with flats to one with sharps, but you'll never see a key signature with both sharps and flats.

Getting to know naturals and accidentals

Many times in music you'll see the symbol ♮, which means a music note should go back to normal. What I mean by normal is that it gets rid of its sharp or flat and goes back to the basic letter, or its natural mode (A, B, C, D, E, F, and G).

For example, say you're playing a song in G, which has one sharp in the key signature. This means that when you see an F note, you should play it in the F♯ position on the fiddle. But what if you come to an F note and it has the natural symbol (♮)? This indicates that you should play the note as an F natural, or normal F, regardless of the key signature.

This change applies to all the F notes in the entire musical measure, so if you see any other F notes in the measure after the F♮, you should also play them as F♮. That doesn't apply to any notes in the previous measure, nor does it apply to any notes in the next measure. If there is no natural sign next to an F in the next measure, you play it as an F♯. Figure 7-17 shows notes that are either F♯ or F♮.

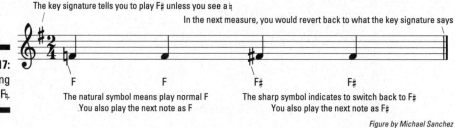

The key signature tells you to play F♯ unless you see a ♮

In the next measure, you would revert back to what the key signature says

Figure 7-17:
Comparing
F♯ and F♮.

F   F   F♯   F♯

The natural symbol means play normal F   The sharp symbol indicates to switch back to F♯
You also play the next note as F   You also play the next note as F♯

Figure by Michael Sanchez

Sometimes in music, the key signature doesn't always cover where some notes should be played on the fiddle. For example, say you're playing a song in the key of G, and you come up to C, which has a sharp sign after it. This note, which is now C♯, is called an *accidental,* and you must play it in a different finger spot than what the key signature asks you to do. When you see an accidental, you continue to play that note sharp or flat for the rest of the measure.

Accidentals can happen with any note on the fiddle, both sharp and flat. Sometimes you'll see a lot of them, while other times you won't see any. The key signature serves as a general rule, but it can easily be broken by the use of accidentals.

Chapter 8

Keeping Rhythm in a Fiddle Tune

In This Chapter

▶ Checking out your rhythm ability

▶ Getting acquainted with some typical rhythms

▶ Introducing time signatures

▶ Using a metronome or your foot to keep the beat

▶ Working with complicated rhythms

▶ Access the audio tracks and video clips for this chapter at www.dummies.com/go/fiddle

Y ou've probably heard the phrase "She's got rhythm," perhaps in reference to someone cutting a rug on the dance floor to, say, Michael Jackson's "Thriller." But what makes that person move her feet in such orderly and rhythmic fashion during such a song? And what does that have to do with playing the fiddle?

Moving your feet in all the right directions seems to be quite different from anything related to playing the fiddle, but everything you do on a dance floor to make all the right moves is the same as playing the fiddle, except your fiddle bow is what actually does all the moving!

I start this chapter by assessing your rhythm ability, and then I go over some common fiddle rhythms. This chapter also covers time signatures, ways to keep the beat, and more complicated rhythms.

Testing Your Rhythm Ability

Everyone is at a different place when it comes to rhythm. Some people have experience with other musical instruments, and it translates to the fiddle, while others pick up the fiddle as their first instrument. Some people find rhythm very easy to understand, while others have more trouble with it.

In this section, you have a chance to evaluate your rhythm experience and ability. Knowing where you stand helps you determine how much time you need to focus on this chapter.

Do you have rhythm?

The following ten questions test your knowledge of rhythm. Questions 1 through 5 ask about your previous experience playing music, which helps your knowledge of rhythm tremendously. Questions 6 and 7 relate to coordination, which is a helpful trait for understanding rhythm. Questions 8 and 9 test your knowledge of rhythm, and the last question relates to confidence. Answer each question with a Yes or a No:

1. Have you played a musical instrument for at least one year?

2. Have you played a musical instrument for at least five years?

3. Have you played a musical instrument for at least ten years?

4. When you play a musical instrument, do you tap your foot often?

5. Have you taken private music lessons?

6. Are you a good dancer?

7. Can you tap your head and rub your stomach at the same time?

8. Do you know what *subdividing* means?

9. Do you know what a *dotted eighth note* is?

10. Do you feel that you won't struggle much with rhythm?

How many questions did you answer Yes to?

8 or more: You'll probably find most of the chapter easy to understand and can skip sections as you see fit. Your rhythm is already excellent!

6–7: You understand a lot about rhythm but may find anything following the section on time signatures helpful.

4–5: You understand basic rhythm but will probably benefit from most of the chapter.

2–3: You definitely want to go over the entire chapter.

0–1: The entire chapter is key for your success on the fiddle.

Can you maintain rhythm?

The following steps show you exactly how to play a basic quarter note as it relates to *rhythm,* the speed at which you play a musical note:

1. **Find a clock that has a second dial.**

   You can also use a stopwatch or some sort of device that measures time in seconds.

2. **Tap your foot lightly to the pace of the second dial.**

3. **Set up in plucking position (refer to Chapter 6).**

4. **Start plucking any string and try to synchronize each time the second hand changes with a musical note.**

   Do this until you feel like you're hitting each pluck almost exactly when the second hand is changing.

5. **Now that you understand the pace of the second hand (which is the same as 60 musical beats per minute, or BPM), try doing this while not having the second hand clock to help you.**

To begin feeling the rhythm of the 60-beat-per-minute quarter note, try the following:

1. **Get a friend to clock 30 seconds for you without you hearing or seeing the count.**

   Your friend should make it clear when the time starts and when it ends. The rest will be blind to you. Closing your eyes would be best. You can also use a stopwatch that indicates the end of the 30 seconds.

2. **When the 30 seconds start, clap from 1 to 30, and when your friend says stop (or the stopwatch goes off), remember what number you ended on.**

3. **Repeat this two more times and then average your three scores.**

4. **Repeat Steps 1 through 3, but now do them while plucking instead of clapping (see Chapter 6 for help).**

5. **Repeat Steps 1 through 3, but this time do them while playing an open string.**

   You want to play a bow stroke in either direction each second of time while keeping track of your count.

6. **Repeat Steps 1 through 3, but do them while playing random notes with random fingers down with the bow (one note played per second).**

This tests your ability to keep proper rhythm while using the bow and placing your fingers down.

Scores:

42 or more: Too fast — you're going too fast and without practice, and this will have a negative effect on your rhythm.

39–41: Below average — you're counting faster than you should, and you need to practice getting each beat (clap, pluck, stroke) slower.

36–38: Average — you counted okay, but the pace was a little fast.

33–35: Acceptable — you counted very well, but a bit on the fast side.

31–32: Great — you counted a little faster than you should have, but still did a great job.

30: Brilliant — you counted absolutely perfectly and deserve some applause!

28–29: Great — you counted a little slower than you should have, but still did a great job.

25–27: Acceptable — you achieved an acceptable score, but a bit on the slow side.

22–24: Average — you counted okay, but your pace was still a little too slow.

19–21: Below average — you counted slower than you should, and you need to practice trying to get each beat (clap, pluck, stroke) faster.

18 or less: Too slow — your tendency is to go too slow; if you don't practice, this will affect your rhythm negatively in music.

Music varies at different speeds (tempos), so if you're wondering how fast a quarter note is played, it all depends on how fast you decide to play it. A good average speed to play a quarter note is close to a second of time (60 BPM). When you're first learning a song, you'll want to take it even slower (like 40 BPM). Play at a slow enough tempo that you aren't pausing between notes to figure out where you should go next. If you see potential road blocks in a few measures along the way, begin at a very slow tempo so you'll be able to smoothly pass through those road blocks.

Concert speed, which is the speed you should learn a piece to perform it or call it "good," is indicated by the composer in the top left-hand corner of the music.

Playing the Most Common Rhythms

Chapter 7 covers the *quarter note,* which is the most common type of note you'll see in music. In this section, you discover a few more rhythms that'll help you in reading many more fiddle tunes.

Sorting out various notes and rests

To make music sound unique, changes in rhythm need to happen. That means that some notes (and rests) are held longer than others and are indicated by a specific musical symbol. While learning a few of these rhythms allows you to play many different songs, you'll need to learn all or most of them at some point in your musical career. Try not to get overwhelmed with understanding them all right away, though — this process takes time.

Half note

Sometimes when you play the fiddle you have to hold notes longer than the standard quarter note. This is indicated by a symbol change and requires you to stroke the bow in a different way.

If you see a note with a white oval instead of a solid black oval, ♩, it's considered a *half note.* These types of notes are played twice as long as quarter notes, and you want to utilize the entire length of the bow in many cases. Each half note is considered two beats/counts.

It's important to use the whole bow while playing every quarter note and half note when you're first starting. With a half note, you move the bow slower than you do with a quarter note. Look at Figure 8-1 and try playing "Twinkle, Twinkle, Little Star," which has half notes in it.

Twinkle, Twinkle, Little Star

Figure 8-1:
"Twinkle, Twinkle, Little Star."

Figure by Michael Sanchez

Now listen to Audio Track 9 to make sure you're playing it right!

Whole note

Sometimes in music, you'll see a white oval without a stem, ○. This is called a *whole note,* and it has four total beats. A whole note is twice as long as a half note and four times as long as a quarter note. While you're playing the whole note, you should be counting to four; otherwise, it's too easy not to play it long enough.

Eighth note

The next important rhythm you must understand is the *eighth note.* It's indicated by a black oval with a stem that has a small flag-like squiggle at the top, ♪. Each eighth note is twice as fast as a quarter note, which means that two eighth notes are the same length as one quarter note.

Eighth notes often come in twos, ♫. Seeing an eighth note by itself is not as common. You'll learn about this rhythm as a single note later in this chapter, but for now, I refer to eighth notes in groups of two.

In Chapter 6, I tell you about putting stickers on your bow at the beginning and end of the bow stroke. Now that you're learning eighth notes, I want you to put a sticker in the very middle of these two stickers, which would make your bow look like Figure 8-2.

Figure 8-2:
Bow with another sticker put on.

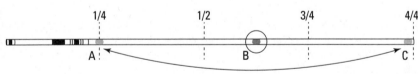

Figure by Rashell Smith

Because eighth notes are played quickly (twice as fast as quarter notes), you only use about half the bow to play them.

Take a look at Video Clip 17, which shows you how to play eighth notes, half notes, and quarter notes properly.

Rests

Often in music, you'll find a ♮ symbol, called a *quarter note rest.* This symbol means that you shouldn't be doing anything (a beat of silence) for the amount of time that it would take to play a quarter note.

Your bow should never leave the strings when you do a rest, and if you have a crossover, you just rock the bow over to the next string while resting. This sort of movement is very similar to the rocking bow drill that I discuss in Chapter 5.

Other types of rests are indicated by different symbols:

Eighth rest (½ beat): ⅞

Half rest (two beats): ▬

Whole rest (four beats): ▬

Staying relaxed with your bow hand is very important to getting a clean sound when doing any sort of rest. While you're stopped, apply a little index-finger pressure onto the bow to help it stay securely on the strings. This can help you get a nice sound when you release the bow for the next note.

Instead of being completely still on a rest, try preparing for the next notes to come. You can actually start crossing strings during a rest and can get your fingers ready for playing the next note. Use the beat of silence for preparation!

If you get any sort of screeching sound while you rock the bow during a rest, or if you have trouble starting the next note cleanly, you're having trouble with bow tension. When you start the next note or you're crossing to another string, make sure you keep the bow on the string and keep your bow grip relaxed.

Comparing the speed of the notes

Here's an exercise I talk about earlier in this chapter that you can also apply to the concept of half notes:

1. **Look at a clock or stopwatch so that you can see the speed of a second.**

2. **Clap up to 10, matching each second change with a clap.**

   There will be 10 total claps.

3. **Now do this again, but clap every other second.**

   This represents the length of a half note, which is twice as slow as a quarter note.

4. **Now clap twice in each second to represent eighth notes.**

There will be 20 total claps in 10 seconds. You can say the word "and" for the second clap or just count up to the number 20.

5. **Now try doing Steps 1 through 4 while plucking any string.**

   Are you keeping up?

6. **Try doing Steps 1 through 4 again using your bow on an open string.**

   Play each note in either direction. It won't be easy to keep up, but stay relaxed and try to get as far down the bow as you can. Remember, if you grip the bow too hard, doing this exercise will be harder. Focus on staying right on the second changes.

7. **Now for the ultimate challenge: Do Steps 1 through 4 while doing the D major scale with the bow going either direction.**

   This time, don't worry about going to 20, but instead just complete the scale up and down.

Getting Familiar with the Time Signature

As I cover in Chapter 7, each measure in music is separated by barlines and is organized in such a way that you have a specific number of notes in each measure. But how do you know exactly how many notes can go into each of the measures? The answer is by looking at the *time signature,* which is an indication of rhythm that's in the form of a fraction. The bottom number shows the division of the whole note, and the top number shows the amount of beats that you should include in each measure.

Starting out with 4/4 (common) time

Refer back to "Twinkle, Twinkle, Little Star" in Figure 8-1, which shows the time signature in a musical piece.

As you can see, the number 4 appears twice, one sitting on top of the other. The 4 on the bottom means that there are four quarter notes or four beats in each measure. The 4 on top means that there are four beats in the measure.

Do you notice that each measure satisfies this requirement? If there were three or five quarter notes in any of these measures, the music would be unbalanced and not written properly.

When you see 4/4, as in Figure 8-1, this is typically called *4/4 time.* Four quarter notes per measure do satisfy this requirement, but you can also have different rhythms/notes that still equal four beats in total.

Here are some potential combinations of notes that can help fill the requirement of a certain amount of beats per measure.

> Two eighth notes = One beat
>
> One quarter note = One beat
>
> One quarter rest = One beat
>
> One half note = Two beats

You can take any of these notes and put them into a measure, but the total beat count in each measure must match the top number in the time signature. "Cotton Eyed Joe" in Figure 8-3 is in 4/4 time. This means there are four beats in every measure.

Cotton Eyed Joe

Figure 8-3:
"Cotton
Eyed Joe."

Figure by Michael Sanchez

Now listen to "Cotton Eyed Joe" on Audio Track 10 to see whether you're playing the rhythms properly. It should take the same amount of time for you to play measure 1 as it takes to play measures 2, 3, and 4.

For the song "Cotton Eyed Joe," make sure you use the whole bow for the quarter notes and half the bow for the eighth notes. If you're at the tip of the bow and you're about to play eighth notes, play them halfway from the tip to the mid-bow. Don't go all the way back to the bottom sticker at the frog, as this is unnecessary. I call this playing organized eighth notes!

You can play eighth notes either at the bottom half of the bow or at the top half of the bow. Every other eighth note group you find in "Cotton Eyed Joe" is played on opposite parts of the bow.

Varying time signatures

You won't always find 4/4 time in music because music can be organized in many different ways. The time signature gives the pulse of the music, or the *meter*. This is chosen by the composer of the song, who wants the music to have a certain rhythmic pattern.

For example, many times you'll see music organized in 2/4 time, which means there are two beats in a measure (or *cut time*). This is often done because the piece is written to be played fast.

Other times you may see the time signature 3/4 because there are a lot of melodies that fit well in groups of three. This means you'd count to 3 when counting each quarter note in a measure instead of 2 or 4. Waltzes are examples of pieces that are often written in 3/4 time.

Take a look at the line of music in Figure 8-4. The first four measures are in 4/4 time, while the last four measures are in 2/4 time.

Changin' Fiddle Time

Figure 8-4:
Music in
4/4 and 2/4
time.

Figure by Michael Sanchez

Most of the time, you'll find music written in only one time signature, although there are exceptions. If the music changes in *meter* (the time signature changes), you'll see a different time signature marking in the music. Everything that follows from that point on will be in that new meter until the end of the piece or until you see another time change.

Keeping the Beat

The most important thing to master in a song is the notes, but a close second is the rhythm. Think about going on to a dance floor, not trying to feel the beat at all, and just running around randomly. It wouldn't look very good, right? If you're just playing notes randomly and not counting properly, your songs won't sound as good as they could, and you'll have a hard time playing with others.

In this section, I go over some ways to help you practice keeping the beat while playing your fiddle.

Using a metronome

A *metronome* is a very useful device that helps to keep meter in a musical piece. There are many different metronomes out there, as discussed in Chapter 2, but all of them serve the same purpose — to help you count and keep proper meter.

Each metronome has a function that clicks when prompted. Every metronome has the option to change the speed of the beat, but the way you change the speed may not be the same. The speed of the clicks depends on the number of BPM (beats per minute) that you set. Recall earlier in this chapter that you used the second hand to represent 60 BPM.

A good speed to set your metronome to first learn a piece is around 40 to 60 BPM. Many fiddle pieces are played much faster than this, but you have to first learn a piece slowly in order to play it fast later. Performance speed for beginner fiddle players is around 80 BPM.

Make sure that the metronome is set at the quarter-note setting. It may have an eighth-note setting or other rhythms you haven't learned yet, but don't use these settings until you build more skill. If you have the metronome set on 60 BPM but you have it on the eighth-note setting, it will actually be the same as if you had it on 120 BPM for a quarter note (double)! If you set the metronome around 60 BPM and it doesn't sound close to a second hand, it's on the wrong setting.

Think about all the numbers that represent each of the notes you've been working with. Every metronome click is considered one beat, so if you see a half note, you should wait for two clicks before you go on to the next note. If you see two eighth notes, you should play them within one metronome click.

Because everyone is at a different level regarding rhythm, it may be very difficult to combine different rhythms and use the metronome at the same time. What I suggest, if you're a newbie to rhythm, is to take a simple song like "Cotton Eyed Joe" and try clapping it with the metronome. Next, try plucking it with the metronome. Last, you can bow it, but only do this if you're sure you're doing the clapping and plucking properly.

Tapping your foot

When you're playing fiddle, you won't always have your metronome around to help. Not to mention you probably wouldn't want to perform for people when they can hear a loud click-click-click! The key is to use the metronome as much as you need and then use other methods of counting to help you.

One such method is tapping your foot. This can work well when you're play-ing a song and you want to keep that nice meter from beat to beat. You don't have to stomp your foot or anything — just lightly tap your foot or even your toe to signify a beat. You can tap your foot throughout an entire song or just during the parts where you feel you need help with the counting. If you're a newer player, you'll want to toe tap or use the metronome almost all the time or your rhythm will be off.

Some less coordinated people may have trouble tapping their foot without a metronome. With everything going on with the fiddle, including different rhythms, notes, and techniques, the tapping may be too much for a beginner player to handle. This is pretty typical, so if this describes you, just use the metronome as much as possible. Eventually, that beat will be ingrained in your head and you'll be able to tap your foot properly.

Go back to the beginning of this chapter and test out your rhythm ability at different speeds. The song "Cotton Eyed Joe" has 4 measures, which is the same as 16 total beats. This means if you were to play the song "Cotton Eyed Joe" at 60 BPM, it should take you exactly 16 seconds. Try tapping your foot to keep a nice beat while playing the song and check to see whether you were quick, slow, or just right. This will give you a clue to whether your tendency is to count too quickly or lag behind on some notes.

You may have trouble counting eighth notes because you have to fit two notes into one tap/metronome click. If you're having trouble with the eighth notes, go back to the basics and count them with the metronome. See whether you can clap steadily and hit every click on every other eighth note.

Playing at the right speed

Playing a piece around 40 BPM is a good general place to start, but your speed really depends on the difficulty of the piece. You don't want to play something too fast, either, as that can sacrifice the song's tone quality.

In many songs, you'll see tempo suggestions, which tell you how fast you should perform a piece. If a piece is written to be played fast, you won't always be able to play it fast enough, but it's something that you can always work toward.

At the beginning of a piece and typically in the top-left corner, you'll see what's called a *tempo marking.* Check out Figure 8-5, called "Arkansas Traveler," which is made to be played at a fast speed.

Arkansas Traveler

Figure 8-5: "Arkansas Traveler."

Figure by Michael Sanchez

Do you see that the song is marked *Allegro?* This indicates that the piece is supposed to be played very fast. This tempo marking suggests that a piece be played between 84 and 144 BPM.

If you're more of a beginner, you should stick to the very bottom of the suggested tempo markings. If you're more advanced, you may want to work up to the suggested tempo marking — even the highest end of it if you think you can do it!

Here's a list of some common tempo markings in music that you may see:

- **Largo:** 42 to 66 BPM
- **Andante:** 56 to 88 BPM
- **Moderato:** 66 to 126 BPM
- **Allegro:** 84 to 144 BPM

There are more than 20 tempo markings, so if you see others that aren't listed here, you can always look them up online.

Don't let your technique suffer because you're trying to play a song too fast. A lot of times when you try to do this, you'll start missing notes and you'll start gripping the bow too hard.

If you're playing a song that's meant to be played allegro, you should still start off playing very slow to master all the fundamentals and musical elements. Even if you know a song in your head goes really fast, don't let that change the way that you practice it. A good way to work up speed is by only going up one to five ticks on the metronome per practice session. Just remember — playing too slow will never hurt you, while playing too fast can.

Playing More Complicated Rhythms

Many songs in fiddle music have rhythms outside of the ones you've already learned in this chapter. If you aren't familiar (or comfortable) with quarter notes, half notes, eighth notes, and quarter rests, review that material earlier in the chapter until you feel you know it. In this section, I cover how to read more complicated rhythms that you'll find in future fiddle pieces.

Working with dotted rhythms

The first rhythm I'd like to cover goes together with another rhythm. It's the *dotted quarter note* and *single eighth note:*

♩. ♪

The dot right next to the quarter note makes the note longer than a typical quarter note — 1.5 beats. The second note you see is a single eighth note, which is .5 beat. Together, these notes equal 2 beats, and they're often seen together.

There's a rule behind the dot after any note that helps explain things clearer for those who like seeing things from a math point of view. Any dot after any note changes the length of the note by adding half the value of the note to the normal value of the note. So in this case, half the value of the quarter note is .5, and the normal value is 1. Together, the note then equals 1.5.

Often, you'll see the dotted quarter note combined with a single eighth note rest. Each eighth note rest is .5 beat. Here are the symbols:

♩. ⁊

Another common rhythm that also uses a dot is the *dotted half note.* This rhythm is a total of 3 musical beats:

♩.

Whenever you see this note, you play it one beat longer than the typical half note. You'll often see this rhythm together with one single quarter note following it, and it completes a typical 4-beat measure.

On the faster side of things, you'll often see notes in music called *16th notes.* They're played twice as fast as an eighth note and utilize a quarter of the bow per 16th note:

A single 16th note by itself would equal .25 beat, or ¼ beat.

Just as there are rests for many other types of notes, there's also one rest the same length as the 16th note called a *16th note rest:*

A more complicated rhythm in music is the *dotted eighth note.* This rhythm is .75 beat, or ¾ beat. You'll find this rhythm combined often with the 16th note. This type of rhythm is common with Scottish music and needs to be played differently from two eighth notes together. I point this out because both pairs equal 1 beat. Listen to Audio Track 11 to get a feel for the difference.

Understanding how to count by subdividing

If rhythms were all quarter notes, half notes, and whole notes, there wouldn't be a reason to count any differently from the obvious way: If you see a quarter note you count to 1, if you see a half note you count to 2, and if you see a whole note you count to 4. But what happens when you're asked to play rhythms that aren't easily counted?

Sometimes you'll come across a situation where you have to count a note that's ¼ or ¾ beat. How would you count that? The only way to do it perfectly is to consider each of these number values (rhythms) more than they actually are for a period of time so that you can count them easier. So if you multiply .25 or .75 by 4, you'd get 1 or 3. That's a lot easier to count, wouldn't you say? This system is called *subdividing.*

Everyone has a different method of counting properly, but I believe subdividing is important because it works perfectly for any type of situation you'll encounter. Sometimes you may have to read things over twice or even a third time to really understand this system, but when you get it, it'll help you in any possible situation.

Figure 8-6 shows an easy rhythm with three different counting options. Line 1 would be taken at a speed of 60 BPM, line 2 would be at 120 BPM, and line 3 at 240 BPM. If you count each line at the specific beats and count the metronome clicks properly, you should clap the exact same way for each of the lines. Listen to Audio Track 12 to understand exactly how this works.

Figure 8-6:
Easy rhythm line.

Counting											
Option 1 (best)	1	1	2	1	2	1	3	1	4	2	2
Option 2	2	2	4	2	4	2	6	2	8	4	4
Option 3	4	4	8	4	8	4	12	4	16	8	8

Figure by Michael Sanchez

I call the first line in Figure 8-6 "counting in quarter notes." This is the basic way to count that works when you're dealing with simple rhythms. The second line is what I call "counting in eighth notes." Use this when you have a lot of eighth notes in a musical passage. I call the third line "counting in 16th notes," which you use when you see a lot of 16th notes in a passage. Because the music line in Figure 8-6 has no eighth or 16th notes, counting quarter notes (the first option) makes the most sense.

The graph in Figure 8-7 breaks down all the rhythms you've learned so far in this chapter. It shows what their values would be if you counted them in quarter notes, eighth notes, or 16th notes.

Do you see where all the values equal 1? This is the base rhythm of each of the ways of counting. So, if you're thinking in quarter notes, the base rhythm would be the quarter note, which equals 1. If you're thinking in eighth notes, the base rhythm would be the eighth note, which equals 1. If you're thinking in 16th notes, the base rhythm would be the 16th note, which equals 1.

Create flash cards of the rhythms in Figure 8-7, which will help you with subdividing difficult rhythm passages. Having this subdividing system embedded in your brain is valuable and will make you a lot better with rhythm, which leads to sounding better on the fiddle. You don't want to be that guy who never knows how to count in a musical passage!

Figure 8-8 shows a musical rhythm example where you may want to count in eighth notes. This means you use line 2.

Musical Rhythm Graph

Note Name		Quarter Notes	Eighth Notes	16th Notes
Dotted whole	○·	6	12	24
Whole	○	4	8	16
Dotted half	♩·	3	6	12
Half	♩	2	4	8
Dotted quarter	♩·	1.5 (1½)	3	6
Quarter	♩	1	2	4
Dotted eighth	♪·	.75 (¾)	1.5 (1½)	3
Eighth	♪	.5 (½)	1	2
Dotted 16th	♬·	.375 (⅜)	.75 (¾)	1.5 (1½)
Triplet eighth	♪³	.333 (⅓)	.667 (⅔)	1.333 (1⅓)
16th	♬	.25 (¼)	.5 (½)	1
Dotted 32nd	♬·	.167 (⅙)	.333 (⅓)	.667 (⅔)
32nd	♬	.125 (⅛)	.25 (¼)	.5 (½)

Figure 8-7:
Musical
rhythm
graph.

Figure by Michael Sanchez

Figure 8-8:
Medium
difficulty
rhythm line.

Counting

Option 1	1	.5	.5	1	.5	.5	.5	1	.5	1	1	1.5	.5	2	.5	.5	1.5	.5	1	4
Option 2 (best)	2	1	1	2	1	1	1	2	1	2	2	3	1	4	1	1	3	1	2	8
Option 3	4	2	2	4	2	2	2	4	2	4	4	6	2	6	2	2	6	2	4	16

Figure by Michael Sanchez

Can you see how the second line makes the most sense? If you tried to count using the first line, you'd find yourself getting stuck because of all the decimal notes. Line 2 avoids all decimal notes and puts every number in a nice layout that anybody can count properly.

Because you're counting in eighth notes, the metronome beat also has to double in speed. Set your metronome at 120 BPM; each click will then represent a number value for line 2. Try clapping along with me in Audio Track 13.

Now that you understand how to count in eighth notes, consider a situation that requires you to count in 16th notes. This happens often in fiddle music, and you'll find it much easier to count many passages in 16th notes.

Use this form of counting to first learn how a rhythm passage works, but don't use it forever. You'd be counting a lot of numbers if you had to count this way every time! Thinking in 16th notes is like taking a microscope and seeing the details of something you wouldn't be able to see with the naked eye.

Take a look at Figure 8-9, which is counted best in 16th notes.

Figure 8-9:
Hard difficulty rhythm line.

Counting

Option 1	1	.75	.25	1.5	.5	.75	.25	1	1	.25	.25	.25	.25	1.5	.5	1	.25	.25	.5
Option 2	2	1.5	.5	3	1	1.5	.5	2	2	.5	.5	.5	.5	3	1	2	.5	.5	1
Option 3 (best)	4	3	1	6	2	3	1	4	4	1	1	1	1	6	2	4	1	1	2

Figure by Michael Sanchez

I've been playing the fiddle for many years, and even I could never count this rhythm line in simple quarter notes. It gives me a headache just looking at the first line! The second line has a bunch of fractions that would be very difficult to count. As you can see in the third line, the numbers are almost all in non-fraction format, and it's a lot easier to count.

Now that you're thinking in 16th notes, you want to increase the tempo of the metronome. Because 240 BPM is just too fast to hear the clicks, choose something more in the range of 180 BPM, which is technically much slower than the piece is supposed to be played. This is fine, because anytime you're thinking in 16th notes, you're breaking down the measure more. Listen to Audio Track 14 to clap Figure 8-9 along with me at 180 BPM.

The key to counting in music is figuring out what counting mode you should be in and then taking a pen and paper and breaking it down. When you begin to progress on the fiddle, you'll be able to do this more on the fly. If you're just starting out, you may even have to break down counting quarter notes, which is fine.

Chapter 9

Starting Easy with Basic Fiddle Tunes

In This Chapter

▶ Figuring out how to move your bow in the right direction

▶ Doing upslides and downslides on beginner fiddle tunes

▶ Changing keys for certain fiddle songs

▶ Practicing various kinds of slurs

▶ Understanding how to use your 4th finger

▶ Access the audio tracks and video clips in this chapter at `www.dummies.com/go/fiddle`

*L*ike many people, you may have wondered about the difference between a violin and a fiddle. They're actually the same instrument — I know, shocking, isn't it? The differences lie in the style of music played on the instrument, the techniques you use, and the types of tunes you play.

This chapter is the first where a violinist would want to stop reading if he didn't have interest in learning the fiddle. I start branching off into the art of learning the fiddle, which includes all the techniques and important aspects of doing it properly. Sit back, relax, and enjoy the ride of learning to play the fiddle that's starting right now!

Fiddlin' in the Right Direction

First I want to show you how to play a tune called "Au claire de la lune." It's a pretty easy tune that has a few basic elements of music I want you to get familiar with. Take a look at the music in Figure 9-1.

Au claire de la lune

Figure by Michael Sanchez

Figure 9-1: "Au claire de la lune."

The mark you see that looks like a table symbol on top of the first note is called a *down-bow mark*. This mark tells you that your bow should be moving downward toward the tip as you play the note. The opposite of the down-bow mark is the *up-bow mark,* which is the V symbol you can see over the second note in the song. Can you see how the bow markings are down-up-down-up-down, and so on? Figure 9-2 further explains the direction of the bow for a down or up bow.

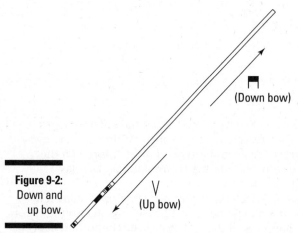

(Down bow)

(Up bow)

Figure 9-2: Down and up bow.

Figure by Rashell Smith

The purpose of down- and up-bow marks is to keep your bow movement organized. One little mistake of not playing a note or playing an extra note can make your bowing backward, so the markings are nice checkpoints to tell whether you're moving your bow the way you're supposed to. Start to get into the habit of following bow markings in a song; doing so leads to proper *phrasing* (the sound you're supposed to make) in a fiddle tune.

Now notice the little *bow-lift mark* in Figure 9-1 that looks like an apostrophe sign at the end of the song. Whenever you see this mark, you should pick up your bow and move it to the other side. In "Au claire de la lune," you should be at the tip of the bow after playing the final note, and the bow lift will bring you back to the frog to play the down bow at the beginning of the line.

Now watch Video Clip 18, where I show you the up bow, down bow, and bow lift done on the fiddle.

Play Audio Track 15 to hear how "Au claire de la lune" should sound.

Sliding with Beginner Fiddle Tunes

The first technique that really shows the fiddle style is called the *fiddle slide*. This technique creates a "droopy" sound that makes any song sound more like a fiddle tune. It's a simple technique that you can add to any note and play a few different ways. Listen to Audio Track 16, which compares a song played in classical (violin) format and then played in fiddle format. You'll notice a big difference!

The first type of slide is the *upslide,* or what I like to call the "happy slide." You can add it to any note that requires you to place a finger down on the fingerboard. It appears as a "/" symbol over the note. The other type of slide is a *downslide,* or what I call the "sad slide." It appears as a "\" symbol over the note.

The following sections go into more detail on each of these fiddle slides.

The upslide

To do the fiddle upslide, follow these steps:

1. **Pick any note on the fiddle that requires finger placement and place your finger where the note is supposed to be played.**

2. **Take the same finger and place it a half step below where you just placed it.**

   So if you picked G, you'd now place your finger where you'd play F♯, or if you chose F, you'd place your finger on E. If you're confused by what a half step means, refer to Chapter 7.

3. **Slide your finger between the two points.**

This means taking your finger and gliding it back and forth without actually picking it up. So if you're working between F♯ and G, slide your finger back and forth between these two points. You don't need your bow to do this yet, and you should be using only one finger.

4. **Now that you're familiar with the distance of the slide, place your finger in the low position.**

If you chose G on the D string, you'd put your ring finger on F♯.

5. **Get your bow ready for a down-bow stroke.**

6. **Slide your finger toward the note you chose while moving the bow.**

Doing so should create a different type of sound compared to just playing the note.

7. **Try moving your finger at different speeds.**

Doing so should create different types of sounds that can flavor certain fiddle tunes.

The downslide

To do the fiddle downslide, follow these steps:

1. **Pick any note and play it normal on the fiddle.**

2. **Aim to glide your finger a half step lower in pitch (toward the nut).**

3. **Set your bow on the strings and move your finger down toward the point while moving the bow.**

By the time you reach the end of the bow, you should have timed it properly to where the half step glide is complete. If you play a long note, the slide will happen slowly. If you play a quick note, you should slide quicker. It's all about timing the slide to match the speed of the note.

Practicing upslides and downslides in fiddle tunes

Try both the upslide and downslide techniques on different notes. Listen to Audio Track 17, which includes upslides and downslides with all the fingers. You can try to make the same sounds on your fiddle!

Figure 9-3 shows a song called "Cripple Creek," which includes some upslides and downslides. Try learning the notes and rhythms first before practicing the slides.

Cripple Creek

Figure 9-3: "Cripple Creek."

Figure by Michael Sanchez

Do you notice the repeat symbols at the end of lines 1 and 2 in Figure 9-3? This means you should play a total of four lines to complete the entire song. Listen to Audio Track 18 to hear the song played with the slides.

Another great tune that you can put slides in is a famous song called "Bile 'em Cabbage Down." Figure 9-4 shows the sheet music for the song for you to follow.

Bile 'em Cabbage Down

Figure 9-4: "Bile 'em Cabbage Down."

Figure by Michael Sanchez

This song has a repetitive rhythm of a quarter note followed by two eighth notes. If you're at the frog, you should play the eighth notes in the bottom half of the bow. If you're at the tip, you should play the eighth notes at the tip of the bow. Take a look at Figure 9-5, which shows the two areas of the bow where you should play the eighth notes in this song.

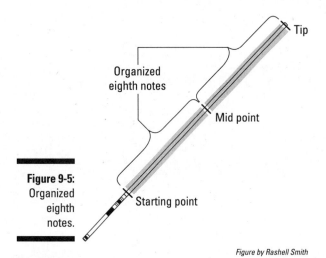

Figure 9-5:
Organized
eighth
notes.

Figure by Rashell Smith

Now listen to Audio Track 19 to hear "Bile 'em Cabbage Down" played with slides. It sure sounds like a fiddle tune when you put those slides in!

Where slides are placed is all up to the fiddler's interpretation. This freedom of choice is much different from classical violin music, which doesn't give you the freedom to play a song differently each time you play it. Fiddling is much more laid back, and I encourage you to open up your imagination to do slides differently each time.

Try adding your own slides to "Bile 'em Cabbage Down," as well as some of the other songs you've learned so far. Play it through a few times, and each time, play it a different way. Record yourself and listen to see which version you like the best!

Varying Keys in Fiddle Tunes

As I discuss in Chapter 7, fiddle pieces contain many different keys — most commonly D, G, C, A, and F. D is a great key to start with because the finger placement is the simplest to play and understand. If you're not sure about what the finger positions are for these keys, check out Chapter 7.

All the songs you've played so far in this chapter are in the key of D. The next song I want to show you is the famous "Oh! Susanna" (see Figure 9-6). It's in the key of A major. Make sure you know the finger placements for this key before you try learning the song; otherwise, it won't sound the way that it should!

Take a look at the sheet music and check the key signature. Do you see how it's in the key of A?

Oh! Susanna

Figure 9-6: "Oh! Susanna."

Figure by Michael Sanchez

Listen to Audio Track 20, which has "Oh! Susanna" played at medium speed with slides.

On Audio Track 20, I play many downslides on 1st-finger notes. I like playing a downslide on my 1st finger because the slide ends when my finger reaches the end of the fingerboard. You can do them on any notes, but this is the way that I like to play them!

Spend at least a week mastering the four previous songs in this chapter. If you're a more advanced player, certainly proceed, but make sure you have the sliding technique mastered.

Playing the Fiddle Slur

Now that you're familiar with some of the basic elements of music, it's time I show you how to do the musical *slur*. This is different from a slide — a slur happens between two or more notes, while a slide involves only one note. Slurring is very important and shows the differences among many of the fiddle styles you learn throughout this chapter.

Take a look at some different types of slurs in Figure 9-7. The slur symbol looks like a smiley face.

Figure 9-7:
The slur
test.

Figure by Michael Sanchez

The first two measures are the easiest regarding slurs. You may only be able to do these for now, which is totally fine! You can always come back to this figure to try out your skills later. The song you'll learn soon requires you to know how to do just the first two measures well. The following steps break down how to play the first four notes in Figure 9-7, which are two sets of slurs.

1. **Take your bow and set it at the contact point.**

2. **Start moving the bow at a slower than normal speed for a quarter note.**

   If you move too fast you won't have room for the second note, which also has to fit in the down-bow stroke.

3. **When you reach the middle of the bow (where you put your eighth note sticker; see Chapter 6), change to using your 1st finger for the E.**

   So in the first half of your bow stroke you play D, and in the second half you play E.

4. **When you reach the tip of the bow, put your 2nd finger down and start moving the bow the other direction (up bow).**

   If you didn't stop your bow at all to do this, you had perfect timing and just completed the perfect slur!

5. **When you reach the middle of the bow again, change to your 3rd finger (G).**

   When you reach the point where you first started, you've just completed two slurs!

Gripping the bow too tight will result in difficulty slurring. You want to be able to move the bow at a constant speed without having to speed up or slow down. Successful slurring is all about preparing your fingers and placing them in the right spots while the bow is moving at a constant pace.

As you move along in Figure 9-7, the slur difficulty gets more and more difficult. Here are some tips to do these slurs . . . eventually!

- ✔ **Crossing while slurring (measures 3–4):** Move your elbow quickly when you're crossing strings and remember the rocking bow drill (relaxing your arm while crossing strings). Doing this well has a lot to do with what you're doing with your right index finger, which I cover in Chapter 5.

- ✔ **Half-note slurring (measures 5–8):** This doesn't look as difficult as the last two measures, but it's played wrong very often. The key is not chopping off the time it takes you to put two half notes into the same bow stroke. Make sure the bottom half of the bow takes up two total beats and the top half takes up another two beats, for a total of four beats. Keep your arm as relaxed as possible.

- ✔ **Four-note slurs (measures 9–10):** Here you see that you sometimes slur more than two notes in one bow stroke. Having your fingers ready to go and close to the fingerboard is key to playing these slurs smoothly and in tune.

- ✔ **Slur crossovers (measures 11–15):** These crossovers take good timing and a good, relaxed bow hand and arm. As you find out in Chapter 5, it's easy to create bad sounds when you don't grip and move the bow properly. Being relaxed here is challenging, but doing so is vital to get the smooth sound you want, even when crossing and timing slurred notes.

Listen to Audio Track 21. Notice the smoothness through each section. If you aren't getting that sound, your technique isn't quite as good as it could be. Refer to Chapter 5 to find ways to get a smoother sound, and don't blame the fiddle!

So how did you do with the slurs? If you're getting frustrated with them, you're not alone — they aren't easy to do at first. Getting slurs to sound smooth and connected takes time, and it's almost impossible to do them perfectly in the first weeks or even months. Give it some time!

Figure 9-8 shows a fiddle song that has some slurs — the famous "Yankee Doodle." You can also listen for the slurs and slides in Audio Track 22.

Yankee Doodle

Figure 9-8: "Yankee Doodle."

Figure by Michael Sanchez

Using the 4th Finger

In case you didn't know, you can place the 4th finger, or pinkie, on the fiddle fingerboard too. Figure 9-9 shows how.

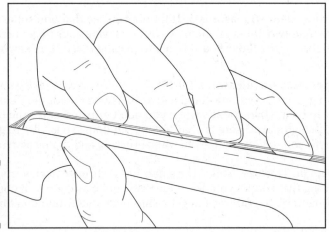

Figure 9-9: Placing the 4th finger.

Figure by Rashell Smith

You can place a sticker in this spot, which would apply to all the 4th fingers on each string. Notice how the space between the 1st and 2nd fingers is similar to the space between the 3rd and 4th fingers. For more on putting stickers on the fingerboard, see Chapter 6.

Understanding when and why to use your 4th finger

So why haven't you used the 4th finger up to this point? The reason is because it's the weakest/hardest finger to use, and it also isn't necessary to learn basic songs on the fiddle. Your 4th finger note is actually the same thing as playing the open string next to it:

- **G4 = D0:** The 4th finger on the G string is D, which should sound the same as your open D string.

- **D4 = A0:** The 4th finger on the D string is A, which should sound the same as your open A string.

- **A4 = E0:** The 4th finger on the A string is E, which should sound the same as your open E string.

So why would you use the 4th finger instead of the open string? The answer is to avoid crossovers in various fiddle passages. Right now it may seem hard to stretch your 4th finger far enough to be in the right spot, but eventually, doing so will seem much easier and will take a lot less energy than crossing over to another string for just one note.

Here are a few instances when you should use the 4th finger to avoid crossover:

D0, D1, D2, D3, D4, D3, D2, D1, D0

D2, D3, D3, D1, D4, D0, A3

In the following passage, playing your 4th finger is unnecessary because you have to cross strings anyway:

D0, D1, D2, D3, E0, E1, E2, E3

In this chapter and Chapter 10, I put the number 4 over notes to tell you when you should use your 4th finger. If you don't see a number 4, that means you should use the open string.

Grasping the fundamentals of using your 4th finger

It's important for you to understand the fundamentals of using the 4th finger. Check out Video Clip 19 for a good explanation.

It will take a while to establish the muscles in your pinkie to stretch far enough comfortably. Typically it takes at least two weeks. You should definitely watch the video to make sure you aren't restricting yourself in any way.

There are a lot of ways to cheat to find the 4th finger, which will make things a lot harder for you down the road. Follow the tips in the video to make sure you establish a great fundamental 4th finger that allows you to play very fast and accurately in the future.

Figure 9-10, "Home on the Range," is a great fiddle song that has some spots where you should use your 4th finger. Those spots are indicated by the 4 above the notes in the music. You can also hear this song on Audio Track 23.

Home on the Range

Figure 9-10: "Home on the Range."

D.C. al Fine

Figure by Michael Sanchez

Chapter 10

Getting into Trickier Fiddlin'

• •

• •

*I*f you have a good handle on the basics of fiddle fundamentals and reading music, you're now ready for the next step. In this chapter, I show you some more difficult songs, and how to make them sound good. Each song is broken down into different areas you can improve on. (If you aren't sure you're ready for this or you're still having trouble with the basics, refer to Chapters 4 through 9.)

Minding the Music's Dynamics

Sometimes, a musical piece can sound really nice if it's played softer in some spots and louder in other spots. These changes in volume are called the *dynamics* of the music. This is another element in music that's like the icing on a cake when it comes to hearing a great sounding piece.

Figuring out how to play more softly

Everything you've played so far has been considered loud — I haven't told you to play anything soft yet. So, the new concept I'm going to show you now is how to play softer than usual!

Take a look at "Fiddlin' with Dynamics" in Figure 10-1.

Figure 10-1:
"Fiddlin'
with
Dynamics."

Figure by Michael Sanchez

Do you see the *f* symbol below the music? That symbol indicates you should play loud — or a better way to explain it is that you should play normal. The reason I say "normal" is that I haven't yet talked about playing louder than you're used to. If you thought the symbol meant you were supposed to just play louder than you've been playing, you'd probably grab the bow way too tight and make sounds you aren't supposed to make! So, for the first two measures, play the song with "normal" loudness.

Next, notice the *p* symbol in the third measure. This symbol indicates that you should play soft. Try out the following steps to play your fiddle more softly and still get a good sound:

1. **Take your bow and set it on the strings.**

2. **Pull the bow about one-quarter the distance that you normally would.**

   This will force you to slow the bow speed down quite a bit. Try to still keep the length of the note the same as if you were to play it with the whole bow.

3. **Go back and forth the one-quarter distance and lighten up your index finger pressure. You shouldn't be gripping tight!**

   Do you notice a much softer sound? If not, you need to loosen things up and possibly use less of the bow.

Listen to Audio Track 24 and pay attention to the dynamic differences. Now, try playing the song yourself and see whether you can make a big difference in dynamic levels between the soft and loud parts. The more difference you can make while keeping a clean sound, the better.

In case you were wondering, *f* stands for *forte,* and *p* stands for *piano.* Many terms in music, like these two, have Italian descent. Also, you'll find the letter "m" in front of these letters at times, which means "medium loud" or "medium soft," or the letters "pp" and "ff," which mean "very loud" and "very soft." These aren't as prevalent in fiddle music as they are in violin music, but they come up occasionally. To play medium loud or medium soft, simply use a little less or more of the bow. For now, though, don't worry about working on medium loudness.

If you're struggling with dynamics, it's a sign that you need work on your index finger. See Chapter 5 for some drills to further develop this finger to put appropriate pressure onto the strings. If you find yourself getting unpleasant sounds while doing dynamics, this is a sign that you're forcing the bow with your big muscles instead of using your small muscles. Again, Chapter 5 can help you with this.

Applying dynamics to a song

Now I want you to take the fiddle tune "Old Joe Clark," shown in Figure 10-2, and put in some dynamic levels. (Remember, you have to learn the notes before attempting to put in dynamics!)

Old Joe Clark

Figure 10-2: "Old Joe Clark."

Figure by Michael Sanchez

Pay attention to the key signature of this piece because you'll have to put your first fingers in a unique position. You play measures 1 and 2 in the lower half of the bow and measures 3 and 4 toward the tip of the bow. Then in measures 5 through 8, you play this entire part soft toward the tip of the bow. This requires you to have a nice relaxed bow hold. Remember, the bow doesn't like to be squeezed hard!

In line 2 you switch off and on playing the eighth notes in different parts of the bow. Make sure you put your 2nd finger on the G string in the correct position because you have a B flat in the key signature. Your 2nd finger should be touching your 1st finger on the G string. Play the second part of line 2 soft at the frog, unlike the first line, where you play the soft notes at the tip.

After you've practiced the piece, listen to me play it on Audio Track 25. I don't take it too fast in order to help you get the dynamics into the song.

Dynamics should always be the last thing you think about in a piece; you have to learn other elements of music first. Think about notes first, rhythms second, slurs third, and then the dynamics. Don't overwhelm yourself with too much if you can't handle it yet!

In Chapter 9, I show you how to put slides into songs. From this point forward, I don't put slide marks in the songs; I want you to express yourself the way you want to. Try putting some slides into any of the following songs where you think they fit the best, and work up speed as your final touch to mastering the song. The faster the sound goes while playing it properly, the more it will sound like a fiddle tune.

Applying Knowledge to Famous Tunes

For the rest of the chapter, I help you apply everything you know to some famous fiddle tunes. For every fiddle tune I show you, I give you some things to think about, including what I think are the most common mistakes for each song. I break up my tips into five main parts, as follows:

The notes: Every piece needs to be in tune and have proper finger placement. I focus on the song's notes and where you may make common mistakes. If you're struggling in this area, see Chapter 7.

The rhythm: You can do many things incorrectly in a piece regarding the rhythm. I give you some tips to help master the rhythm of each of the songs. If you're struggling in this area, check out Chapter 8.

The slurs/slides: Slurs are very important in a song but are tricky to do at times. I help you get the best tone out of your slurs and offer some suggestions regarding a few places to slide.

The dynamics: In this chapter, I explain how to play louder and softer in a piece. I give you some tips on how to do this for each song.

The tone: Here I help you get the best overall sound out of each piece. I talk about places where you may struggle to keep your bow grip relaxed and why you may be making some bad screeching sounds in certain areas.

Don't expect to play these songs perfectly the first day you start working on them. Building a good sound takes time. Even if you've played other songs well in the past, that doesn't mean you'll get a great sound out of new songs right away. Patience and practice are the key to success!

I recommend you always work on technique in the first part of your practice session and then work on at least one or two pieces in the second half of your practice session. You should spend an average of between one and two weeks on pieces like the ones in this chapter. If you're a more advanced player, you may be able to fly through them, but you should work on any song that first challenges you for at least a week.

"America the Beautiful"

I start out with the famous "America the Beautiful," shown in Figure 10-3.

America the Beautiful

Figure 10-3: "America the Beautiful."

Figure by Michael Sanchez

The notes: This song is in the key of C, which means your fingers will follow the C major pattern. Make sure your 1st and 2nd fingers are touching on the A and D strings; these are both half steps. An example of this is in the third measure, when the F note follows the E note. Later in the song, you have an accidental C♯ in measure 7, which you should play with the 2nd finger next to your 3rd finger on the A string.

The rhythm: This piece has many dotted quarter note rhythms. (If you need a refresher on how to count these rhythms properly, see Chapter 8.) Each time you get to a measure that has a dotted quarter note, you should count it in eighth notes. For example, in measure 1, count 123-1-12-12. This pattern comes up quite a few times in the song. Make sure you count rests properly in this song and also that you don't cut half notes too short.

The slurs/slides: This piece has no written slurs, which makes things a bit easier to learn. My suggestion is to put upslides on any of the long notes in the song, which will make the tune sound more fiddle-like.

The dynamics: This piece is designed to be played loud or at a normal volume. Use the whole bow whenever possible to get a nice loud tone.

The tone: Make sure you pay attention to the 4th finger marks in this song; they're important to the tone of the piece. Relax your bow grip and make sure you don't tense up when you have the quick eighth notes. Start off slow enough so that you can learn the song well and then work up speed.

Now listen to the final result of "America the Beautiful" on Audio Track 26.

"Amazing Grace"

Another famous tune I want to show you is "Amazing Grace." Take a look at the sheet music in Figure 10-4.

Amazing Grace

Figure 10-4: "Amazing Grace."

Figure by Michael Sanchez

The notes: "Amazing Grace" is in the key of G, which means any F notes in the song would be played sharp. Because no F notes are in this piece (refer to Figure 10-4), this song is similar to playing in the key of C. In the first measure, watch your finger spots going from B to G and then back to B again. I suggest leaving your 1st finger (B) down while going to the G; picking it up isn't necessary. Because your bow will be moving quickly back and forth, try matching these notes with the tuner before attempting to do the slur.

The rhythm: This song has three main types of rhythms: quarter notes, eighth notes, and half notes. Each of these rhythms needs to be a certain length, so make sure you count them properly. If you are unsure how long they should be played, refer to Audio Track 27. Use half the bow for the eighth notes, the whole bow for the quarter notes, and make sure you move the bow slower for the half notes which are twice as long as a quarter note. Also notice two D notes that are tied together in the first line, and two G notes that are tied similarly in the second line. Hold each of these ties for 5 total beats (the same amount of time that it would take to play 5 quarter notes).

The slurs/slides: In the first measure, the slur between the B and G is tricky. Make sure you don't tense up your bow hand to do this, and keep a relaxed shoulder. I suggest doing this passage over and over until you feel you're playing it cleanly. Slide the second note (G) and some B notes in the piece. You can also slide the long D at the end of the line.

The dynamics: The sheet music has you playing the notes in this song loud, so make sure you use the entire bow. You can use less bow for the slur, but make sure you use more bow than you probably feel comfortable using. Doing so will make the slur smooth, clean, and loud.

The tone: To get a nice clean sound, it's important that you work on the tough slur and use as much bow as possible. If you're getting some squeak sounds or bow bounces, refer to Chapter 5 for help in fixing whatever it is you're doing incorrectly. Bad sound is almost always caused by bow tension.

Now listen to "Amazing Grace" on Audio Track 27.

"Little Brown Jug"

The next song is "Little Brown Jug," shown in Figure 10-5. You'll know it when you hear it.

Here's the five-part breakdown for "Little Brown Jug" to help you through it:

The notes: This piece requires a bit of jumping around between fiddle strings, so make sure you have a grasp of the notes. Figure 10-5 shows that the song is in D. It's very easy to dip your hand when going over the E string, so make sure you keep your knuckles up. I suggest matching up any E string notes with the tuner. Also, make sure you don't ignore all the spots where you see the number 4 over the note. This means to play your 4th finger instead of an open string.

The rhythm: This song has a lot of 16th notes. If you aren't sure how to count them, see Chapter 8. You can always take the song slow so you aren't caught off guard when you get to all the 16th note parts. Any quarter note in the piece is the same length of time as four 16th notes, so make sure to hold them long enough.

Little Brown Jug

Figure 10-5: "Little Brown Jug."

The slurs/slides: "Little Brown Jug" has no slurs, but you can put a fair number of slides in the song. Moving your finger as quickly as possible through any slide will give the piece a certain sound that fits it well. It's difficult to slide on any 16th note, so try to slide on some of the eighth and quarter notes.

The dynamics: This song is supposed to be played loud at the beginning and then soft in measures 5 to 8. Remember to use a little bit of bow and press down less with your index finger to get a softer sound.

The tone: You won't be able to use the whole bow for each note in this song, but you can try to guide the bow as much as possible with your index finger for a quick, clean sound. This will help you play fast and efficiently.

A good practice habit to get into is to attempt to memorize any piece. Because "Little Brown Jug" isn't very long, it's a good choice to play repeatedly and then attempt to memorize and play it. What's nice about memorizing a piece is that it allows you to concentrate more on your technique while playing the song. Memorizing a piece also helps with performing if you ever feel up to it.

Now listen to "Little Brown Jug" played at a slow speed on Audio Track 28. If you feel you're doing all the elements of playing properly and getting a good sound, start working with the metronome to build speed.

"Turkey in the Straw"

Now it's time to learn the bluegrass piece called "Turkey in the Straw." If you don't know this one, I'd be really surprised. Take a look at the sheet music in Figure 10-6.

Take your time on this song; it has a lot of things to learn and master.

> **The notes:** There are many versions of this song in different keys; I chose a harder version for you. This version is in the key of F. Make sure you keep your knuckles up in this piece and don't reach toward notes with your left hand. If you aren't sure what this means, review the fundamentals of the left hand in Chapter 6. Watch those low notes and don't dip your hand back to play them. Also pay attention to the 4th finger marks in this song. There are spots where 4s should be played, while in others it's okay to use open strings. Using 4s in the spots that I recommend will help you from crossing strings unnecessarily.

Turkey in the Straw

Figure 10-6: "Turkey in the Straw."

Figure by Michael Sanchez

> **The rhythm:** This song has a tricky rhythm in many spots, where the eighth note lies on off beats of a measure. An example of this would be in measure 5, where you see an eighth note at the beginning of the measure, followed by a quarter note. To do this properly, you need to move your bow quickly for the single eighth note, and make sure you get the bow far enough so that you can play the following quarter note in the up bow. If you are unsure how to play this rhythm, I suggest referring to the second half of Chapter 8, which breaks down rhythms like this in detail. You can also listen to Audio Track 29 if you prefer to just hear what it's supposed to sound like.

The slurs/slides: This song has some slurs to do after you learn the notes. Pay attention to the bow markings to see whether you missed a note or slur in the song. If you aren't sure what bow markings are, check out Chapter 9. In one spot, you have to cross strings while slurring, so make sure you have a relaxed shoulder.

The dynamics: Some fiddle songs, like this one, won't have a dynamic marking. This means that there are no indicators for you to play either loud or soft. If this is the case (like in this song), you should lean on the side of playing loud.

The tone: Staying in good parts of the bow is key to good tone in the song. With the eighth notes being in tricky spots, it's easy to navigate the bow to the frog, close to where your bow hold is. You will find it a lot harder to create a clean sound at the frog, so focus on using your index finger to adjust the bow to stay in the range discussed in Chapter 5. This chapter also has great tutorials on how to move the bow quickly, which is really helpful in the tricky eighth note spots.

Ready to hear how this song is supposed to be played? Listen to Audio Track 29 to hear the song played at a slow speed.

"Slurrin' Dixie"

The final song I want you to learn completes your journey through famous and popular songs that every fiddle player should know. It's called "Slurrin' Dixie" — check it out in Figure 10-7.

This is my unique arrangement of the popular fiddle tune "Dixie." I tried to include lots of the elements I've gone over so far in this book, all in this one song. Good luck, and here are some tips:

The notes: The key isn't too bad; the song is to be played in D major. Make sure you watch your 2nd fingers. This song has a lot of 4th fingers to watch out for. Don't skip over them!

The rhythm: The rhythm is somewhat challenging in this song, but it's not too bad if you know the song.

The slurs/slides: This is by far the hardest tune I've put together for you regarding slurs. Most arrangements aren't as full of slurs as this one — now you see why I titled it so! Learn the song first with no slurs and then go ahead and challenge yourself by trying to do the slurs. You need to have excellent technique to get a clean sound on each of the slurs. Think about keeping the bow speed consistent and using your index finger as much as possible through the slur. You can put slides anywhere on long notes. Try sliding on the 4th finger, which sounds cool, although it's difficult!

Slurrin' Dixie

Figure by Michael Sanchez

Figure 10-7:
"Slurrin'
Dixie."

The dynamics: As you can see, the beginning of this song has both a *p* and an *f*. This means the first time you play up to measure 8, you can play it loud, and then the second time (because of the repeat sign), you can play it soft. I suggest playing the rest of the piece loud.

The tone: This is the hardest piece so far to get a good tone on. Remember, practice makes perfect, and you can't go fast until you have enough attempts under your belt. I consider this song another one in the category of performance pieces after you get the hang of it.

Now listen to "Slurrin' Dixie" on Audio Track 30.

Part IV
Working with the Various Fiddle Styles

Betty Liken

Check out www.dummies.com/extras/fiddle to find an article that offers tips on how to improve your sound with various fiddle techniques.

In this part . . .

- Discover the different types of ornamentation that give Irish music its unique sound and practice playing jigs, polkas, reels, and rolls.

- Practice the techniques that give Scottish music its heavy, rhythmic sound.

- Find out what goes into playing the old-time music that you probably associate most with the fiddle. Practice syncopated beat patterns, long and short bowing, droning, and alternate tuning to get the old-time sound.

- Have some fun learning to play the bluegrass style by understanding how a bluegrass song is structured, practicing bluegrass bowing patterns, and playing chops behind a melody.

Chapter 11

Developing the Irish Fiddle Style

Irish fiddle is one of the most well-known fiddle styles in the world and is the first stop on your journey to learn how to play specific styles of fiddle. For a classical violinist, this is a great starting point to see the differences between playing classical violin music and fiddle music.

If you're a classical violinist, the biggest difference you'll find is that Irish fiddle is all about *ornamentation* — little elements that are added to a fiddle piece that make it sound unique from just the base melody. I compare this concept to decorating a house. If you just purchased a house and put nothing inside of it to decorate it, there wouldn't be much character to it, right? The same would be true if you just play the base melody of a fiddle tune without putting any ornamentation into it.

The ornaments I show you throughout this chapter are accents, slurs, grace notes, triplet runs, and rolls. These all exist in classical violin as well, but the difference is that it's up to fiddlers to learn them so well that they become part of interpreting the piece to make it their own.

Throughout this chapter, I give you my suggestions of ornaments for Irish music. But it's all up to you to put in ornaments to make your music sound cool and unique. If you're a classical violinist, this thought process won't be easy, but it will actually make you open up your brain to a different type of creativity. You'll play something other than what's written on the page, and that's a big deal for classical violinists!

Getting Started with Learning Jigs

If you've never heard or played an Irish jig before, you're in for quite the treat. The jig is one of my favorite styles of fiddle music and one of the easiest to play. This style of music started in 16th-century Ireland and Scotland as the first type of dance music. Today, jigs are very popular across the world and still popular in their countries of origin.

There are many different types of jigs, including slip jigs, light jigs, simple jigs, and treble jigs. They're all a little different in meter (some are in 9/8 time), but they're all great songs for dancing and having a good ol' time! In this section, I show you a few simple jigs out of the thousands that you can find in the world.

Irish jigs commonly use 6/8 time (see Chapter 8 for the lowdown on time signatures). This means that each measure has six beats, with some eighth notes, quarter notes, or dotted quarter notes.

Many Irish jigs have two parts. Typically, you play both part A and part B twice.

Figure 11-1, "Swallowtail Jig," is a famous jig in 6/8 time. This tune is one of the simpler Irish tunes and one of the most recognizable.

Learn the notes for "Swallowtail Jig" first before going on to the next section. Then in the next section, you take the song and put some Irish elements into it.

Make sure you pay attention to the key signature stating that the song is in D major. This means that your 2nd finger will be touching your 3rd finger on the A and D strings. If you're unsure how to play in D major, refer to Chapter 7.

Although Irish music sounds best when played fast, don't try to play any song fast when you first start playing it. Your focus should be to play the song perfectly at a slow speed. The more you play it, the faster it will get. Because you'll be adding some new elements in the next section, you definitely want to master playing the notes at a slow to moderate speed first. You can use a tuner on each note to match pitches for the first few days.

"Swallowtail Jig" has a few spots where using a 4th finger (pinky) would be more useful than an open string. Although using the 4th finger can be more difficult than using an open string, it is a good habit to get into. The places I have indicated using 4th fingers in Figure 11-1 will help you avoid crossing strings unnecessarily and is highly recommended.

Swallowtail Jig

Figure 11-1: "Swallowtail Jig."

Figure by Michael Sanchez

Accenting in Irish music

In music, an *accent* is an emphasized note, which, in Irish music, is located in spots that you try to emphasize to create a unique sound. The accent symbol looks like a sideways up-bow symbol: >. In this section I show you how to play these accents and where to put them.

To create the accent sound, you want to pull the bow farther than you normally do while still maintaining a clean sound. Figure 11-2 has a set of accented eighth notes; follow these steps to play them.

Figure 11-2:
Eighth note
accents.

Figure by Michael Sanchez

1. **Take your bow and set it at the contact point.**

2. **Play basic eighth notes back and forth using half the bow to warm up.**

   Take the eighth notes at about 60 BPM, which is two eighth notes per second. You can use a metronome or a watch.

3. **Use your index finger to move the bow faster, especially at the start of each stroke, to create an accent.**

   Going a little bit farther on the bow than the distance you went to warm up can help create this different sound.

4. **Go back and forth by playing basic eighth notes and then accented eighth notes. Are you able to create an emphasized sound?**

If you're having trouble envisioning how this works, think about what you would do in a tug-of-war match when you're first allowed to tug the rope. That initial energy you put into the first tug is sort of what you do in the beginning of the accented note.

Anytime you have to pull the bow faster, it's natural to want to grab on for dear life. You may feel comfortable using your shoulder or gripping harder to tug the bow. The key is to use only your index finger and have all your other muscles relaxed, as I talk about in Chapter 5. This is a little different from the muscles you'd use in a tug-of-war match!

The amount of bow you use on an accent varies widely depending on the speed of the note and the speed at which you're playing a certain song. You really can't stick to a particular amount of bow because of these variables.

Just remember when you have an accent to tug the bow farther than you normally would. The goal is to create a different sound from the way you'd normally play the note.

Now try to do the accenting pattern in Figure 11-3, which accents beats 1 and 4. These are the typical spots you want to accent in Irish music. Play the other eighth notes that aren't accented with a smaller bow than normal. This isn't the same as loud versus soft — you just use very little bow for the other eighth notes to make the accented notes sound more Irish. If you normally use about half the bow for a regular eighth note, use much less in this case. You aren't trying to play the notes softer — just less emphasized. The key is for the accented notes to stick out.

Figure 11-3: Irish accenting pattern.

Figure by Michael Sanchez

Using very little bow for beats 2, 3, 5, and 6 requires controlling the speed of the bow with your index finger. Here's an example of what you should be thinking:

BIG – small – small – BIG – small – small

Watch Video Clip 20 to make sure you're doing the Irish accent technique properly.

Remember everything you had to learn when you first started the fiddle? All the techniques seemed very difficult at the time because they were brand-new concepts. Now that you're adding in new techniques like accents, it's important that you review Chapter 5 to reinforce the fundamentals. Chapter 5 talks a lot about creating a clean sound by using the index finger, which is also what you should use to move the bow with accents.

Now it's time to put your accent ability to the test! Take a look at the first measure of "Swallowtail Jig" in Figure 11-4, which has the same pattern as Figure 11-3. You can do this pattern in any measure that follows, as it creates a dancing feel.

Swallowtail Jig

Figure 11-4: "Swallowtail Jig" with accents.

Figure by Michael Sanchez

Accents are considered *ornamentation,* meaning they can be added to a jig to flavor the song. If you're used to classical violin, every element of music is included in a piece, including where you should accent. In Irish fiddle, however, these symbols aren't always placed because it's left up to musicians to put in accents where they feel the accents best fit their style. Anytime you see an Irish jig in 6/8 time, you can add accents, and beats 1 and 4 are the best places to put them.

If you want to hear my version of "Swallowtail Jig" played slow, listen to Audio Track 31. If you want to hear it played fast, listen to Audio Track 32. I put accents in on every first and fourth beat.

Slurring properly in Irish jigs

One of the most important aspects of playing Irish fiddle is getting familiar with the slur patterns. This is much different from classical violin playing because Irish slurs happen in unique spots. Take a look at the line in Figure 11-5, which shows a classical violin slur pattern.

Figure 11-5:
Classical violin slur pattern.

Figure by Michael Sanchez

Now take a look at Figure 11-6 to see what slurs look like in Irish music. This is an example of where slurs often happen, but by no means do they need to happen every time. Variation is key to getting a unique fiddle sound! The spots you see in Figure 11-6 are good spots to at least start with and show you the difference between classical and Irish styles.

Figure 11-6:
Irish fiddle bow pattern.

Figure by Michael Sanchez

Creating your own unique sound is very important when getting into the Irish style. In other words, each time you play a piece, it's okay to do the ornamentation a little differently. For example, you could slur a total of four times the first time through the tune and then the second time only do it once.

Bowings are much more laid-back in Irish fiddling. You can start doing a piece up-bow one time and then do it down-bow another time. This can give different flavors to the way a song sounds and makes Irish fiddling much more flexible than classical violin.

Figure 11-7 shows one of the most famous Irish jigs, "The Irish Washerwoman." This is a song every Irish fiddler should memorize, and I'm sure you'll get asked to play it at some point!

As you can see, I haven't put any ornamentation into this jig. Listen to Audio Track 33 to hear what the jig sounds like with no ornamentation. I play it nice and slow for you!

The Irish Washerwoman

Figure 11-7: "The Irish Washer-woman."

Figure by Michael Sanchez

Hopefully, you have the notes memorized after some intense practice and are ready to put in some ornamentation. That means it's up to you to put in the slurs and accents in spots you deem fit. Here's a recap of the best spots to put in accents and slurs:

Slurs: Beats 6 and 1; beats 3 and 4

Accents: Beats 1 and 4

On Audio Track 34, you can hear a version of "The Irish Washerwoman" with a few slurs put in. This is the way that many fiddlers play this song, with the 6th beat of a measure often slurred to the first beat of the next measure.

Including ornamentation in some jigs is a little tricky. Figure 11-8 — a jig called "Haste to the Wedding" that's famous all across Ireland — is one such piece.

Haste to the Wedding

Figure 11-8: "Haste to the Wedding."

Figure by Michael Sanchez

The tricky part about putting ornamentation in this song is that the spots I showed you to put accents in are identical notes. This means you should use your index finger to press down into the bow to create a difference in sound between two notes played in the same bow stroke. Here's how to do this:

1. **Set the bow at the contact point.**

2. **Play quarter notes back and forth to warm up.**

   Take them at about 60 BPM, using the whole bow.

3. **In the middle of the stroke, ease off on the index finger pressure a little, followed by quick pressure downward to achieve the same pressure as when you started.**

   Do this while moving the bow at the same speed.

   Listen to Audio Track 35 to hear what this is supposed to sound like. Remember, the bow has to be moving at the same speed back and forth.

4. **Go back and forth a few times, trying to imitate the sound of the audio clip.**

   This is the slur sound you want to make when ornamenting "Haste to the Wedding."

Now, listen to Audio Track 36 to hear "Haste to the Wedding" at a slow speed with the ornamentation of the same note.

No jig sounds good when it's slow, trust me. When you start to get the hang of the notes and have played "Haste to the Wedding" over and over, you'll want to speed it up so it sounds like Audio Track 37. Good luck!

Playing the Irish Polka

Another type of dance music, which focuses on couples dancing, is the Irish polka. This kind of music is a little bit different from jigs regarding where the accents lie and also the time signature, which is typically 2/4. Figure 11-9 shows where these accents should be when you see four consecutive eighth notes.

Figure 11-9: Polka accents.

Figure by Michael Sanchez

The arrangement of accents in Figure 11-9 is called *off-the-beat*. If accents were placed in the opposite spots, it would be called *on-the-beat*. The off-the-beat arrangement creates a sound that is unique to the Irish polka.

Figure 11-10 shows a very popular Irish polka called "Bill Sullivan's Polka" with places to put these unique accents.

Accenting the sound of music on the off-beats is simple when you have a simple eighth note pattern, like four eighth notes in a row. In this situation, you would accent the second and fourth beats by moving the bow quicker than normal with your index finger. Now I want you to think about the timing when you accent these eighth notes (on beats 2 and 4). If you replace the measure with a quarter note to start (like in "Bill Sullivan's Polka"), you would accent at the last half of the quarter note instead of the beginning. This gives the polka a danceable feel!

Bill Sullivan's Polka

Figure 11-10: "Bill Sullivan's Polka."

Figure by Michael Sanchez

"Bill Sullivan's Polka" starts on a quarter note. Now split it into two parts:

The first half of the quarter note – Played normal

The second half of the quarter note – Accented

So the speed of the bow will start going normal speed, and then in the same bow stroke, you would speed up the second half to create an accented sound.

Listen to Audio Track 38, where I will show you what accenting on the second half of a quarter note sounds like. You can try to imitate this sound. Now listen to Audio Track 39, which breaks down how to do this accent in the first measure of "Bill Sullivan's Polka."

In Irish music, it's often appropriate to slide into notes. This is normally done on just a few select notes that are typically longer in length. Notice where I put the slide markings on the quarter notes in the song.

Now listen to the beautiful "Bill Sullivan's Polka" on Audio Track 40.

Creating a Great Sounding Reel

The most popular type of Irish fiddle style (by far) is the reel. This style is played often in Irish sessions and is called a reel because the time signature is played in "real" time, which is 2/4 or 4/4. This is different from jigs, which are typically written in 6/8 or 9/8 time.

Putting in grace notes

To create a great sounding reel, you must first understand where the accents lie. The arrangement is much different from the polka style in the preceding section because in reels the accents lie on the beat, as shown in Figure 11-11.

Figure 11-11:
Reel
accents.

Figure by Michael Sanchez

A *grace note* is a very quick note that happens right before a base note and fits well in different musical styles, including Irish reels. Take a look at the musical line in Figure 11-12. It has two grace notes, which are indicated by the smaller than usual notes.

Figure 11-12:
Grace notes.

Figure by Michael Sanchez

When putting in grace notes, it's important to understand the base structure of the musical part. Here's how to play the line in Figure 11-12:

1. **Play the musical line without adding any grace notes.**

   Tap your foot each time you play one of the notes.

2. **Now notice where the grace notes are placed on the musical line.**

   They are different pitches than the base D notes. Right before you play the first note of each measure, you should "grace" the E right before you play the D. Do this as quickly as possible.

3. **Listen to Audio Track 41 to make sure you aren't holding the grace notes too long.**

   Also, notice how the base notes are still being hit in the same spots, with the only difference being a very quick (almost sounds like a mistake) note played right before the base note.

Having your fingers close to the fingerboard is very important to play the grace note quickly. Also, having good fundamentals in your left hand is important so you don't have to work harder than you really need to. If you're struggling with the grace note, review Chapter 6 to reinforce your left-hand technique.

Figure 11-13 is an Irish reel called "The Mason's Apron." This song has some grace notes and includes some of my suggested slurs.

This piece has a lot of tricky crossover slurs. Start by just learning the base notes of the piece, and even take the grace notes out at first if you need to. The slurs and grace notes are considered ornaments, so they're just extra parts that make the song sound more like the Irish style. If you're more of a beginner player, you especially want to work on notes and rhythms first, and then the ornamentation.

The Mason's Apron

Figure 11-13: "The Mason's Apron."

Figure by Michael Sanchez

Make sure you don't skip the 4th fingers to avoid unnecessary crossovers in the song.

Now, listen to "The Mason's Apron" on Audio Track 42. Notice how the emphasis (accents) is on the off beats.

Adding triplet runs

One thing you can add to "The Mason's Apron" and other songs to add a little different flavor is triplet runs at the beginning of the song. A *triplet* is three notes that are combined together to equal one beat. So, instead of two eighth notes to start a piece (which also equals one beat), you can do a triplet run (three notes). Figure 11-14 shows how the first two measures would look if you added a triplet run.

Figure 11-14:
The triplet run.

Figure by Michael Sanchez

As you can see, Figure 11-14 also has a triplet run added to the end of the line. This shows that you can add triplet runs anywhere in an Irish piece for more variation.

Now listen to Audio Track 43 to hear how the line in Figure 11-14 should sound. Notice that the triplet notes are played a little bit faster than if you were to play two eighth notes (you have to fit three notes into one beat instead of two).

Introducing the Irish Roll with the Hornpipe

The last type of Irish style I show you in this chapter is called the *Irish hornpipe*. This style incorporates a swing-type rhythm that you haven't learned yet in this book. The Irish hornpipe is typically in 4/4 time and has a lot of grace notes and triplet runs.

The first line of Figure 11-15 shows a set of eighth notes, which you can assume as a swing rhythm in a hornpipe. Because you're assuming this is a swing rhythm, you are going to play it differently from what's written. You should hold the first eighth note twice as long as the second eighth note to create the proper swing rhythm.

In the second line of Figure 11-15, I show you the literal rhythm that should be played when swinging eighth notes. This will sound the same as what I show you in the first line. The second line can be explained as a pair of eighth notes played with a triplet feel created by tying the first two notes of the triplet and playing the 3rd note.

By seeing eighth notes in a hornpipe, you can generally assume the notes are played in a swing rhythm. You won't see it written out like I did in line two of Figure 11-15, as this is just to show you what it looks like in literal form.

It is possible to see the swing pattern illustrated as a dotted eighth note followed by a 16th note, but the swing feel is more subtle than that.

Figure 11-15:
Swing rhythm with eighth notes.

Figure by Michael Sanchez

Listen to Audio Track 44 to hear me play Figure 11-15. Both lines will sound exactly the same.

Figure 11-16, "The Derry Hornpipe," is an example of an Irish hornpipe. It includes suggestions for the Irish roll, which I talk about later in this section.

The Derry Hornpipe

Figure by Michael Sanchez

Figure 11-16: "The Derry Hornpipe."

In Figure 11-16, measures 6 and 15 incorporate what in Irish music is called the *cut-grace note*. This is simply a grace note that cuts the pitch between two notes of the same pitch. Without this grace note, the notes would tie together and not sound like two different pitches.

Measures 6 and 15 are especially tricky because you're combining swing rhythm, grace notes, and slurs. Listen to Audio Track 45 to hear measures 6 and 15 played slowly.

Because you're doing one note separately followed by three slurred notes in these measures, pull the bow as far as you can on the first eighth note. This will give you enough bow room to play the three eighth notes that follow the first eighth note.

In measures 1, 4, and 10, there's a little symbol above each note called an *Irish roll*. The Irish roll is a unique ornamentation that's very common in Irish melodies. This symbol creates extra notes played very fast around the target note. Take a look at what finger pattern you'll play based on the finger number that you see the roll over.

1st finger roll: 1-2-1-0-1 finger pattern

2nd finger roll: 2-3-2-1-2

3rd finger roll: 3-4-3-2-3

As you can see, an Irish roll starts on the base note, goes up a finger spot, goes back to the base note, goes down a finger spot, and goes back to the base note.

You want to do the Irish roll as fast as possible, and you don't want it to sound similar to the way you play other notes. Listen to Audio Track 46, which demonstrates how to play the rolls found in "The Derry Hornpipe."

Now listen to "The Derry Hornpipe" with the Irish roll played at medium speed on Audio Track 47.

Chapter 12

Scottish-Style Fiddling

People have fallen in love with the Scottish fiddling style for over 500 years. Scottish fiddling is different from other fiddling styles because of the lively and vibrant sound of the notes and rhythms. This style is a lot heavier sounding (some refer to it as "dirtier") and much more rhythmic than the Irish style that I cover in Chapter 11.

Several different styles of Scottish fiddling exist. In this chapter, I look briefly at some of them and the characteristics of each one. I also explore the various types of Scottish fiddling tunes and how to play them. At the end of this chapter you'll have a better understanding of the different Scottish fiddling styles and a basic grasp of the techniques involved.

Branching into the Scottish Tradition

Fiddles were first introduced in Scotland in the 1660s and were popular instruments for the upper class and nobility who could afford them. Soon the popularity of the fiddle spread throughout Scotland as a source of recreation and entertainment for all the Scottish people.

Like many fiddling styles, Scottish fiddling has sub-styles that originated from the main style but have different characteristics. Here are the various regional styles of Scottish fiddling:

- **Highland/West Coast:** This style is what many people think of when they think of Scottish fiddling. Marches and jigs are common pieces for this style of playing. The strathspey is also popular in the Highlands area. Don't worry — I explain the strathspey later in the chapter!

- **Shetland:** Before the Shetland Islands were part of Scotland, they were claimed as Norwegian territory. Because of this, the Shetland style has both Norwegian and Scottish influences. The Shetland style is bouncy and very energetic.

- **North-East:** The North-East style is very graceful and elegant sounding and focuses on technique and showmanship. The strathspey is also a common feature in this style of playing.

- **Cape Breton:** During the 1770s, many Scottish people living in the Highlands moved to Nova Scotia to create a better life for themselves. Some people don't feel the Cape Breton style is part of the Scottish music tradition because Cape Breton is part of Nova Scotia and not Scotland. However, the Scottish people who moved to Nova Scotia still came from Scotland. This style of fiddling is upbeat and has a good dance rhythm. Most of the Cape Breton-style of playing is accompanied by a piano.

Even with the different regional styles of Scottish fiddling, common techniques are used. Throughout the rest of the chapter, I show you how to do some of these techniques and provide a lot of music for you to learn from.

Irish fiddling and Scottish fiddling have many similarities, which is why you see much of the same music here that's in Chapter 11. Get ready to play some fun songs!

Jammin' to Scottish Jigs

Today, jigs are associated more with Irish fiddling than with Scottish fiddling, but that wasn't always the case. Jigs in the early 17th century were an important part of Scottish fiddling. *Jigs* are lively, energetic tunes typically written in 6/8 time. They can also be written in 9/8 time; these are known as *slip jigs*. Jigs have a pattern of groups of eighth notes, with each group containing three eighth notes. The first note of each group of three is accented or emphasized. However, the notes are still played evenly. You may also notice other ornamentations used, such as grace notes.

Before teaching you the Scottish jig, I first want to be sure you understand how to play grace notes. If you aren't sure, refer to Chapter 11. Playing grace notes in Scottish music is similar to Irish fiddling in that you play a quick note before a regular base note. The difference in the Scottish style is that these grace notes are a bit quicker than in the Irish style. I know this sounds crazy, as you may think that the grace notes in Irish fiddling are very fast!

Listen to the difference between an Irish grace note measure and a Scottish grace note measure on Audio Track 48 to see what I mean.

As you discover in Chapter 11, an Irish jig is a song in 6/8 time where beats 1 and 4 are emphasized. Scottish jigs are similar, except the bow patterns are a little different, and they typically have more ornaments. Take a look at "The Jig of Slurs" in Figure 12-1.

Try to play the grace notes as fast as you can. Remember, you can add them in anywhere; playing the fiddle is all about embracing your own style. The pattern of slurs is only a suggestion; you can do more or fewer if you prefer.

Don't get ahead of yourself trying to learn the ornaments until you have a solid foundation of the notes. Eventually, the more you play this piece, the faster you'll get. And this piece goes very fast!

Now listen to "The Jig of Slurs" played at a moderate speed on Audio Track 49.

Notice how beats 1 and 4 are emphasized in this tune. That's very important to get the jig feeling in a song, and the Irish style follows the same concept. Remember, it's all about controlling your index finger — flip to Chapter 11 if you need a refresher.

Another song I want to show you how to play is a jig called "Cock o' the North" (see Figure 12-2). This song is a bit tougher, with a larger variety of rhythms and slurs.

The Jig of Slurs

Figure 12-1:
"The Jig of Slurs."

Cock o' the North

Figure by Michael Sanchez

Figure 12-2: "Cock o' the North."

Now listen to Audio Track 50 and see whether you can imitate the sound I'm making with the ornaments. Can you tell it's a little bit different from the Irish-style sound?

Keeping It Real with Scottish Reels

Reels originated in Scotland and later became part of other styles of fiddling, such as Irish fiddling. Reels are played fairly quickly and crisply. A Scottish reel has an even-structured driving rhythm, and the time signature is written in either 4/4 or 2/4.

As I discuss in Chapter 11, reels accent beat 1 and 3 of each measure. This applies to Scottish reels as well. But Scottish reels differ from others in the type of rhythms used, the bowing patterns, and the quickness of the grace notes. The first song I show you is the simplest and most well-known reel out of the three I'll have you play. It's called "The Devil's Dream" (see Figure 12-3).

As you can see, I've suggested some slurs in this song. Because this tune is played very fast, you'll find that many of the notes are played separately, but it's okay to slur here and there. Make sure you accent beats 1 and 3.

Now listen to the song played at slow and fast speeds on Audio Tracks 51 and 52. You won't believe how fast this one is eventually supposed to go!

One technique that's similar to the Irish style is the *Scottish triplet.* This is characterized by three quick notes typically played before the first beat of a measure. You'll notice this in the next song I show you, "The Flowers of Edinburgh" (see Figure 12-4). This tune has a lot of ornaments added, including grace notes, slurs, and turns.

Usually, these triplets are played near the tip of the bow, starting with a down-bow. Having a loose and relaxed bow hand will help you tremendously. Review the bow-hand exercises in Chapter 5 if you're finding that you're not getting the type of sound you want from your triplet notes.

Not sure what the symbols at the end of the piece mean? These are *turns,* which I discuss in Chapter 11.

Scottish music is meant to be bold and heavy, so make sure that you aren't getting any airy type of sound when you play this piece. Really dig in with your index finger into the bow, making good contact to get that "dirty" type of sound. You don't want to squeak, but getting a thick sound is what this style is all about.

Now listen to Audio Track 53 to hear "The Flowers of Edinburgh" played at moderate speed.

The Devil's Dream

Figure 12-3: "The Devil's Dream."

Figure by Michael Sanchez

The Flowers of Edinburgh

Figure 12-4: "The Flowers of Edinburgh."

Figure by Michael Sanchez

Perfecting the Strathspey with Scottish Snaps

The *strathspey* is a dance tune in 4/4 meter that usually includes the Scottish snap. Many times it occurs in a major key. The strathspey is a type of reel, but played much slower. However, some styles, including the Cape Breton style, play strathspeys much quicker.

One of the most common rhythms used in Scottish fiddling is the *Scottish snap,* also called the *Lombard rhythm.* The Scottish snap consists of 16th notes and dotted eighth notes. Because the Scottish snap is a quick rhythm, you should make only a small movement with your bow hand, using only the small muscles in your bow hand to achieve the correct sound (just a flick of your wrist and fingers). Because the rhythm is quick, it's also important to keep your bow hand relaxed and not tense.

The Scottish snap is much different from anything in Chapter 11. Take a look at the line in Figure 12-5.

Figure 12-5:
Musical
line with
the Scottish
snap.

Figure by Michael Sanchez

Scottish music has a lot of Scottish snaps. One way to get the hang of them is to listen to Audio Track 54, but you can also refer to Chapter 8, which talks about how to count this sort of rhythm, thinking in 16th notes.

Can you hear the bite I'm playing in this audio recording at the beginning of each measure? This is the style you want to include in Scottish music compared to other styles. It's very harsh sounding at the beginning of many strokes and has quick up-bow strokes.

You may have trouble playing the 16th notes in Figure 12-5 fast enough. It's all about having a relaxed hand and not forcing the fast notes with your big muscles. See Chapter 5 for a refresher on *not* using your big muscles. This is important to be able to do the Scottish snap most effectively.

In Figure 12-6, you can put the Scottish snap into the strathspey style with "Boyne Strathspey."

If you've never played the dotted eighth rhythm before, this song will be hard for you. If the rhythm isn't hard for you, try to put the harshness into the notes. You can lift the bow off the strings and land harshly, especially when you're playing beat 1 of each measure.

Now listen to "Boyne Strathspey" played slow and then fast on Audio Tracks 55 and 56.

Boyne Strathspey

Figure 12-6: "Boyne Strathspey."

Figure by Michael Sanchez

Playing Marches with Driving Up-Bows

Marches are fun tunes to play. They can be played fast or slow, but all have a steady beat. Many fiddle marches are actually pipe marches that have been adapted to play on the fiddle.

One thing that's unique to Scottish fiddling is the *up-bow* technique. Getting a harsh and full sound by pressing into the string is key. It's also very appropriate to move your up-bows farther and faster than you normally do. These are called *driving up-bows* and are unique to the Scottish fiddle style. Listen to Audio Track 57 for a comparison between a normal quarter-note pattern and the way it's done in Scottish fiddling.

The driving up-bow is an important part of Scottish fiddling — especially the Cape Breton style. Instead of pulling the bow up and down, this style focuses on just moving the bow up. If you're reading a piece of Scottish music, you may see several notes in a row that should be played with up-bows. The focus on the driving up-bows helps to accent the music, which is another characteristic of this style of fiddling.

Figure 12-7, "The Barren Rocks of Aden," is a march on which you can include driving up-bows. Keep in mind that you can include driving up-bows on all the tunes you've learned so far as well.

The Barren Rocks of Aden

Figure 12-7: "The Barren Rocks of Aden."

Figure by Michael Sanchez

The bowings you see in Figure 12-7, as well as in other songs, are suggestions only. Try and create your own bowing pattern now that you're starting to see the trend. Are you noticing that the bowings are more random than in Irish music? See what you can do if you eventually memorize a tune, play it by heart, and do the slurs differently each time.

Working with Slow Airs

The final Scottish style I want to show you is the *slow air*. This style is much different from any of the styles I've shown you so far, as it's played at a slow tempo and with feeling. These types of tunes have a lot of ornamentation and can eventually be played with *vibrato* (shaking your finger to create a more musical sound), a technique I discuss in Chapter 15. For now you can just learn a slow air the way it's written, unless you know how to do the vibrato technique already.

Check out Figure 12-8, a Scottish air called "Sally Air."

Sally Air

Figure 12-8: "Sally Air."

Figure by Michael Sanchez

Do you notice the Scottish snap throughout this piece? This is still done rhythmically, the same way it is in the other Scottish styles, but it's played slower overall.

Listen to Audio Track 58 to hear what the song sounds like at normal tempo, which is slow.

If you're having trouble getting that nice sweet feeling out of this piece, you may want to turn to Chapter 5 to brush up on your technique.

Embellishing Tunes with Ornaments

You have many different ways to *ornament,* or embellish, Scottish tunes. It's very important to build these sorts of ornaments into your repertoire so that if you ever play in a jam session, you can create variations on the tunes you're playing.

Here's a list of the different types of embellishments I cover in this chapter and Chapter 11:

- **Accents:** Emphasizing certain beats to give drive to a piece
- **Grace notes:** Adding little notes before base notes, played very fast
- **Rolls:** Going up from a note, back to the note, down from the note, and back again, to add a different flavor to a note
- **Slurs:** Grouping notes together in unique ways to create a different sort of sound
- **Snaps:** Changing rhythm slightly to be in snap format instead of a basic rhythm
- **Triplet runs:** Attaching three notes at the beginning of a phrase that equal one beat of time

With all these possibilities, the sky is the limit! What I suggest you do is take any piece, master the notes/rhythm, and then begin experimenting with doing different things. Obviously, various styles have typical patterns, but you can still experiment to create your own unique sound. The more ornamentation you put into songs, the better they'll sound.

One of the most well-known Scottish tunes that can be played a number of different ways is "Largo's Fairy Dance." This tune was written by Nathaniel Gow and has been recorded in many different ways over the years. Figure 12-9 shows the sheet music for this song, with some suggested slurs.

Largo's Fairy Dance

Figure 12-9:
"Largo's Fairy Dance."

Figure by Michael Sanchez

You can listen to me play this piece three different ways on Audio Tracks 59, 60, and 61. After hearing each way, try to put your own style into it based on the ornamentation possibilities I've discussed.

Chapter 13

Fiddling to Old-Time Music

In This Chapter

▶ Introducing old-time fiddle music

▶ Getting acquainted with syncopation

▶ Driving the pulse by accenting beats 2 and 4

▶ Playing songs with short and long bowings

▶ Understanding droning and alternative tuning

▶ Access the audio tracks and video clips in this chapter at www.dummies.com/go/ fiddle

*O*ld-time music is, ironically, not that old. It's traditional American music that got its name in the 1920s. This style of music, often called *old-timey* or *mountain music,* has traditions from many different regions in the United States. States that made old-time music popular include Alabama, Georgia, Kentucky, Mississippi, North Carolina, Tennessee, Virginia, and West Virginia. Although old-time music has roots in Ireland, Scotland, and England, it's very different from the music introduced in Chapters 11 and 12.

Throughout this chapter, I go over some great old-time music and some of the main features of the style.

Getting to Know the Old-Time Fiddle Style

Some of the basics of old-time music include various types of bowings, syncopation, and shuffles. Another important part of this style is the *drone,* which is playing two strings at once. This is an exciting style to learn!

The fiddle is often tuned differently in old-time fiddling to give the instrument a unique sound.

Unlike Scottish and Irish music, ornamentation isn't as important, and many old-time fiddlers learn tunes by ear, not by reading music. They may not use a chin rest or shoulder rest when they play, and it's common for them to have their bridge shaved down flat. This allows them to hit double-stops and chords, which I show you how to do in Chapter 15.

You'll find that some of the most recognizable fiddle music is classified as old-time music. For instance, "Cripple Creek" and "Turkey in the Straw," in Chapters 9 and 10, respectively, are considered to be old-time tunes.

Old-time music and bluegrass (which I cover in Chapter 14) are similar but different in some ways. The biggest difference is in the way the melody is played. Old-time music doesn't have a lot of soloing, while in bluegrass, each player typically plays a solo, or *break,* at least once. Still, a lot of the techniques I discuss in this chapter are applicable to bluegrass.

The remaining sections in the chapter each cover a different aspect of the old-time fiddle. I start by showing you syncopation, which is very common in old-time tunes, followed by how to play accents, bowings, and some unique elements like droning and alternative string tunings.

Understanding the Syncopated Pattern

Old-time music often has an off-beat pattern called *syncopation* — when notes being played deviate in certain places from a typical beat pattern. Take a look at Figure 13-1 to see what a typical beat pattern looks like.

Figure 13-1: Standard beat pattern.

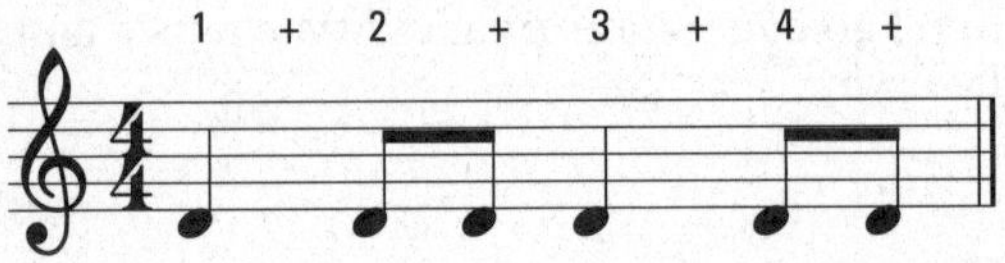

Figure by Michael Sanchez

Notice the numbers and plus signs in Figure 13-1. The numbers show when the beats are happening in the measure, and the plus signs signify the in-between spots. Also, notice that there's a note starting on beats 1, 2, 3, and 4.

Now take a look at Figure 13-2, which shows a syncopated pattern different from the standard beat pattern in Figure 13-1.

Do you notice that there's no note starting on beat 2? Unlike the standard beat pattern, the syncopated pattern has notes in the in-between spots instead of right on the beat. Beats 1, 3, and 4 are standard, but beat 2 is syncopated. The notes labeled "off" are played off the beat instead of on beats 1, 2, 3, or 4, which would make the pattern standard.

Figure 13-2:
Syncopated
beat pattern.

Figure by Michael Sanchez

Now listen to both the standard beat pattern and the syncopated pattern on Audio Track 62.

Thinking of this rhythm pattern in eighth notes is a good idea. If you're confused, flip to Chapter 8, which talks about counting rhythm in music.

Now take a look at the song "Mississippi Sawyer" in Figure 13-3 to see when a syncopated rhythm might happen in old-time music.

As you can see in measures 8, 9, 17, and 18 (the first and second endings), there's a rhythm pattern that's syncopated. Listen to Audio Track 63 to hear "Mississippi Sawyer" played at a moderate speed.

Sometimes syncopation is tough because you can easily run out of bow. The eighth note that's syncopated can sometimes cause your bow to be cramped at either end if you don't move it fast enough. Chapter 5 covers moving the bow and how to do it fast by using more of your index finger. If you're getting stuck in the syncopated parts, turn to Chapter 5 to really get a grasp on the index finger.

You can play "Mississippi Sawyer" and many other songs in this chapter in a number of different ways. Changing up rhythms and even notes in some spots is totally acceptable when you play. The way the notes and rhythms are placed is just a suggestion. Putting in slides in certain spots is very acceptable in old-time music. Any quarter note or half note would be a good spot, but you can really put them anywhere in the song.

Mississippi Sawyer

Figure 13-3: "Mississippi Sawyer."

Figure by Michael Sanchez

Emphasizing Beats 2 and 4

In old-time music, a certain pulse drives the music, unlike other styles. The driving pulse happens on the second and fourth beat of each measure, where you can accent these notes to sound different from the first and third beats. Figure 13-4 shows where the accents should happen in old-time music.

Figure 13-4: Old-time accent pattern.

Figure by Michael Sanchez

Try playing the rhythm in Figure 13-4 four times, until you get the hang of where the accent lies. You can also hear it on Audio Track 64. If you aren't sure how to do accents, refer to Chapter 11.

Now apply this technique on the old-time song "Wildwood Flower," shown in Figure 13-5.

Wildwood Flower

Figure 13-5: "Wildwood Flower."

Figure by Michael Sanchez

Listen to Audio Track 65 to hear how "Wildwood Flower" should sound at a moderate speed. After you learn the song, try to put accents on beats 2 and 4. Do you notice the syncopation in measure 7?

Many rhythms in the song "Wildwood Flower" are classified as a *shuffle rhythm*. This is when you play a quarter note followed by two eighth notes. This rhythm is very common in old-time and bluegrass music.

Mastering Short and Long Bowings

Old-time music features two different types of bowings:

  ✔ **Short bowing,** which means you play a song with no slurs.
  ✔ **Long bowing,** which means you play a song with various slurs.

The following sections cover the ins and outs of short and long bowing.

Short bowing

The song "Angelina the Baker" in Figure 13-6 is a famous song with short bowings.

Listen to "Angelina the Baker" on Audio Track 66, paying attention to the short bowings and accents.

Sometimes, as in the song "Angelina the Baker," there are dotted quarter notes that carry over the second or fourth beat of each measure. You want to put pressure down with your index finger to still get the accent sound toward the end of the dotted quarter note. You don't need to have a note start on the second or fourth beat to create the accents.

Listen to Audio Track 67 to hear how to apply accents in the first measure of "Angelina the Baker."

Now try the song "Martha Campbell" in Figure 13-7, which is also written in a short bowings format.

See if you can make "Martha Campbell" sound like Audio Track 68.

Angelina the Baker

Figure 13-6: "Angelina the Baker."

Figure by Michael Sanchez

Long bowing

After you have a handle on short bowings, you're ready to try long bowings. Get started by trying the song "Bitter Creek" in Figure 13-8.

As you can see, "Bitter Creek" has a lot of three-note slur patterns. These are pretty common in old-time music and really can be put in at many different spots. On Audio Track 69, you can hear "Bitter Creek" first played the way the sheet music is written and then played with some variations.

Martha Campbell

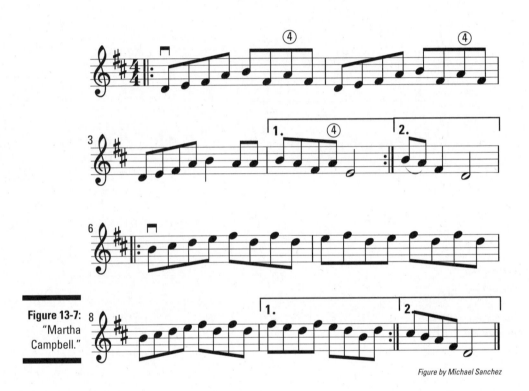

Figure 13-7: "Martha Campbell."

Figure by Michael Sanchez

Now try the song "Liberty" in Figure 13-9, which has a common three-slur pattern.

Audio Track 70 shows how "Liberty" should sound at a moderate speed. Remember, it takes practice to play it slow first to be able to play it up to speed later!

"Liberty" has a lot of string crossings that can make it hard to play the song fast. As I discuss in Chapter 5, it's important to have a relaxed shoulder to do bow crossings fast. Make sure you aren't gripping the bow too hard. Doing some of the drills in Chapter 5 will help you stay relaxed enough to play many different parts of the song.

Bitter Creek

Figure 13-8: "Bitter Creek."

Figure by Michael Sanchez

Liberty

Figure 13-9: "Liberty."

Figure by Michael Sanchez

Getting the Old-Time Droning Sound

The *drone sound* is unique to the old-time fiddle style and happens often in certain places to give the music flavor. A drone sound happens when you play two notes at the same time — an open string and the string adjacent to it, which can also be open or fingered.

Getting the classic drone sound takes some practice. Up to this point I've only asked you to play one string at once, so playing two notes at the same time will take some getting used to. In this section, I start with the fundamentals, and then I show you how to do some basic drones followed by how to play them in some fiddle tunes.

Working on hitting two strings at once

In Chapter 5, I explain the importance of applying proper technique to get a clean sound when moving the bow back and forth. Just like I show you in that chapter to stroke one note at a time, the process is similar to stroking two notes at the same time. The only difference is that your bow will be in a slightly different spot (in between strings). Start by trying to create a good sound hitting one string at a time:

1. **Set your bow on the strings.**
2. **Play the D string four times and then the A string four times with no fingers down.**
3. **Now put your bow in the center of these two positions and try to hit both strings at the same time.**

Try to get as clean of a sound as possible, thinking about the concepts from Chapter 5. If you aren't getting the same sound as you got on open strings D and A, you're probably using the big muscles instead of the small muscles. This is easy to do when you first start trying to hit two strings at once.

You don't need to apply extra force to hit two strings at once. If you apply extra force, you'll get an unwanted sound instead of a clean sound. Keep the bow speed constant and think about Chapter 5 and/or what you did to get a clean sound in Step 2.

Watch Video Clip 21, which shows you how to hit two strings cleanly at the same time.

Playing your first few drones

Now that you understand how to hit two strings at once, you're ready to start droning. Don't let your left hand tense up at all through this process, as that's a common reason for unwanted sounds.

Droning is when you play a note on the fiddle with a finger down and play it together with a string with no fingers down. When you place your fingered note down, it's important to place your finger as far away as possible from the open string that you're playing with the drone. The reason for this is that if your finger even just ticks the open string, it will make an awful noise. By keeping your finger away from the open string, you create space between the finger being placed and the open string, a process called *tunneling*. Creating a nice big tunnel between your finger and the open string creates a nice clear sound.

To further understand this, check out Video Clip 22, which shows you what tunneling looks like and gives you some important tips.

If you're struggling with avoiding hitting the open string during drones, you may want to refer to Chapter 6, which talks about left-hand technique. Having your knuckles up high and finger angles back is very important to create proper tunnels.

Next, I want to show you a measure that requires droning. Try to see whether you can get a clean sound while playing Figure 13-10. If you can't, refer back to the previous steps on getting a clean sound hitting two strings at once. There's no change from that except that you're adding in the steps of putting a finger down.

Figure 13-10:
Droning
measure 1.

Figure by Michael Sanchez

The line in Figure 13-10 shows that you should play the D string while playing all the higher notes on the A string. To do this, you have to set your bow in between the strings to hit two strings at once. A little added pressure on the index finger will help.

Now listen to Audio Track 71 to hear what the drone measure in Figure 13-10 sounds like.

You may have a bow speed problem while doing drones. Try to keep the bow moving at the same speed at all times because slowing down and speeding up makes it hard to get a clean sound.

You can also play the open string on the opposite side to do drones. This is a little bit harder because it requires you to avoid touching the open drone string with your finger. Figure 13-11 shows a second drone measure, playing open E, along with the A string notes.

Figure 13-11:
Droning
measure 2.

Figure by Michael Sanchez

Now listen to Audio Track 72 to hear what droning measure 2 sounds like. Sliding into the fourth finger creates a cool sound, but if you can't do it yet, that's fine.

Figure 13-12 shows how the hand should look when playing notes on the D string while playing open A. Try to stay as far away as possible from the string that's being used for droning (the open string). Touching it will cause the sound to be off. You'll know it when you hear it.

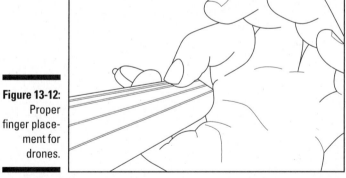

Figure 13-12:
Proper
finger place-
ment for
drones.

Figure by Rashell Smith

In each of these droning measures, you should find that the fourth finger note has the same pitch as the open string. If you notice that this isn't the case, then either your strings are out of tune or you aren't reaching far enough.

Droning can be one of the most frustrating things to learn if you don't have proper technique. Like anything else, it takes practice, so be patient! This is a great time to go back and try to do some of the drills in previous chapters. You'll see a difference in the way your drones sound if you do!

Playing drones in fiddle tunes

There's nothing like getting that classic drone sound in a fiddle tune. Now that you've learned the basics, I want you to try putting that training into action!

Figure 13-13 shows a song called "Betty Likens," which is a good tune in which to put the drone.

Betty Likens

Figure 13-13: "Betty Likens."

Figure by Michael Sanchez

Audio Track 73 takes measure 4 of "Betty Likens" and breaks it down very slowly to include some drones. Only do this when you feel familiar with the entire song first.

Audio Track 74 puts the drone technique into the song played slowly. Each time through, you'll notice a different variation.

Figure 13-14 shows another famous song, called "Whiskey Before Breakfast."

Whiskey Before Breakfast

Figure 13-14: "Whiskey Before Breakfast."

Figure by Michael Sanchez

Audio Track 75 takes the first measure of "Whiskey Before Breakfast" and plays it while droning with open A. Listen to how this should sound played slow.

Now listen to how I put in various drones throughout the song each time through.

Droning is different from double-stopping (covered in Chapter 15). The difference is that droning is playing an open string along with a note, while a double-stop is playing two notes with fingers down. As you might guess, double-stopping is a much harder technique. A lot of old-timey music has double-stops.

Tackling Alternative Tuning

Many old-time songs require alternative tuning rather than the typical way of tuning. Standard tuning is when the strings on your fiddle are tuned to G-D-A-E, with G being the lowest string and E being the highest. This tuning works for most old-time fiddle music, but sometimes you'll find other tunings that give songs a unique flavor.

The following steps show you how to do the alternative tuning D-D-A-D, which requires you to use the pegs to change string pitches. If you're unsure how to tune the fiddle, refer to Chapter 3.

1. **Make sure your strings are near standard tuning so that you have an idea of your pitch.**

2. **The middle two letters in this alternative tuning are the same as in standard tuning, so you only change the outside strings.**

3. **Start with the E string. Take the fine tuner or peg and move the E pitch down to a D pitch.**

   Use a tuner to make sure you're precisely on a D pitch.

4. **Now do the same thing with the G string, but technically, it goes down farther than what you did on the E string (two pitches).**

   So now, every string should be tuned to a D pitch except for the A string.

Pretty interesting, huh? This tuning allows a cool droning sound while playing on the middle two strings. So when you're playing on the typical D string, you can drone with the new low D string (used to be G). When you're playing notes on the A string, you can drone with the new high D string (used to be D). Figure 13-15 gives you an opportunity to practice this technique with the song "Bonaparte's Retreat."

Bonaparte's Retreat

Figure 13-15: "Bonaparte's Retreat."

Figure by Michael Sanchez

As you can see, I labeled the tuning in the sheet music D-D-A-D, which is different from standard tuning. You can play the song just as you'd normally read it in standard tuning, but now you can use the strings on both sides to create drones along with the melody. Listen to what this sounds like slow on Audio Track 76.

You may encounter many other tunings in old-time music, so it's important to pay attention to the sheet music. For example, other tunings include G-D-A-D, A-E-A-E, and A-E-A-C♯.

Chapter 14

Learning Bluegrass Fiddle

In This Chapter

▶ Playing bluegrass kick-offs and tags on the fiddle

▶ Trying some bluegrass bowing patterns

▶ Chopping behind the melody

▶ Access the audio tracks and video clips in this chapter at www.dummies.com/go/
fiddle

*B*luegrass music is an American tradition that was created by the famous mandolin player Bill Monroe (1911–1996). He formed a band called the Bluegrass Boys that started to become famous around the Great Depression via airplay on radio stations throughout the country. After some time, Monroe got his debut at the Grand Ole Opry and never looked back.

Monroe combined old-time Appalachian music with a little bit of blues and gospel music from the American South to create this very unique sound.

In this chapter, you discover how bluegrass music is structured, some common bluegrass bowing patterns, and a technique called *chops* that turns your fiddle into a percussive instrument.

Understanding the Bluegrass Structure

If you've ever been to a bluegrass concert, you may recall the scene as a bunch of musicians getting together and trying to outduel one another. The common instruments you see in a bluegrass band are fiddle, mandolin, banjo, dobro, guitar, and bass.

One of the musicians (usually a fiddler) begins a tune by playing a kick-off. Next comes the melody, which consists of a verse and chorus. The verse is sung by a solo vocalist, and the group sings the chorus, hopefully employing good harmonies.

Next, each band member takes a solo that resembles the melody and conforms to the chord structure of the song. Here's where the fiddler can really shine. Then the vocalist returns and sings the verse again, followed by the group chorus. The piece ends with a tag, which is often played by the fiddler.

In this section, I give you the lowdown on the kick-off and the tag as they pertain to fiddle.

The kick-off

Bluegrass has a unique structure that includes many parts. The first part of a bluegrass song usually consists of the *kick-off* — when one of the musicians in the group (usually the fiddler) plays a few measures of music before the song officially starts.

The kick-off must be played in the key of the actual song, so it's important not to just play any ol' kick-off. It also tells the other band members what the tempo of the song will be. Figure 14-1 shows you a few different kick-offs you can use to start a piece. You can also hear these kick-offs on Audio Track 77.

Figure 14-1:
Kick-offs.

Figure by Michael Sanchez

You have many different ways to play a kick-off, so the kick-offs in Figure 14-1 aren't your only options. Chapter 17 covers improvisation, which you can refer to in order to create your own personal kick-offs.

If you decide to do the kick-off in a group, everyone must know what the rhythm will be. In Chapter 8, I discuss keeping rhythm steady in a tune, and this is especially important when you're playing with others. I suggest tapping your foot for at least two measures so that you get a good start to the kick-off.

The famous bluegrass tag

In bluegrass, a *tag* is when one of the players closes a song with a unique ending. You can play tags in many ways, and they're typically about four measures long.

Check out some simple tags in Figure 14-2. Pay attention to the key signatures; you want to match one of these tags with a song you play in a similar key.

Figure 14-2: Common tags.

Figure by Michael Sanchez

On Audio Track 78, I play these tags slowly, so that you can start getting the hang of what they're supposed to sound like. Notice some of the slides that I put in as well for flavor.

Some tags are a little more complex, as shown by the ones in Figure 14-3.

Figure 14-3: More complex tags.

Figure by Michael Sanchez

Now listen to the audio clip of each of these tags played at medium speed on Audio Track 79.

I always recommend incorporating the droning technique with your tags. This can really end the piece well if you create a clean-sounding drone. If you're unsure how to do the droning technique, refer to Chapter 13.

The way you decide to play a tag is totally up to you, but remember to follow the key signature of the song you're in.

The Blue Grass "Fiddle" Boys

Some of the most famous fiddlers in the world got their name from playing music with Bill Monroe and the Blue Grass Boys. As a leader, Bill recruited some of the best fiddlers in the country to play music in his band. Even though Monroe didn't actually play fiddle, he still made it a very important part of his music. Some of the fiddlers who got famous from playing in the Blue Grass Boys include Tommy Magness, Chubby Wise, and Glen Duncan.

Picking Up Bluegrass Bowing Patterns

Bowing is very important in bluegrass fiddling, as it flavors the music to sound unique to the style. By combining certain notes in a bow and then separating others, you'll find certain patterns that you can generally follow in a lot of music.

The two most popular bowing patterns, which are categorized as *shuffles,* are the Nashville shuffle and the Georgia shuffle. These are both bluegrass bowings, but they're different bow patterns. The Nashville shuffle is the easier of the two; the Georgia shuffle is much more difficult to master.

Playing the Nashville shuffle

The *Nashville shuffle,* which is often called the *simple shuffle,* is a very common bow pattern in bluegrass fiddling. This is an important bowing to do properly, as it really gives songs a hoedown feel.

To play the Nashville shuffle, you do a simple down-bow stroke followed by two small strokes, and then you do an up-bow stroke followed by two small strokes. If you have a set of four eighth notes, you slur the first two and then play the next two as separate bows.

You can see what these rhythms look like in Figure 14-4 and listen to them on Audio Track 80.

Figure 14-4: Rhythms used with the Nashville shuffle.

Figure by Michael Sanchez

Do you hear how the second and fourth beats are emphasized? This is the style you should try to achieve by pressing more into the bow than usual (called *accenting*).

Playing the Nashville shuffle in "Durham's Bull"

Take a look at the song called "Durham's Bull" in Figure 14-5, which has Nashville shuffle bowings.

Durham's Bull

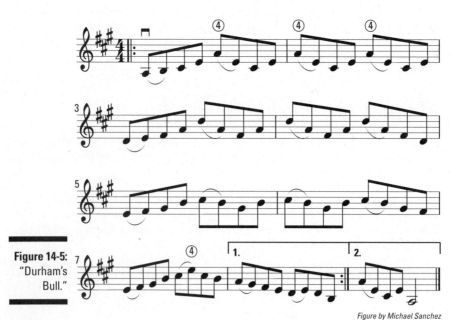

Figure 14-5: "Durham's Bull."

Figure by Michael Sanchez

Now listen to "Durham's Bull" on Audio Track 81 and hear how it incorporates the Nashville shuffle bowing.

Because "Durham's Bull" is in the key of A, make sure you don't miss any of the sharps (F, C, and G). Play the song slow to start; you'll naturally build up speed. The faster this song is played accurately, the better it will sound.

Playing the Nashville shuffle in "Bill Cheatham"

Figure 14-6 shows another famous bluegrass tune with the Nashville shuffle. The tune is called "Bill Cheatham."

Bill Cheatham

Figure 14-6: "Bill Cheatham."

Figure by Michael Sanchez

Now listen to "Bill Cheatham" on Audio Track 82. Doesn't the Nashville shuffle really flavor the piece?

Putting in your own Nashville shuffle to "Blackberry Blossom"

Now check out another fiddle tune, "Blackberry Blossom," in Figure 14-7. I want you to incorporate the Nashville shuffle.

Blackberry Blossom

Figure 14-7: "Blackberry Blossom."

Figure by Michael Sanchez

Now listen to Audio Track 83 to hear "Blackberry Blossom" played at a medium speed.

Getting into the Georgia shuffle

In bluegrass, a unique bow pattern that really brings out the style of the music is called the *Georgia shuffle*. This bow pattern accents the off-beats and has three notes slurred into one bow stroke. Take a look at Figure 14-8, which shows the bow pattern for this shuffle and where the accents and bowings lie.

The Georgia Shuffle

Figure 14-8: The Georgia shuffle.

Figure by Michael Sanchez

To get the best sound out of the Georgia shuffle, make sure your bow grip and wrist are very relaxed. Having flexibility makes it possible to get a clean sound instead of a scratchy sound with the accents. Because the emphasized note is often a single note by itself, you have to use your index finger to move the bow quickly while keeping the rest of your hand relaxed.

Video Clip 23 shows the popular Georgia shuffle bow pattern.

Applying the Georgia shuffle to "Ragtime Joe"

Figure 14-9 shows the music for the song "Ragtime Joe."

Now listen to Audio Track 84 to hear me playing "Ragtime Joe" and applying the George shuffle bow stroke throughout the piece.

Ragtime Joe

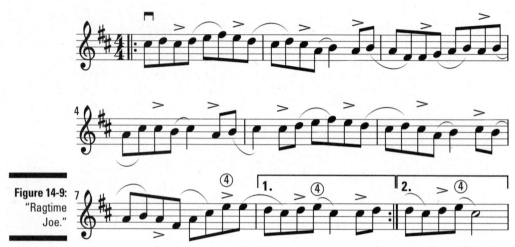

Figure 14-9: "Ragtime Joe."

Figure by Michael Sanchez

I recommend learning the notes of "Ragtime Joe" first before attempting to put in the accents and slurs. The ornamentation makes the song much more difficult to play and create a clean sound. Just play the notes for a few days without the ornamentation to get the hang of the tune.

Putting the Georgia shuffle into "Fire on the Mountain"

Figure 14-10 shows another song that uses the Georgia shuffle technique, "Fire on the Mountain."

I recommend playing this song first with no slurs, as the Georgia shuffle can really complicate the bowing. You can also try to play the entire song with the Nashville shuffle bowing instead, which is easier. Make sure that you work on the notes first though!

Now listen to me playing "Fire on the Mountain" on Audio Track 85.

Fire on the Mountain

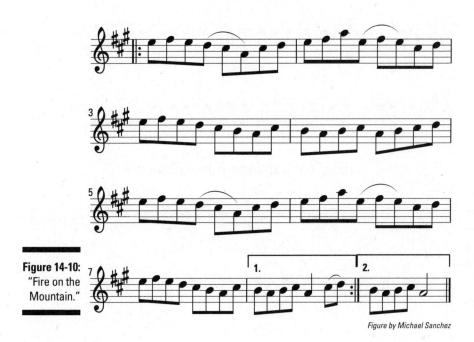

Figure 14-10: "Fire on the Mountain."

Playing Chops

The final part of bluegrass music that I want to show you how to do is the *chop*. In a chop, you play single notes or chords underneath the melody. This is basically what you would play when somebody else is playing the melody or soloing. The best places to do these chops are on the off-beats of each measure. They should be short and percussive.

Usually, when I do chops in a band, I play them with an up bow. It looks cool to continue to lift your bow back to the same point while doing a chop. Whether you play up or down bow, chops are typically done at the frog.

I show you how to play chops in Video Clip 24.

Figure 14-11 shows a musical piece with melody and what you'd play behind the melody.

Bile 'em Cabbage Down (Melody)

Bile 'em Cabbage Down (Chops)

Figure 14-11:
Adding
chops
behind a
melody.

Figure by Michael Sanchez

Make sure you keep your volume at a minimum when playing chops, as you
don't want to disturb the melody. The point is to complement the melody and
provide a rhythmic background, not be the center of attention. When all the
musicians play chops at a moderate level, it contributes a lot to the bluegrass
sound.

Part V
Taking Fiddling to the Next Level

Cacklin' Hen

Improvisation is really fun, especially when you play with someone else like a guitar player. Head to www.dummies.com/extras/fiddle for an article that covers safe notes to play over guitar chords to help you jam with a friend.

In this part . . .

- ✔ Add some more difficult fiddle techniques to your repertoire, including shifting, vibrato, and double-stops to advanced tunes.

- ✔ Get out of your comfort zone by playing in front of others, joining a jam session, or attending a camp.

- ✔ Find out how to create tunes by understanding improvisation and get an introduction to the world of electric fiddles.

Chapter 15

Shifting, Vibrato, and Double-Stops

In This Chapter

▶ Playing in second and third positions

▶ Adding flavor to your sound with vibrato

▶ Developing your double-stop skills

▶ Access the audio tracks and video clips in this chapter at www.dummies.com/go/
fiddle

A re you ready to take your fiddling skills up a notch? In this chapter, I introduce you to shifting, vibrato, and double-stops. When you get through with this chapter, you'll have a bunch of tricks up your sleeve to apply to the fiddle!

Make sure you have a good handle on the basics covered in Chapters 3 through 6 and Chapters 9 and 10 before you attempt the techniques in this chapter. You need solid fundamentals before you can really start to add some of these new techniques.

Changing Positions by Shifting

So far, all the songs I've gone over in this book have been in what's called the *first position*. This refers to the standard position of your left hand on the neck of the instrument.

The range in first position is from the open G string (the lowest note you can play) all the way up to B on the E string (the highest note you can play in that position). Sometimes you'll see notes that are a little bit higher than first position that require you to move your hand up, or *shift*. A couple of the notes that exceed this range are C and D on the E string, which are shown in Figure 15-1. You don't see these notes often in fiddle tunes, but you have to be prepared when they do come up.

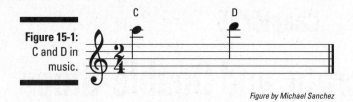

Figure 15-1:
C and D in
music.

Figure by Michael Sanchez

Now take a look at the diagram in Figure 15-2, which shows you where these
notes are located on the fingerboard.

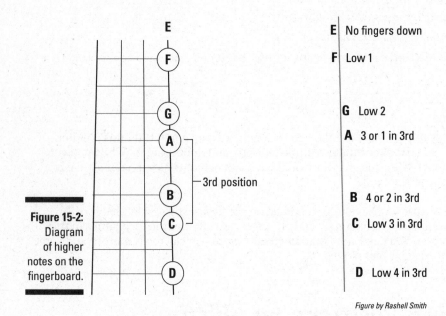

E	No fingers down
F	Low 1
G	Low 2
A	3 or 1 in 3rd
B	4 or 2 in 3rd
C	Low 3 in 3rd
D	Low 4 in 3rd

Figure 15-2:
Diagram
of higher
notes on the
fingerboard.

Figure by Rashell Smith

Moving into second and third positions

To be able to play the C and D notes, you need to have your hand in a position other than first position. To help reach the C, you can go into second
position, and to reach the D, you can go into third position.

I recommend focusing first on third position, as it covers not just C but C and
D both. If you shift into second position, you may find that you can't reach
the D without excessive stretching of the fourth finger, but shifting into third

covers both the C and the D. You'd think that learning second position first would make more sense, but trust me that learning third position will be much more helpful!

You still need to understand where both the second and third positions are. Here's a guide:

1. **Grab a tuner and make sure your E string is tuned properly.**

   If you're unsure how to tune, see Chapter 3.

2. **Play all the notes in first position on the E string in the key of C (no sharps or flats).**

   The notes are F with your 1st finger, G with your 2nd finger, A with your 3rd finger, and B with your 4th finger. Match these notes with the tuner.

3. **Now move your thumb and 1st finger up to where your 2nd finger played G.**

   This is *second position,* which allows you to reach one note higher with your 4th finger (C). The notes to match with the tuner are G, A, B, and C.

4. **Next, move into third position by moving your 1st finger and thumb where your 3rd finger originally played A.**

   The notes you can match with the tuner are A, B, C, and D.

A good way to practice these positions is to play the C major and D major scales. Both of these sets of notes bring you into the high C and D notes I've been talking about. In the D major scale, you actually play C♯, which is a half-step higher than C. Follow the fingerings in the music in Figure 15-3 to shift from first position to third position.

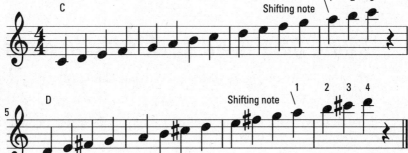

Figure 15-3: C major and D major scales in two octaves.

Figure by Michael Sanchez

Confused about all this shifting stuff? You aren't the first! Shifting is one of the tougher concepts to learn because it's a completely different way to find notes. Watch Video Clip 25, which shows me playing the C major and D major scales, to see how to shift your hand.

In the C major scale, your 2nd and 3rd fingers should be touching in third position (B and C). In the D major scale, your 3rd and 4th fingers should be touching (C♯ and D).

As you shift into second or third position, move your whole hand, especially the thumb. Moving your thumb is very important to find exactly what position you're in on the neck. Also, make sure you don't grip the neck too hard or shifting will be harder.

Have you ever noticed that the raised marks (frets) on a guitar fingerboard get smaller and smaller from top to bottom? This concept is the same on the fiddle — it's just invisible because the fiddle has no frets. So, a space between notes in third position is slightly shorter than a space between notes in first position. If you want to really get the concept of this, play C and D in third position (on the E string) and compare that to C and D in first position (on the A string). See how the spacing is slightly different? This will take time to master, as it's all muscle memory.

Are you wondering why you can't just stretch for these notes in first position? When songs start speeding up, you'll find that it takes too much time to stretch for a C or D note on the E string. Also, when you stretch you're more likely to not hit the notes in tune. Your playing will be much more consistent if you shift the hand.

Violin music has a lot more spots where you'll need to shift than the fiddle music has. Some violin songs require you to go as high as 11th position. Yikes! You may be feeling glad you chose to learn the fiddle over the violin.

Trying your hand at shifting in a song

"Song of Christy" in Figure 15-4 requires some shifting of your hand into third position.

Now listen to "Song of Christy" played at moderate speed on Audio Track 86.

Song of Christy

Figure 15-4: "Song of Christy."

Figure by Michael Sanchez

Developing the Perfect Vibrato

Creating a good fiddle sound starts with learning the basics of playing. But after you get the basics down, what can you add to make the music sound even better? In this section, I show you how to do the *vibrato* technique, which is basically the rapid fluctuation of pitch produced on a sustained note by a back and forth movement of the left hand.

Most musical instruments, including the human voice, have the ability to do vibrato. Think about opera singers when they hold a note for a long period of time; they aren't just singing the pitch but going up and down rapidly with their voice around that note, almost as if their voice is vibrating on that one note. Any musical sound can be improved and given flavor by applying this technique.

To give you a better idea of what vibrato is, listen to a musical phrase with vibrato and then without vibrato on Audio Track 87.

Vibrato isn't easy. In fact, it's one of the most difficult techniques to learn on the fiddle, and many people struggle with it. Throughout this section, I give you tips on how to do it properly, but remember that it will take patience and time. This process can only be done well if done one step at a time over a period of a couple of months.

Moving your hand consistently

The first thing you need to understand with vibrato is that it's all about consistency. This means that every movement that you make with your hand back and forth should be exactly the same, with no variation in the distance or speed. Audio Track 88 shows what I mean by consistency versus inconsistency.

One problem you'll face is that you'll want to move your hand too quickly, which is the worst thing you can do. Although vibrato sounds best when you master a quick movement, it's virtually impossible to do at first. You need to make slow consistent movements, and over time, the speed of the vibrato will increase. Forcing the speed is not good.

Choosing your wrist or forearm to create the vibrato movement

There are two different ways to create vibrato movements:

- ✔ Using your left-hand wrist
- ✔ Using your left forearm

Which one you choose is totally up to you; some people find one way easier than the other. Personally, I find forearm vibrato to be easier to do consistently than wrist vibrato. In my opinion, forearm vibrato is safer if you want to develop a consistent, beautiful vibrato, but either one takes time and practice. The guide in the next section is for forearm vibrato, but you can also try to imitate those movements with your wrist.

Whatever method you choose, never combine the movements of both the forearm and the wrist — it's either one or the other.

The statement I just made about vibrato can be controversial. Some of the best fiddle players in the world do wrist vibrato, but keep in mind that they've spent a lot of time mastering the movements with the wrist. You can be successful with either one, but not forcing the speed too soon and maintaining consistency is key in both types of vibrato. Don't choose wrist vibrato just because you can move your wrist faster — choose whichever one comes naturally to you, and stick to it.

Laying a foundation with proper arm movement

A good way to start with the forearm vibrato is to shake someone's hand. When you do this, you don't move your wrist or fingers, do you? It would be a little creepy if you were to move your fingers in a handshake! The movement you make with your forearm and hand during a handshake is very similar to the movement of vibrato, only your arm is vertical instead of horizontal.

Now follow these steps to help lay the foundation for forearm vibrato. This process doesn't add the bow into the equation yet — doing too much at first can be too challenging.

1. **Set up your left hand properly by putting your thumb in the proper spot on the fingerboard, positioning your hand in a high position, and turning your hand so that it's an inch away from the neck (refer to Chapter 4 if you need a refresher).**

   Take a look at this hand position in Figure 15-5.

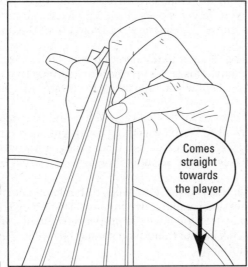

Comes straight towards the player

Figure 15-5: Proper position of the left hand.

Figure by Rashell Smith

2. **With a loose hold on the fingerboard, move your hand toward you and away from you very slightly but don't slide your thumb — only rock your thumb.**

Make sure you maintain your hand position. Each movement back and forth should go about a centimeter and should go at the same speed forward and back. A good speed to start with is to complete two movements in one second. This is probably a lot slower than you'll want to go, but try it anyway!

If you're holding the fingerboard too tight, you'll have a hard time moving your hand for vibrato. It's important to have a loose hold, so make sure you're holding the fiddle correctly with your chin and shoulder. Otherwise, you may rely too much on your hand to hold the fiddle, which can restrict movement of the vibrato. See Chapter 4 if you need a refresher on the correct way to hold your fiddle.

3. **Look at your hand and try to bring it directly toward you back and forth.**

   The incorrect movement is opening up your hand instead, which will seem more natural to you. This is the hardest and most awkward movement, and it takes time to master.

4. **When you feel like you've mastered the proper movement of your hand, put a finger down on the fingerboard while doing the same movement as described in the previous steps.**

   The finger that you just put down should rock back and forth like a rocking chair. Make sure the finger never slides, but only rocks. Because your forearm is moving, your finger moves along with it. You should never force your finger to move. Remember what I said about the handshake?

Was that process confusing? If so, watch Video Clip 26, which will guide you through the steps one by one. This is the first part on learning how to master vibrato. In the next section, I show you how to apply vibrato with the bow.

Developing a consistent vibrato takes a lot of patience and practice. Like anything else, you may want to learn everything overnight and rush through the process. If you really want to create a great sounding vibrato though, the process in Video Clip 26 is what you should follow.

I suggest working through this process for a week or two minimum, before and after each practice session for about five minutes. Don't move on to the next section until you really feel you have the proper movements, which takes time. Take a look at this checklist of things you should be thinking about when doing the first steps of vibrato:

   ✔ Is my hand relaxed?

   ✔ Is my hand in the proper position, including my thumb and knuckles up high?

✔ Am I holding the fiddle properly with my chin and shoulder?

✔ Am I going slow enough so that I'm able to create consistent movements?

✔ Are my fingers rocking instead of sliding?

✔ Am I being patient and understanding the process?

Putting the bow together with vibrato

To begin this section, I want you to try patting your head while rubbing your stomach at the same time. Do you notice that your hands want to do similar movements instead of doing separate things? It's a lot easier to do one thing with both hands than to do two different things with your hands at the same time. This is why putting the bow together with vibrato is so tough. Your hands will want to do similar things, which is totally incorrect if you want to do vibrato properly.

As I go over in Chapter 5, your right hand should do very specific things when pulling the bow back and forth. Your index finger should be guiding the bow along, while your left-hand fingers should be pressing down on the string. Everything from that chapter applies when putting vibrato together with bowing. Nothing changes, but you may find it difficult to keep your right hand relaxed while moving the bow with vibrato.

To start putting vibrato together with the bow, follow these steps:

1. **Play the notes on the two lines in Figure 15-6, focusing on using the entire bow throughout this process.**

   Play the piece at 60 BPM, or two eighth notes per second. The goal is to try to create a similar sound to what vibrato should sound like.

Figure 15-6: Vibrato music lines.

Figure by Michael Sanchez

As you play the line in Figure 15-6, you shouldn't have much trouble putting the correct number of notes per bow (four or eight). Unfortunately, as you go into the next step, it won't be as easy. In vibrato you may find yourself doing seven movements because it's easier to skip the last movement needed to make the vibrato consistent (seven instead of eight). Comparing the musical line in Figure 15-6 to vibrato can help you think about the consistency you need when you start moving the bow.

2. **Imitate the sound you just made with the G/F♯ with your 3rd finger vibrato on the D string.**

   Although the sound shouldn't be exactly the same, the concept of how the vibrato goes back and forth is very similar. Try to do four vibrato movements per bow or eight vibrato movements per bow, making sure you aren't missing any of the movements.

   Most students try to make the vibrato movements back and forth as fast as they can and have no organization. When you do G/F♯ and are actually following a musical line, you're following an organized structure (you aren't just doing as many G/F♯s as you can).

   Using the whole bow is tough when you're doing vibrato because your hand will want to tense up.

3. **Focus on keeping your bow movement consistent through the process of doing the vibrato movements.**

   This may be more difficult to do toward the end of the bow, especially if you haven't worked a lot with your index finger. Your bow needs to move at the same speed back and forth to really get a smooth sounding vibrato. Check out Chapter 5 to really get a grasp on this.

   Being relaxed while playing at the tip is pretty difficult in general, and now that you're doing this with vibrato, it's going to be that much more challenging. Vibrato brings a whole new aspect to tension that you haven't seen before, and you may need to do some of the drills again from Chapter 5.

Try this process with all your fingers on different strings. Mix it up; you want to master this movement with any finger down. Watch Video Clip 27 to see these steps in action.

Doing vibrato with fingers 1, 2, and 3 is much easier than with the 4th finger (pinkie). You may find that your hand tenses up more than usual when you put your 4th finger down. You can avoid this by laying your 4th finger down very gently on the fingerboard. This will help you establish a good moving vibrato with your 4th finger.

After you build enough skill, you may be able to do 16 movements of vibrato per bow, but just remember how important it is to do 16 and not 15. That last little movement is the hardest one to get because you'll probably be more focused on moving a finger to change the note. This is a timing thing that's easier to do when you're doing eight or four movements/notes per bow.

Listen to Audio Track 89 to hear me going back and forth between the F#/G and the vibrato movement. Try to imitate the exact sounds I make.

It's helpful to a lot of people to understand the process of how vibrato develops over time. It's kind of like understanding how a baby can only speak so many words in the first few years of life but over time is able to speak fluently and be easily understood. Listen to Audio Track 90 to understand the progression that you'll see over time if you start by learning the vibrato slowly.

Over the next few days/weeks, you'll notice that creating consistent movements is getting easier, but don't force the speed. Speed will come naturally, and the more you don't force it, the better your vibrato will sound.

Understand that your hands are doing two different things during vibrato. If you're getting a scratchy sound, it could very easily be the right bow hand and not the left fingers/forearm movement that's causing the bad sound. Remember, it's important to keep your bow relaxed through the process.

Make sure you have a good grasp of combing the bowing with vibrato before moving on to the next section. Generally, working for at least a month (five minutes a day average) is good enough for you to move on. Jumping into the next section without having a solid grasp on vibrato may create bad habits with consistency.

Appling vibrato in fiddle tunes

After you have a grasp of vibrato fundamentals, you can start putting the technique into songs. In this section, you work on learning a song that will sound excellent with the vibrato technique.

The best place to put vibrato is on long notes, especially notes that you hold for at least two beats. Take a look at the musical line in Figure 15-7.

Figure 15-7:
Vibrato line.

Figure by Michael Sanchez

On the half note, try to do a consistent movement of your hand to create a nice vibrato sound. Listen to the way I do this on Audio Track 91.

Now try the song "Au claire de la lune," which you learned in Chapter 9, and apply vibrato on any of the half notes. Listen to the consistency of the vibrato in Audio Track 92 and then try it yourself to see how you do.

Vibrato is one of the most frustrating and easily disregarded elements of playing the fiddle. It can be overlooked because many songs on the fiddle are played fast. But vibrato adds a significant element to playing songs and can make a huge difference between sounding decent on a slow piece and sounding great on a slow piece.

I hope you make some beautiful music with your new skill of playing vibrato!

Sharpening Your Double-Stop Skills

Double-stops are when you play two notes at once, but you play both of the notes with a finger down. You can also call double-stops *chords.* As you've found with the fiddle, it isn't always easy to put your finger down in the right spot, but now with double-stops, you have to do two down at the same time. Sounds fun, doesn't it?

When you put a finger down on one string, and play it along with an open string, this is considered a *drone.* Drones are easier to play than double-stops because you don't have to get the accuracy of two finger placements proper (you only have to focus on one being right).

In this section, I show you how to play some tricky double-stops that you'll often encounter in intermediate fiddle tunes. Learning this concept will help you create a more mature fiddle sound that really adds a lot to the instrument.

Developing proper fiddle placement with double-stops

If you're a beginner player, you can always choose not to play a double-stop and instead play just the top note. This is the easy way out, but it's definitely what you should do if you don't feel comfortable playing the double-stop yet. Adding in the double-stop, though, gives your tone a fuller sound.

Listen to Audio Track 93 to hear the difference between a passage that has a double-stop and the same passage without a double-stop. Do you notice how the double-stop adds to the music?

Take a look at the musical line in Figure 15-8 to see how to start learning double-stops.

Figure by Michael Sanchez

Figure 15-8:
Double-stop
line.

As you can see, the first measure has two notes on top of each other. This means that you play both notes at the same time. Do you see where the black dot is on each of the lines? This shows you which notes should be played at the same time. The first measure has all fiddle drones; one of the notes is played with an open string (see Chapter 13 for more on fiddle drones). The second measure has all double-stops; you need to put two fingers down at once.

Follow these steps to play the fiddle line in Figure 15-8:

1. **Put your 2nd finger on the D string (F♯), making sure you curve the finger over and far away from the A string.**

    You don't want your finger to touch the A string when you play both notes together.

2. **Play four of the F♯s without combining it with the open A yet.**

    The speed of your bow and relaxed grip will be the same going into the next step.

3. **Combine playing the open A with the F♯ and do it four times.**

    You've just played the first measure.

4. **Put your 3rd finger down on the D string (G) and make sure you're in tune.**

    You can always use a tuner to make sure you're putting your finger in the right spot.

5. **Put your 1st finger down on the A string (B) while keeping your 3rd finger down on the D string.**

    It's very important that your 3rd finger on D doesn't touch the A string or it will create a very bad sound. Lean your 3rd finger more toward the G string to stay away from the A.

6. **Play both the 3rd finger and 1st finger separately to make sure you're in tune and not touching the strings improperly.**

    If you hear a clash of sound, your 3rd finger may be slightly hitting the A string accidentally.

7. **With a relaxed bow grip, play both strings together.**

    Forcing this will cause a bad sound, so it's important to apply the bow just like you would with any other note.

8. Now go from measure 1 to measure 2 without stopping.

Try to imitate what you hear on Audio Track 94.

If you're struggling to get a similar sound to the one on Audio Track 94, it's almost always because of bad technique. You could be doing any of the following things, which may be causing the bad sound:

- You aren't placing your fingers in the right spots to create the proper note.
- Your 3rd finger may be hitting the A string instead of staying away from this string.
- You may be gripping the bow too tightly to create the double-stop.
- You may only be using a little bow, which makes it harder to create a clear sound.
- You may be using too much arm instead of guiding the bow with your index finger.

Watch Video Clip 28 to fully understand these points and how to get the best possible sounds out of your double-stops.

Getting proper contact with the bow is the most important thing to create a clear sound with double-stops and drones. It's easy to try to force the sound of the double-stop by gripping harder or applying your big muscles into the stroke instead of the small muscles. If you're having a hard time with this, refer to Chapter 5 and apply the same techniques with double-stops.

It's especially important to have your fingers in the correct spots when playing a double-stop compared to just a single note. The reason for this is that if one of the notes is off, you'll hear a clash of sound between both notes that sounds very unmusical. Think of two singers trying to sing a harmony line together, but one of them is out of tune. Even though one of them is singing in tune, it will sound off because they aren't both in tune.

Applying double-stops in fiddle tunes

As I tell you throughout this book, you can change a fiddle tune each time you play it. With this in mind, understand that you can add or subtract double-stops in fiddle pieces whenever it fits your mood. Figure 15-9 is an example of a tune with all the basic notes.

Listen to Audio Track 95 to hear the simplicity of "Galesburg Tune."

Galesburg Tune

Figure 15-9:
"Galesburg
Tune,"
part 1.

Figure by Michael Sanchez

Playing the musical line in Figure 15-9 shouldn't be too hard for you. (If it is, don't continue on to Figure 15-10 until you've mastered it!) Figure 15-10 takes "Galesburg Tune" and adds some double-stops and drones.

Galesburg Tune

Figure 15-10:
"Galesburg
Tune,"
part 2.

Figure by Michael Sanchez

Figure 15-10 has a double-stop in the first and last measure. Listen to me play it at a slow speed on Audio Track 96.

One thing you may want to try, which is a level above simply doing a double-stop, is to slide into the double-stop. I cover slides in Chapter 11 and the concept is the same, only you do it with two notes. This is considered an advanced concept, so if you're more of an intermediate player, sliding into a double-stop may be difficult for you to accomplish (especially sliding into the notes in tune). Start first with just trying to play the double-stops without sliding before trying to apply a slide into them. You can technically slide both notes or just one.

Check out the tune "Cacklin' Hen" in Figure 15-11, which has some suggested double-stops.

Now listen to "Cacklin' Hen" at a moderate speed on Audio Track 97.

Try to replace some of the suggestions in the piece with some of your own. I put some suggested slides in, but you can always vary these throughout the tune.

I've been using the same double-stop so far in this section, but it's not the only one you can play. In the next section, I show you some other combinations of double-stops that are more difficult.

Cacklin' Hen

Figure 15-11: "Cacklin' Hen."

Trying out some advanced double-stops

Sometimes you'll see various combinations of double-stops in fiddle tunes. Some are harder than others to play, and the difficulty isn't just because of the notes but the rhythms and notes you have to play *before* the double-stop. Jumping around is possible, as well as using different finger positions to satisfy certain double-stops.

Figure 15-12 is a popular intro in fiddle music that sounds best when you combine double-stops. Doing so requires some unique positioning of your fingers, which I explain.

Figure 15-12:
Fiddle intro
line with
double-
stops.

Figure by Michael Sanchez

Follow these steps to play this intro line with double-stops:

1. **Put your 2nd finger down on the E string (G).**

   This finger will stay in this position throughout the intro. Make sure you keep your knuckles up high so that you can do the next part properly.

2. **Put down your 1st finger on the A string (B) without hitting the E string.**

   Your 1st finger on the A string and your 2nd finger on the E string should be close together.

3. **Play two eighth notes, as shown in Figure 15-12.**

4. **Now take your 2nd finger, which is currently on the E string, and put it over not just the E but also the A string.**

   This is a tricky swap that takes having your finger down just right so that you get proper contact against the fingerboard.

5. **Play the 2nd finger on the A and E together.**

   This is the toughest part of the intro; you need to make sure you're pressing down properly on both strings.

6. **To play the final note of the intro, leave your 2nd finger down (even on both strings; like it was just positioned is fine) and place your 3rd finger on C♯ on the A string.**

   Normally, you play C♯ with your 2nd finger, but because it's covering the G on the E string, you need to use your 3rd finger. Your 2nd and 3rd fingers should be close together.

Listen to Audio Track 98 to hear the intro played slow.

The double-stop that usually follows this intro is done by taking your 3rd finger, which was on C♯, and sliding it up to D. You'll see this in the song that's coming up. After you play the first ending, you'll play the first note of the song, which is the double-stop that I'm talking about.

Figure 15-13 is a tune with some difficult double-stops, including the intro that you just learned. The song is called "Fairview County."

Fairview County

Figure 15-13: "Fairview County."

Figure by Michael Sanchez

As you can see, the intro doesn't always have to happen at the beginning of the piece. In this case, you play it at the end of the first ending. Technically, though, you can also play it at the very beginning of the piece.

Now listen to "Fairview County" played at a slow speed on Audio Track 99. Apply the double-stops if you can.

It's totally fine to learn just the top notes of a piece before applying the double-stops. It takes time to develop a clean sound with them, and sometimes you have to work on the rhythms and basic notes first before adding in double-stops. The more you do them, the easier they'll get. Don't just disregard them either; they really add flavor to a fiddle tune!

Chapter 16

Expanding Your Ability

. . . .

. . . .

Following everything I've shown you so far in this book will help you succeed in many areas of playing the fiddle. But one area I haven't really talked about yet is performing.

Every musician goes through a period where she thinks she's not good enough to perform for other people. This is pretty normal because when you're first starting out, many sounds come out of your fiddle that you don't want others to hear!

You may wonder why you can't just go through life only playing by and for yourself. The reason is that doing so will stop you from expressing yourself and building musicality. Simply playing by yourself will result in perfecting some songs to get the best possible sound. Eventually, you'll start working on putting your own interpretation into those songs. However, if you play for and with other people, this process will happen much sooner. You'll quickly learn how to express notes and rhythms in a uniquely different way.

Playing for others typically starts with playing for friends and family, which helps build your confidence. I start this chapter by talking about playing for friends and family and also playing in a recital.

Other ways to build confidence that I discuss in this chapter include attending a camp/workshop, joining a jam session, and attending an open mic night. These are all ways to build your experience outside of just playing by yourself at home. You'll find accelerated progress by making these some of your goals and then doing what you can to achieve them.

Playing for Others

One way to expand your ability on the fiddle is to start playing for friends and family. This is a great way to build your playing skills without showcasing yourself to the whole world.

If you've only been playing for a few years and want to start doing something other than just playing or practicing by yourself, here's something for you to try: Get out your fiddle the next time one of your friends or family members is over and show the person the latest tune you've learned and mastered. If you haven't been playing that long, the person you're playing for should understand if you make mistakes, and you'll probably be surprised at how much your listener likes hearing you play!

One way you can get involved with playing for others (if you don't want to organize it on your own) is to join a *recital* — a gathering of musicians with roughly the same ability level who perform songs in front of an audience. What's nice about a recital is that the people listening aren't usually judgmental — they just attend to hear their special someone play. This is a great way to make your debut in front of others, and many recitals are very low-key, with no pressure. Most teachers have recitals they put on for students, but if you don't take lessons, you can still call and see whether a teacher would include you in his recitals.

Getting Involved with a Workshop or Camp

One of the best ways to improve your ability on the fiddle is to listen to and learn from other fiddle players. You'll find many different workshops and camps around the United States that are great for even beginner fiddlers looking to improve their skills. Some programs are aimed at specific ability levels, while others offer a wide array of classes for all ages and ability levels.

This section provides a list of some of the most well-known fiddle camps and workshops in the United States. I highly recommend finding one that's closest to you and seeing how fun it can be. Each program I've listed is a great opportunity to meet others, improve your skills, and learn from some of the best instructors in the world.

What to expect

Every camp/workshop offers different types of classes. Some focus on specific genres of fiddle, while others cover more general styles of fiddling. If you have interest in mastering only one style of fiddle, make sure the camp/workshop you choose is suited to that style.

Typically, each camp lasts about a week, and food and housing are generally part of a package deal. Check out each website for information on how to enroll and what the requirements are as far as ability level. Each camp/workshop has an enrollment fee, and some are nonprofit.

Finding the best summer camps

Many camps happen in the summer, as you'll see by the following list. The biggest things I suggest you look for in a camp are the ability level, the types of classes offered, and whether jamming happens at the camp.

Acadia School of Traditional Music & Arts

www.acadiatradschool.com

This program has many classes, workshops, jam sessions, and more. It's a good program to consider if you're interested in Irish music and old-time. The classes are held in Bar Harbor, Maine, on the campus of the College of the Atlantic.

Alasdair Fraser Scottish Fiddle Camp

www.alasdairfraser.com

Alasdair Fraser is one of the most highly regarded Scottish fiddle players in the world, and his camp is held in California around June. This is a terrific camp if you're a serious Scottish fiddle player and want to improve your skills.

Blue Ridge Old-Time Music Week

www.mhu.edu/oldtimemusic

This program hosted by Mars Hill University features many classes for beginner to advanced fiddle players. The old-time tradition is the main focus of this program, held every June in North Carolina.

California Bluegrass Association Music Camp

http://cbamusiccamp.com

This bluegrass camp for all ages has classes for beginner to intermediate fiddlers. Classes are separated into three levels and are taught by some talented bluegrass instructors. This program is a great way for beginner players to improve their skills.

Cascadia Irish Music Week

www.cascadiairish.org

This program is a fine choice for beginner to advanced players looking to improve their skills in the style of Irish fiddle. This camp is held one week in August in Washington State.

Colorado Roots Music Camp

www.coloradorootsmusic.com/index.htm

This camp features all different styles of fiddle, including old-time, Irish, Scottish, bluegrass, and more. The classes offered are for all ages and ability levels and are taught by some of the most prestigious fiddlers in the world.

Julian Family Fiddle Camp

www.familyfiddlecamp.com

This is a highly recommended camp that offers general to master classes for the fiddle in various styles. Many well-known instructors teach at this camp, and it's a family-friendly atmosphere. The camp is held in California in April of each year.

Live Oak Fiddle Camp

www.liveoakfiddlecamp.com

Held in Texas each May, this camp has many classes focused on more advanced instruction in the styles of old-time fiddling, bluegrass, and more. This camp is a great way to connect with other fiddle players and attend various workshops.

Maine Fiddle Camp

www.mainefiddle.org

This camp, held every summer in Maine, is a good choice for those interested in the Scottish tradition. About 100 different instructors teach from June through August, with all ages and ability levels welcome.

Mark O'Connor/Berklee College of Music Summer String Program

www.berklee.edu/summer/mark-oconnor-berklee-summer-string

This program has been going on each summer for the last 20 years and is a great program for intermediate to advanced fiddle players. It's mostly for teenage students but doesn't have an age restriction. Mark O'Connor is one of the most prestigious fiddle players in the world. Mark discusses his method of learning fiddle, accompanied by many other well-known instructors.

National Oldtime Fiddlers Contest & Festival

`www.fiddlecontest.com`

This national competition for advanced fiddlers happens in Idaho each year in June. It's a great event to attend even if you aren't participating, as some of the best fiddlers from around the world go here to compete.

Reiner Family Band Workshops

`www.reinerfamilyband.com/introduction.html`

This is a great program held in Massachusetts throughout the year that features over 150 different types of fiddling workshops taught by many different instructors from all over the world.

Rolland Fiddle Camp

`www.peterrolland.com/Rolland_Fiddle_Camp.html`

This camp is ideal for those interested in learning fiddle in a small group setting. It's located in Colorado and is taught by fiddler Paul Rolland. It's a great value for the price.

These camps are by no means the only ones to choose from. You can do research in your local area or ask various fiddle instructors what camps or workshops they recommend for students. There are hundreds out there each year!

Joining a Local Jam Session

One way you can expand your skill on the fiddle is to join or attend a local *jam session.* This is typically a regularly scheduled gathering where people get together to play various styles of music. Many times you'll find the musicians gathered in a circle, following various rules of etiquette, depending on the style of music being played and the culture of the group.

Jam sessions are much different from *rehearsals,* where musicians get together with the common goal of taking a piece to the next level. Rehearsing is more about fixing mistakes and not moving forward until you have things in order. In jam sessions, you certainly hope to play a song better each time you play it, but you're also there to have fun — the emphasis is on the interplay and camaraderie among musicians.

To start, you must find out whether a group you're considering is open, where anyone can join, or closed, where the musicians only want to play with those who are already part of the group. You can find out by calling the group leader and asking her what type of group it is. If it's a closed group, the leader may have some suggestions for you based on what you're interested in joining.

Some jam sessions are interested in growing as large as possible, while others prefer to only accept a few new members. Try to get a feel for whether a group is interested in accepting new members and/or whether the group prefers more visitors. Every situation is different, but don't assume that a closed group has something against you.

Being badly out of tune can cause you to be the outcast of a jam session really fast! I talk about tuning in Chapter 3, and before you start playing with any group, make sure you're as close to perfectly in tune as possible. Tuning during a song is bad form; you should tune your fiddle before you come. If you need to tune it when you get there, go to a room far away from the group, if possible.

Jam sessions aren't designed to be freebie music lessons. It's important to respect other musicians and know when it's appropriate to get tips and advice from them. The safest way to get tips from some of the best musicians in the jam is to ask whether they, or others they know, would recommend private lessons. Otherwise, asking for too many specific tips at the jam can be inappropriate.

Don't underestimate the power of listening when it comes to a jam session. Although the goal is to play music, you sometimes have to listen to the group you're interested in for a while first to get the hang of what the musicians are doing. Listening to a few songs or even to an entire session before stepping in to play with a new group is totally acceptable and is even considered good etiquette when you first join, even if you're an advanced player.

It's important to know your level of expertise before getting into a group. Tell the group leader what your experience is and how long you've been playing. I suggest modesty when answering questions about yourself. It would look bad if you exaggerated your skill and then didn't live up to it with the other musicians. Groups are typically friendly to those who are just starting out. As long as a group knows what level you're at, the group will likely be accepting of your mistakes. Be respectful at all times.

All types of music can be played at jam sessions, and the type of music influences how the music is played and what the proper etiquette is for the session. The following sections give you info on how to find and get involved in these groups, as well as some do's and don'ts.

Playing in a bluegrass jam

The primary goal of a bluegrass jam is to have a good time making music together. These jams showcase great bluegrass music, and you're likely only a phone call away from getting involved if you have the ability and desire. Bluegrass jams aren't always limited to bluegrass music; some groups add other types of music into the rotation.

Unlike other types of jam sessions, bluegrass sessions typically consist of many players that come and go. In other words, it's pretty common for musicians not to know one another, whereas other sessions are weekly gatherings with a lot of regulars.

Finding a jam

Bluegrass jam sessions often happen around bluegrass festivals, which are held at various times of the year. Common instruments you'll find in these types of jams are fiddles, mandolins, guitars, and dobros, but they're not limited to these. Because bluegrass music requires precise rhythms and involves soloing by each musician, this type of jam is normally separated by ability levels. Generally, advanced players like to play with advanced players, and beginners like to play with beginners.

The best way to find a bluegrass group is to do a search on the Internet or talk with other fiddle players or teachers in the area. Many times, getting into a group is a matter of knowing someone who can help you get in, but you can also find many open groups. Here are some questions you'll want to ask when you call for information:

- ✔ How long has this group been meeting?
- ✔ What's the ability range of players in this jam?
- ✔ Is there a list of music I should memorize before joining the jam?
- ✔ How often does this jam meet?
- ✔ Should I come check it out as an audience member first?
- ✔ Where do you meet?
- ✔ Is there a group leader?

A great resource for finding a bluegrass group in your area is the website http://simplybluegrass.com/jams. This site has a list of bluegrass jam sessions and festivals from all over the United States. Most of the listings have phone numbers so you can begin calling various groups to see which one may fit you best!

Unlike other types of jam sessions, bluegrass jams are typically limited to two players per instrument. If there are more fiddlers in the jam, they may double up on a solo instead of each taking a turn. Don't take it personally if a group already has too many players and asks you to just come as an audience member to start.

General etiquette

In a bluegrass jam, everyone usually takes a turn playing each tune at least one time. (Check out Chapter 14 to find out about the different parts you may be playing while the solo is happening.)

Here are things considered to be bad etiquette for someone playing in a bluegrass jam (known as a *picker*):

- ✔ Playing too loudly, especially during someone's solo.

- ✔ Asking too many questions while others are playing. It's best to know etiquette before you come into a jam session; try to do as much research as you can.

- ✔ Tuning or making noise while in the circle. If you want to do this, proper etiquette is to step away from the circle.

- ✔ Not allowing everyone to play. Even if you're a more advanced player, let everyone take a part in the jam and allow even the weaker players to take a turn.

- ✔ Not taking part in solos. Bluegrass music is written to be inclusive, so not taking part in solos is considered bad form. It's best to join another jam session or practice on your own until you feel comfortable playing the solo when it comes your way.

- ✔ Playing the tune more than once when it's your turn. Don't get carried away and show off all the versions of the tune that you know. Chances are you'll get several opportunities to display another variation when it's your turn again.

There are also rules for audience members who are just at a bluegrass jam to listen (known as *grinners*). For example, talking too close to the players is considered bad form. Whispering is preferred if you have to say something to your neighbor, but whatever you do, don't talk or whisper loud enough for the players to hear. This is not only distracting, but rude! The other important thing as an audience member is not to try to meet the musicians until every song is over.

If you find yourself not playing up to par in a bluegrass jam or not following proper etiquette, you may be considered a *jam-buster*. These are people who cause others to quit because they prevent the jam from being fun. It's not fun when people break the rules and aren't as good as the other players. The best thing you can do if you have a jam-buster in your group is to leave the group.

Try to look up at the group leader as much as possible; staring at your fingerboard can cause you to sometimes miss your part. Don't be upset if this happens, but try to be as attentive as possible to your surroundings so you're ready when the time comes.

Getting into an Irish session

At Irish sessions, musicians play traditional Irish music and some other genres like Scottish. Unlike many types of jams, the music is mostly played for the pleasure of the musicians and not as much to perform for others. Irish sessions often occur in pubs, and although the musicians play in front of people, the sessions are very casual in nature. The feel of a music concert is definitely not what an Irish session is all about.

Notice that I use the word *session,* not *jam.* Irish sessions aren't considered "Irish jams," although they're very similar to the types of jams I talk about in this chapter. Just remember that in this style of music they're called sessions — don't call them jams!

The types of instruments you may find at an Irish session are fiddles, flutes, accordions, banjos, whistles, and more. In an Irish session, each instrument plays the direct melody of the tune without any sort of improvisation. As I discuss in Chapters 11 and 12, this type of music is heavily reliant on ornamentation, which is what varies each time you play a tune.

Finding a session

The best way to get into an Irish session is to introduce yourself to the session leader and tell him what type of instrument you play. Typically, Irish sessions are pretty casual and easy to get into, although some sessions are stricter than others. Usually, session members will let you sit in and jam to a few tunes, and over time, they may even have you start or lead a tune.

A good way to find Irish sessions is to research local Irish pubs in your area. Even if they don't host Irish sessions in their pub, they may know of other places that do or people to talk to. Get to know people that play Irish sessions as they can be your connection to new ones that pop up in your area.

General etiquette

Compared to bluegrass jams, Irish sessions are much easier to keep up with. They stick to a pretty formal structure and don't feature soloing.

Here are some notes on bad etiquette in an Irish session:

✔ Don't fake it if you don't know it. Many times, players like to drone on under an unknown melody, but that's considered bad form in an Irish session.

✔ Never play more than one instrument in the same song. Wait until the song is over to change instruments if you prefer to do so.

✔ Don't play loudly when someone else is singing. This can happen easily in Irish sessions, so make sure you change your dynamic level, especially for vocals.

✔ Don't deviate from the melody on fiddle. Remember that Irish sessions are formatted differently from other styles; the melody is the priority. Straying from the melody is considered bad form.

✔ Never play more than one rhythm instrument at a time. This can distract from the melody and is considered bad form.

It's very common for an Irish session to have a *set list* — a list of songs that are grouped in a predetermined manner. Instead of asking what song is up next, get hold of the set list so you know exactly what songs are to come and which ones you may want to participate in.

Although I wouldn't consider this bad etiquette, bringing music to a session is commonly looked down on. Doing so shows that you're unprepared, and although it's not a reason for dismissal, you should instead memorize the tunes that the group is playing. If you're working in more of a beginner session, bringing music may be more acceptable, but if nobody else has music, don't join until you feel more prepared.

Fiddlin' in an old-time jam session

Old-time music has been an American tradition for many years, and there are plenty of places that keep the tradition going with ongoing jam sessions. Hearing old-time music is a great experience, but you won't really understand the tradition and how the music sounds until you play in one of these jam sessions.

The type of instruments you'll find at old-time jams are mainly fiddle, mandolin, guitar, and banjo, but they're not limited to these instruments. Typically, each group has a rotation of old-time tunes that it plays during the sessions and usually has a set list.

Every old-time jam is different in the way that things are done and the rules that apply. For example, some groups may be very strict regarding how people should join the group if they're late, whereas others may be more laid-back about it. Some groups are particular about who starts a tune, while others are not.

Finding a jam

The Internet is a great place to start if you're interested in finding an old-time jam. Because bluegrass and old-time tunes are both typically played at jams, you may be better off searching online for "bluegrass jams."

Another way you may find a jam is to go on Craigslist and find someone who teaches fiddle, banjo, mandolin, or dobro. These players are typically connected to the jam community and may be able to lead you in the right direction.

Some jam websites have a list of tunes you should know to be in the group and any other information associated with the jam. Here's a website that really impressed me and consists of intermediate and advanced players: www.pegramjam.com/.

Some old-time jams call for singing instead of instrumental music. The amount of singing varies depending on the group. Personally, I prefer groups that are mostly instrumental, as they allow me to listen to other instruments instead of mixing in vocals. Mixing in vocals can be confusing at times and can cause others not to always know when to come in.

Every jam has a different personality, and it may take you some time to find out which type of jam is best for you. Some people prefer a laid-back approach, while others like a more formal and organized approach. You may also find that the size of the group is important to you, so trying out different groups allows you to see what you like best in a group. You won't know until you try various ones!

General etiquette

In an old-time jam session, someone chooses the tune that's going to be played and also selects a musician to start the kick-off. It's important for the person starting the kick-off to give everyone an organized tempo.

Here are some things considered to be bad etiquette in an old-time jam:

- ✔ Coming unprepared. Ask questions before joining an old-time jam to get used to the habits and rules related to the group. Remember, every group is different, so asking questions is important.

- ✔ Stopping the tune before it should end. Typically, the person who starts the tune should end the tune.

- ✔ Not sticking to the speed of the tune.

- ✔ Playing too loud. Just like with other jams, it's never fun to always hear someone play much louder than everyone else.

- ✔ Being in your own world. It's much better to listen to others and try to get a feel for the tune instead of only listening to yourself. This will cause the overall sound of the group to suffer.

In an old-time jam, it's a good idea to vary your dynamics in a song. If you aren't sure how to do this, see Chapter 10, which talks about dynamics. Varying your dynamics makes the song sound more interesting and sounds much better than everyone playing loud all the time.

Checking out Coffee Shops and Open Mic Nights

Another way to expand your ability on the fiddle is to get out and play at a coffee shop or an open microphone (mic) night. These are opportunities for musicians to play music they've prepared in front of others. In the case of a coffee shop, it may only be one song, whereas an open mic night may allow you to play various songs, sometimes jamming with others. These are great ways to network with other musicians as well.

To play in a coffee shop, all you have to do is speak with the owner or manager, who will typically schedule an audition for you. Some are more laid-back and don't require an audition, but it really depends on the quality of music they want to have in their place.

An open mic night is very similar to playing in a coffee shop. It's basically an event where any musician can get up and play in front of others. Open mic nights are typically held at (but certainly not limited to) bars. Lots of times, you'll find multiple musicians jamming in front of a microphone and trading solos. This is similar to a jam session except it has the feel of a performance rather than just a jam. Open mic nights sometimes have paid leaders, and if they like you, they'll tell you about others in the area that you can join.

To get involved in an open mic night, I suggest finding bars where bands play regularly, because they're more likely to have open mic nights. Call the bar and ask whether it or any nearby bars hold these events, and find out when you can go check it out.

Playing at open mic nights or coffee shops is usually for those with more experience and confidence playing in front of others, but it's not limited to those people. You can also find a partner to play with, whether it be a guitarist backing you up or another fiddler playing a duet with you. Having a partner can sometimes help calm your nerves.

Ask yourself what type of environment you prefer if you can't decide between a coffee shop and an open mic night at a bar. Although both can help improve your ability, it's important to be around like-minded people who make you feel comfortable.

If you're interested in joining a band, open mic nights are a great way to get noticed by band leaders. Bands are often looking for a fiddle player to complete their band (or replace their last fiddle player), so this is a good way to expose yourself to the community as a fiddle player in the area. You don't have to be interested in joining a band to join an open mic night, but this does give you the opportunity if you're good enough and you're discovered.

Chapter 17

Improvising and Playing Electric Fiddle

. . . .

In This Chapter

▶ Improvising music over chord structures

▶ Getting acquainted with the electric fiddle

. . . .

A big part of playing the fiddle is playing with others or putting your own spin on music. In this chapter, I go over the basics of improvisation so that you can jam along with other players like guitarists. I also introduce you to the electric fiddle, which really comes in handy if you want to perform or record your playing.

After reading this chapter, you may just be ready to play in a band or at least rock out to some electric fiddle in your home. You could be creating your own tunes before you know it!

Introducing Improvisation

Improvisation is the changing of existing music or creating new music based on the chord structures of a tune. It really opens up your ability to play endless amounts of music.

Have you ever heard a great fiddle tune on the radio or the Internet that had music besides just a fiddle? During these musical recordings, different layers make up the final product. You start with a melody and then get different parts of music, such as the following, to fit in around that melody:

✔ **Harmony:** An arrangement of notes that's different from the melody but done in a way to accompany the sound of the melody. If you've ever played a duet with another fiddle player, the second or bottom line is the harmony line.

✔ **Fills:** During spots where the melody/harmony is at a rest, you can play notes to help fill the song with more music. It's common to see fills from any instrument other than the one playing the melody.

✔ **Rhythm:** The chords being played that fit the musical structure of the melody.

I consider harmony and fills to be more advanced concepts and not something you really need to do unless you're playing in a professional band. Rhythm is usually taken care of by instruments other than the fiddle — most commonly the guitar.

Say that you go to a cookout and someone there happens to play guitar. She finds out that you play fiddle and asks whether you want to jam together. All the guests at the cookout get excited because they'd love to hear some great fiddle and guitar playing! This same kind of situation could also happen at a jam session or an open mic night where a guitar player wants to jam with you. If you want to jam with someone, you need some skills you haven't learned about in this book yet — improvisation!

Jammin' with a guitarist is all about the guitarist playing certain chords that sound good (match up) alongside the melody you decide to play. It sounds great together when done right.

If you're a classical player, this process will be challenging for you because you're accustomed to just reading the music. You need to open up your musical brain and be more imaginative, or, in musical language, be more improvisational. You actually have to create music in your head instead of reading it on paper.

Understanding chord structure

Chord structure consists of the various chords a guitarist would play at different points in a song to match well with the notes you're playing. You can plan your own chord structure ahead of time and then use improvisation to create your own melodies based on that chord structure.

Take a look at the following chord structure. Each of these letters represents a chord a guitarist would play for one measure of music, or four beats. An uppercase letter indicates a major key, and a lowercase letter indicates a minor key. To keep things simple, I cover only major keys in this book.

D-G-C-D

Following this chord structure, a guitarist would play a D chord for one measure, transition to a G chord for the second measure, transition to a C chord for the third measure, and then go back to a D chord for the last measure. This would make up four measures of music.

To make sure the guitarist understands what to do in the preceding chord progression, tell him to play a D chord for four beats, a G chord for four beats, a C chord for four beats, and then a D chord for four beats.

Here's another example of a musical chord structure:

D-D-D-D-G-G-G-G

With this chord structure, the guitarist would play a D chord for four measures (16 total beats) and then transition to a G chord for the next four measures (16 more beats). So this entire musical structure would take up eight measures, or 32 beats.

Here's another example of a musical structure:

D-D-G-G-C-C

This chord structure has three chord changes consisting of D chords, G chords, and C chords. The guitarist would play a D chord to start the structure for two measures, followed by a G chord for another two measures, and then finally a C chord for the last two measures.

Getting used to the notes that can be played during chords

Guitarists can play a number of different chords. Some are easier to understand than others, but for now I'm going to show you the most popular ones, which they should know how to play. Having knowledge of these chords allows you to play a bunch of different songs with the guitar.

All the chords in the following list have three different letters from A through G that make up the chord. These are the letters a guitar would play during various chord changes. Because a guitar has six strings, each of the three notes can be played different ways. Don't worry about understanding that part, though; hopefully, the guitar player knows how to create the chords! Here are the most popular chords, along with the letters that make up the chord:

D chord: Made up of notes D, F♯, and A

G chord: Made up of notes G, B, and D

C chord: Made up of notes C, E, and G

When you hear country music on the radio, 95 percent of the chords you're hearing are based on chords D, G, and C. This is great for beginner guitar players because they can start jammin' to country music rather quickly with knowledge of these chords.

Take a look at the free Cheat Sheet at `www.dummies.com/cheatsheet/fiddle` for explanations of more chord structures you may be interested in learning.

Starting with the safe notes

I want to first talk about the D chord structure. Because the D chord is made up of the notes D, F♯, and A, these are the notes that I want you to think of as "safe notes." What this means is that during any D chord that's being played, these are the notes that you can play on the fiddle that match perfectly with it.

When you start jammin' with a guitar player, you'll notice times when the notes you're playing don't quite sound right with the chords the guitarist is playing. That's why I'm showing you the safe notes — they'll always work with the chord. You don't want to play these notes all the time during a chord, but they're good to include in certain spots to start to build a melody that works.

Take a look at the musical line in Figure 17-1, which shows you all the safe notes in a D chord that can be played on the fiddle.

Figure 17-1:
Safe notes
you can play
during a D
chord.

Figure by Michael Sanchez

Now, let's say the guitarist plays the following musical structure, and you want to play a melody on top of it:

D-D-D-D

A good spot to put the safe notes in this structure would be the first beat of every measure. I show you what this would look like in Figure 17-2.

Figure 17-2:
Safe notes
on beat 1
of each
measure.

Figure by Michael Sanchez

Do you see how each of the first beats of the four measures has a note that's part of the D major chord or a safe note of the chord (D, F♯, A)?

Adding more notes

Now I show you more of what you can play during the musical structure. This is just a foundation for what you can do, but there are many variations, and eventually, you'll expand on what you can do with more practice.

Figure 17-3 shows some notes that you can add to the third beat of each measure. Adding to beats 1 and 3 is a good system to follow when you're first trying to play improv.

Figure 17-3:
Safe notes
on beat 3
of each
measure.

Figure by Michael Sanchez

Now it's time to fill in beats 2 and 4 of the musical structure. Safe notes would work in each of these spots, but I want you to expand your thinking a little and fill in different notes outside of the safe notes. First you have to understand what key you're in.

Understanding the key of a song helps to fill in certain spots. In Chapter 7, I show you in detail what notes you can play during various key signatures. Say that the musical line you're trying to fill in Figure 17-3 is in the key of G. Some good notes to play to fill in beats 2 and 4 are any of the notes in Figure 17-4.

Figure 17-4:
Notes in G
major that
can work as
note fills.

Figure by Michael Sanchez

Figure 17-5 shows some notes you can add to beat 2 from the G major chord progression in Figure 17-4.

Figure 17-5:
Further
progression.

Figure by Michael Sanchez

Now you have everything filled in but the fourth beat of each measure. I want you to try to expand your musical mind by filling in the rest. Remember, you can use any notes from the G major scale to fill in the spots where you see the rests.

Figure 17-6 shows what I came up with.

Figure 17-6:
Final
progression.

Figure by Michael Sanchez

This particular progression would work when a guitar player plays chords D-D-D-D. Pretty cool, huh? There are endless possibilities, so remember that there isn't one right answer to a perfect solo. Use your imagination and your ear to tell yourself what sounds the best.

TIP

Did you find that some attempts sounded better than others? This is common because improvisation is very experimental. Some things you do will sound very musical, while others — not so much. Allow yourself to mess up a few times — it's totally fine and expected!

Now try another progression: D-G-G-C, in the key of G again. Take a look at Figure 17-7 to see what I came up with using safe notes.

Figure 17-7:
D-G-G-C
progression.

Figure by Michael Sanchez

Do you see how the notes I put in this line are based on the notes of the chord? For example, the notes of a G chord are G, B, and D. Do you see how measures 2 and 3 are filled with these notes? Measure 4 also has two safe notes from the C chord.

Take the line in Figure 17-7 and try to create your own quarter notes to complete the musical line. Try doing this a few times first before you see what I came up with. Use notes from the G major scale to fill in where the rests are.

Figure 17-8 shows what I came up with.

Figure 17-8:
D-G-G-C
progression,
part 2.

Figure by Michael Sanchez

Adding in rhythms in improvisation

So far, I've stuck to the basics of changing notes, but I haven't talked about the rhythms. This section goes over improv with rhythms, which adds a lot to playing a melody line.

Figure 17-9 shows another chord progression, D-D-G-G. All the notes are from the notes of each chord.

Figure 17-9:
D-D-G-G
progression.

Figure by Michael Sanchez

Instead of filling in the rest with quarter notes, try to use eighth notes. Take a look at what I came up with in Figure 17-10.

Figure 17-10:
D-D-G-G
progression,
part 2.

Figure by Michael Sanchez

Now I'm going to switch some notes around and plug in some half notes to show you another variation. Remember, there has to be a total of four beats in each measure. Take a look at Figure 17-11.

Figure 17-11:
D-D-G-G
final
progression.

Figure by Michael Sanchez

This progression is much closer to a "cool" melody compared to the ones before, which were based on too many rules. Sticking to a safe note for the first note of each measure is a good rule of thumb, but after that, it's much better to have a free mind and find your way back to the safe note.

Listen to Audio Track 100 to hear the line in Figure 17-11, followed by some other suggested melodies. Then go ahead and try one yourself!

Even more important than hitting a safe note per measure is hitting the right note when the guitar player changes his chord. Say you have a D progression for a few measures. You could "wander" away from the safe note for the entire two measures and aim to hit the chord change in the next measure. That's what's going to make your sound musical and get the applause you want from the audience.

Make sure that, at minimum, you hit a safe note on each chord change. Try tapping your foot to know when the chord changes are happening so that you and the guitarist hit the change at exactly the same time.

Using the Electric Fiddle

If you're interested in adding another dimension to your fiddle playing, you might consider getting an electric fiddle. This is a great investment if you plan on playing in a band or group or want to experiment with creating different dynamics and tones on the fiddle.

Electric fiddles and acoustic fiddles are exactly the same as far as the way they're played. There's no difference in the way the fiddle is tuned or the technique you apply to make a sound. Everything I show you throughout this book applies to playing the electric fiddle.

There are, however, many benefits to getting an electric fiddle, including the fact that it's really cool! Here are a few of the benefits:

- ✓ **Having an alternate instrument:** It's always nice to have more than one instrument just in case one or the other has a problem.

- ✓ **It's better outdoors:** An electric fiddle typically costs less than a nice quality acoustic, so it's always a good alternative for playing outside or in places where you don't want to risk damaging your nice wood instrument.

- ✓ **The ability to play with headphones:** Most electric fiddles have the capability of plugging in headphones. This allows you to hear the music as long as you want in your ear, while not disturbing others nearby. When played without headphones, the electric fiddle sound is very soft.

- ✓ **The ability to be heard with other musicians:** Guitar players can get loud, so having an electric fiddle is the only way to compete for sound. You wouldn't stand a chance of being heard with just an acoustic fiddle!

- ✓ **It's a lot of fun:** Playing electric fiddle creates a different sort of sound, and you actually adjust the tone with an amp. You can blast music in any area like you never have before with an acoustic.

Although you can get the electric fiddle to sound good, it won't produce as natural and clean of a sound as an acoustic. I highly recommend learning on an acoustic first and using it as your primary instrument.

Steel strings work best on an electric fiddle because steel strings are most durable and typically go well with the sound of the electric fiddle. I wouldn't suggest getting $50 strings with an electric fiddle, or purchasing an expensive electric fiddle over $1,000, because sound is more dependent on the quality of the pickup and the ability of the player, not the strings or instrument.

Using the pickup

One thing that's very different between an acoustic fiddle and an electric fiddle is the use of a *pickup,* which captures vibrations from electric stringed instruments and converts them to an electrical signal that is amplified. Each electric fiddle has an internal mechanism that allows it to be plugged in electronically. This gives you the ability to do a lot of things you weren't able to do before.

There are many different types of pickups out there, but all have the same thing in common — one end is usually hooked onto the bridge of the fiddle. This allows the pickup to work properly so it's able to "pick up" the vibrations from the bridge, which can then translate them into musical sounds.

Think for a second how the bridge works on an acoustic fiddle. The bridge works the same on an electric fiddle, but the acoustic fiddle uses the wood of the fiddle to translate music into the air, while the pickup replaces this process on an electric fiddle.

An alternative to getting an electric fiddle is to purchase a pickup that you can hook on to your acoustic fiddle. This will allow you to hook into an amplifier, which I talk about in the next section. My favorite type of electric fiddle pickup is the Yamaha VNP-2. This pickup comes with the pickup already attached to the bridge as part of a complete system.

Plugging into headphones or an amplifier

If you play an electric fiddle by itself, it won't be very loud at all. This isn't really the way it's meant to be played because it's used most effectively when combined with headphones or an amplifier.

By plugging into an input on the fiddle, you're able to hear yourself through headphones without disturbing others around you. Normally, you have a volume control that can be adjusted right on the fiddle, as well as a tone control. You can adjust these two features to get the sound you like in your ear.

You can also plug an electric fiddle into an amplifier or even an entire PA (public address) system. This allows the fiddle sound to be as loud as the amplifier or PA system allows. There are some amps that, if brought outside, could be heard for thousands of feet! This works great when you want to get a louder sound when you play at a live event because you can turn the volume up or down as needed. Using an amp is also fun to do when playing at home as you experiment with different tone controls. You can also set it at a low volume level to practice.

So, how do you plug into an amplifier? You use a cable to connect the amplifier to the electric fiddle's input. Every electric fiddle should have this input.

Typically, you'd use a quarter-inch cable to connect an electric fiddle to an amplifier. You can find these at Radio Shack or online by doing a search for "quarter inch mic/fiddle cable." The length you need depends on the distance you want to be from an amplifier when you play. Generally, when playing with an amp, anything closer than 10 feet should work. You may need a longer cable if you're connecting to a PA system that's far away from where you're playing the fiddle.

Many electric fiddle outfits come with cables. You'll find some of the cables to be unique, so pay attention to the type you have if you need to replace it. If an electric fiddle doesn't have the input jack, one end of the cable may hook into a similar input like you'd use for headphones. It just depends on what electric fiddle you have.

Every amplifier is different, and there are many variations of quality. The three things that factor into the cost of an amp are the size, the features, and the brand name.

- **Size:** If you're just looking to play in your home, a small amp under $100 will usually do the trick. I've used the Fender mini-amps, which, at under $50, still pack a punch; although they're small, they can fill a room pretty well. These amps are sufficient for some, but not if you want to play in a live group.

- **Features:** Amps can have so many features that choosing one can be somewhat overwhelming at first. Generally, the more capability it has, the higher the price. If you're interested in creating a very warm, sweet sound and getting the most variation of tone, an amp with lots of different buttons/options is best. I explain the buttons on an amp in the next section.

- **Brand:** I tend to think the best amps are from the companies Fender or Fishman. There are many others out there though, and the best way to test them out is to go to a place like Guitar Center, which has many to choose from. The online store Electric Violin Shop is also a good source for amps and is very helpful with questions.

You can use any sort of amp with an electric fiddle, even ones that say they're for a guitar. Don't get caught up in what instrument the amp says it should be used with because they all work in the same manner. You can spend a lot of money on an amp, but I don't think it's necessary to spend more than $600.

In the following list, I explain what various amplifier features do:

- **Volume:** This controls the overall volume you want to come out of the amp.

- ✔ **Gain:** This is similar to volume but related to distortion. Because distortion doesn't sound the best on the fiddle and doesn't really fit the style of fiddle music, the gain should be lower than the volume. Guitar players in a rock or metal band heavily use distortion. To the fiddle player, this is considered a dirty, unnatural sound.

- ✔ **Mid:** This feature controls the middle tones on the fiddle and how loud they are compared to the high notes and low notes. If set too high, it can sound distorted. This is one of the features that you experiment with quite a bit to find the optimal tone.

- ✔ **Treble:** Just like the feature when you're adjusting the sound on the radio, this controls the tone of upper notes. Because the E string can potentially sound scratchy on an amp, it's important to manage the treble at a certain point. Typically, the optimal point is in the middle range.

- ✔ **Bass:** This feature controls the low notes on the fiddle and gives body to the sound. You don't want the bass down all the way or you'll get a thin sound. You also don't want it too high or it can cause distortion.

- ✔ **Reverb:** This feature can create a warmer sound for the fiddle if maintained at a low level. If you have it up too high, however, it can create an unpleasant metallic sound.

Watch Video Clip 29 to see me experimenting with an electric fiddle and an amp. You'll see how I adjust certain features to get the optimal sound. Ultimately, the goal is to get a clean/natural sound, which gets harder to do when you require more and more volume.

Hooking into a PA system

A PA system is something you'd see at a live event that contains an entire system of sound equipment. It's used to control and project the sound of multiple musicians at the same time. PA systems are common at churches, restaurants that play live music, open mic nights, and anywhere else you'd hear a live group or band. Because these systems can be complex, a sound engineer, or "sound guy," usually sets up and controls them.

PA systems have many different parts:

- ✔ **Soundboard:** Instead of hooking your cable into an amp, you connect it directly into the sound board, where the tone and volume of your fiddle can be adjusted to mix properly with other instruments that are playing in the group.

✔ **Speakers:** The overall sound that a PA system creates comes out of the main speakers.

✔ **Floor monitors:** These are typically placed on the floor in front of you when you play and are adjusted on the soundboard. They're used to help you hear your own sound when you play, because it may be hard to hear yourself with the surrounding noise. This is similar to the sound that's coming out of the speakers, but because you usually can't hear that sound clearly enough, having a monitor is important.

A really great option, especially if you plan on moving around when you play, is an *ear monitor.* This is an ear bud, along with a battery pack, that's used in place of a floor monitor. What's great about an ear monitor is that you can adjust how loud you want your sound to be while playing with others and not disturb other musicians with your floor monitor. You'll be a guitar player's best friend if you use an ear monitor! This is definitely a great investment if you commit to joining a live band that you'll play music with frequently.

If you want closer control of how you sound to an audience, using an amp is best. Sometimes, though, an event will require the PA system to adjust how your fiddle sounds with the overall sound of the band. A PA system allows for more flexibility — the sound man can turn up your volume during a solo if needed or turn down your sound if you're blasting over someone else's part!

Part VI
The Part of Tens

No matter how much you love playing the fiddle, practicing is bound to become a drag every now and then. Head to www.dummies.com/extras/fiddle for a list of ten ways to get out of a practice slump.

In this part . . .

✔ Discover ten famous fiddle players who shaped the fiddling world into what it is today.

✔ Get suggestions on the best ways to find a good music teacher who can help you continue to improve your fiddle playing.

Chapter 18

Ten Great Fiddle Players You Need to Hear

▶ Considering some pioneering fiddle players

▶ Looking at fiddlers in different musical styles

Many famous fiddlers have influenced the history of fiddle playing throughout many generations. In this chapter, I name ten fiddlers who've contributed to the history of fiddle music either through famous compositions they've written or through their art of playing. All these fiddlers have mastered their skills in music and in playing the fiddle. They're known not only for their musical abilities but also for their love of playing fiddle and sharing their passion with the world.

Charlie Daniels (1936–present)

Charlie Daniels is probably best known for his country hit "The Devil Went Down to Georgia." Charlie is not only a talented fiddle player but also a talented singer and guitarist. His unique style of music combines rock, country, bluegrass, blues, and gospel. Charlie is the son of a lumberjack and was born and raised in North Carolina.

At the age of 21, Charlie pursued his dream of becoming a professional musician. After starting a group called the Jaguars, Charlie was encouraged to move to Nashville and pursue work as a session musician. He found success moving to Nashville in the 1960s, and his career began to explode. In 1962, he co-wrote the song "It Hurts Me," which was recorded and released by Elvis Presley in 1964.

Charlie Daniels holds several title awards. He was named the BMI Icon at the BMI Country Awards in 2005. He was inducted into the Grand Ole Opry in 2008 and into the Musicians Hall of Fame and Museum in 2009. Charlie continues to be a hit today and still influences fiddle music.

Mark O'Connor (1961–present)

Mark O'Connor was born on August 5, 1961, in Seattle, Washington. Mark is not only a well-known fiddler performer but also a well-known music teacher and composer. His music career started at an early age, and by the time he was a teenager, he had won national titles on fiddle, guitar, and mandolin. At 13, Mark was named the youngest person to win the Grand Master Fiddler Championship.

Mark's musical compositions have been embraced by many other famous musicians and performers, including cellist Yo-Yo Ma and singer Renée Fleming. Selling over 2 million CDs, Mark's music has been a huge success. In 2001, he won a Grammy Award for his CD *Appalachian Journey*.

Mark is also known for his fiddle and violin teaching method. He first introduced the O'Connor method in 2009, and it's very popular with many violinists. It gives violinists a technical foundation using a variety of songs and exercises. Mark regularly gives lectures, string camps, and workshops around the United States throughout the year. For more information about his musical works or events, check out his website at www.markoconnor.com.

Bob Wills (1905–1975)

Bob Wills is best known for his influence on Western swing. Bob grew up on a cotton farm, and when he wasn't picking cotton, he was learning to play the guitar, mandolin, and fiddle. At a young age, he began performing regularly, mainly for dances and radio stations.

Eventually, Bob started his own band called the Texas Playboys and recorded with several different publishers. He received many music awards throughout his life, including the honor of being inducted into the Country Music Hall of Fame in 1968.

Bob suffered with his health throughout his music career, having several heart attacks. In 1973, while working on an album that would feature the Texas Playboys, he suffered a stroke that left him in a coma. Bob was never able to finish that last album and died from his stroke on May 15, 1975. The Texas Playboys finished the album without Bob. Even through all his health difficulties, Bob always continued his dream, and for that he will never be forgotten.

Craig Duncan (1954–present)

Craig Duncan is both a classical- and country-trained musician. He started playing the violin when he was 8 and continued his studies at Appalachian State University in Boone, North Carolina. Craig is a talented fiddler who also plays viola, mandolin, rhythm and electric guitar, and several other instruments.

Craig has also written books and produced and arranged music. Some of his books include *Famous Fiddlin' Tunes, Fiddling Chord Book,* and *You Can Teach Yourself Fiddling* (all by Mel Bay Publications). Craig has also been a featured instrumentalist on more than 60 albums.

A member of the North American Fiddlers' Hall of Fame and Who's Who in Music and Musicians, Craig's music has been featured on many TV shows. He has appeared on *The Oprah Winfrey Show* and programs on A&E, BET, PBS, History, and other TV channels. Craig Duncan continues to perform today and enjoys sharing his love of music with the world.

Jay Ungar (1946–present)

Jay Ungar was born in the Bronx in New York City and started violin lessons at the age of 7. The son of immigrant parents, Jay mainly listened to traditional Hungarian and Macedonian music growing up. However, when he entered high school, Jay was introduced to bluegrass and traditional folk music. In the 1960s, he became a member of Cat Mother and the All Night News Boys, and shortly thereafter, the Putnam String County Band. Later in his career Jay was a member of Fiddle Fever and the David Bromberg Band. He continues to perform today doing duets with his wife, Molly Mason.

Jay is best known for his composition "Ashokan Farewell," the Grammy Award-winning and Emmy Award-nominated theme song from the Ken Burns PBS documentary series *The Civil War.* In 1992, Jay and his wife were featured on the soundtrack to the documentary film *Brother's Keeper,* music from which was later released on a CD called *Waltzing with You.*

Justin Branum (1984–present)

Justin Branum started learning the fiddle at age 12 and began competing in fiddle contests around the country shortly after. His playing was influenced by bluegrass, Texas fiddling, Western swing, and jazz violin. This talented musician also plays the mandolin, guitar, cello, and bass, and sings. Justin is a composer and arranger of music and an adjunct professor of jazz violin at Webster University, where he received his master's degree in jazz performance.

Some of Justin's championship titles include the 2010 Grand Master Fiddler, 2010 Tennessee State Fiddler, 2010 Gone to Texas Fiddler, and the 2008 Young Adult Fiddle contest. He has played in many bands, including the swing band Swing DeVille, Colonel Ford, the Palominos, the Notable Haberdashers, and others around the St. Louis area. Justin owns a private music studio and teaches lessons in St. Louis, where he currently resides.

Bobby Hicks (1933–present)

Born in Newton, North Carolina, Bobby Hicks started learning the fiddle at age 9 and by the age of 11 had won the North Carolina State Championship. Bobby started working for Jim Eanes and began his career in bluegrass and fiddle. At 21, Bobby joined Jim Eanes's band, but he left in the 1950s to join Bill Monroe and the Blue Grass Boys. He was originally hired as a bass player, but shortly after he switched to fiddle. Bobby quit the band in 1956 to join the Army, rejoining in 1958 and going on to record ten more songs with them.

After playing with the Blue Grass Boys for a while, Bobby decided to move on and became a member of Porter Wagoner's band in 1959. Later, he became a member of several other bands around the country. Bobby Hicks was admitted into the National Fiddler Hall of Fame in 2002 and is a ten-time Grammy Award-winner whose music can be heard on over 50 CDs.

Alasdair Fraser (1955–present)

Alasdair Fraser is a Scottish fiddler player currently residing in northern California, where the *San Francisco Examiner* has called him "the Michael Jordan of Scottish fiddling." He has won numerous awards, has many TV credits, and has been the featured performer on many soundtracks. If you've listened to the soundtracks from the movies *Last of the Mohicans, Titanic, The*

Spitfire Grill, or *Braveheart,* you've heard him play. Alasdair has performed more than 50 times on BBC Radio and is a two-time winner of the Scottish National Fiddle Championship.

In 1996, Alasdair's album *Dawn Dance* received a National Association of Independent Record Distributors (NAIRD) award as best Celtic album of the year. Shortly after, Alasdair formed a band called Skyedance with the group members featured on *Dawn Dance.* He performs regularly with Natalie Haas, a cello player who graduated from the Julliard School of Music. The two musicians combine the violin and cello to create cutting edge Scottish fiddle music. Alasdair also operates Culburnie Records and, wanting to share his love of fiddling, founded three summer fiddling programs in California: The Valley of the Moon, Sierra Fiddle Camp, and Isle of Skye.

Natalie MacMaster (1972–present)

Natalie MacMaster is an award-winning Cape Breton-style musician born in Nova Scotia, Canada. She started learning the fiddle at age 9, and by the time she was 16, she had started her fiddling career and released her first album, *Four on the Floor.* Natalie has toured with artists Faith Hill, Carlos Santana, and Alison Krauss and has recorded with Yo-Yo Ma. She has received the "Artist of the Year" award from the East Coast Music Association several times and two Juno Awards for best instrumental album. The Canadian Country Music Association named her "Fiddler of the Year."

Natalie has released 11 albums and performed thousands of shows. She enjoys playing as a soloist or with her band, touring throughout Canada and the United States. As a professional musician, Natalie is very outspoken about her priorities. She believes her family and faith are important, and she continues to arrange her busy life in a way that keeps these aspects prioritized. Natalie currently resides on a farm in Douro, Ontario, with her husband and five children.

Martin Hayes (1961–present)

Born in Maghera, Ireland, Martin Hayes is a well-known Irish fiddler who has won the All Ireland Fiddle Championship six times. Martin's passion for music came from his family. He began playing the fiddle when he was 7. His father was a fiddler and leader of the 50-year-old Tulla Ceili Band. Martin's grandmother played concertina, and his uncle was a national fiddle champion.

This talented fiddler has recorded five albums and has won an Irish National Entertainment Award and the BBC Radio 2 Folk Awards' 2000 award for Instrumentalist of the Year. Martin is a member of the Irish music band the Gloaming and continues to carry on his father's legacy, playing regularly with the Tulla Ceili Band. He is also director of the Masters of Tradition festival held in Ireland every summer since 2003. Martin's expressive style of Irish fiddling continues to inspire other fiddlers around the world.

Chapter 19

(More Than) Ten Tips on Finding the Right Teacher

In This Chapter

▶ Knowing the traits of a good teacher

▶ Looking for a teacher locally or online

▶ Matching a teacher with your personality and goals

F inding a good teacher is very important to your development as a fiddle player. Some of the best fiddlers in the world trace their roots back to great instructors who inspired them and taught them how to play. Throughout this chapter, I go over some tips on how to find a good instructor. By the end of the chapter, you'll feel comfortable taking the first steps to walking into your very first private lesson — and many more to come!

Seeing the Value of a Private Lesson

Hopefully, you've learned a lot from this book, but it's up to you to apply the knowledge and use it to your advantage. What's nice about taking private lessons on top of reading this book is that you get live feedback about what you're doing incorrectly. Having a professional point out your mistakes can give you confidence in what you need to practice to get better, and professionals may pick up on certain things that you otherwise wouldn't have figured out. Even the littlest bad habit that you form by learning on your own can result in a big problem later without you even knowing you're doing it!

Another thing that's really helpful about taking private lessons is the accountability factor. Having a live teacher to report to can do a lot toward helping you continue your journey of learning the fiddle and sharpening your skills. If you're learning all on your own, you may find it harder to progress, especially when you get stuck and feel discouraged. Take it from me that the accountability goes a long way, even if you only take lessons once a month.

Understanding What Makes a Good Teacher

Some people may think that a good fiddle teacher is someone who knows a lot about the fiddle and has the most experience playing it. Being able to play well is certainly a good trait to have as a teacher, but it's only one of the many things you'll want to look for when taking private lessons. I believe the four most important areas you want to evaluate in a teacher are playing ability, teaching experience, personality, and adjustability.

✔ **Playing ability:** If you're just starting, this criterion isn't as important as if you were a more advanced player. Still, you don't want to hire someone who teaches you the wrong habits but someone who can teach the drills that are necessary for you to improve.

A good rule of thumb is to make sure the teacher has played at least ten more years than you.

✔ **Teaching experience:** Having a degree in music education is great, but don't rely on the degree to tell the whole story. Just because someone has a degree doesn't mean she's a good teacher. Many people without music degrees still make great teachers. Look at the number of years the person has spent teaching the fiddle. If she has more than 20 students, that's a sign that she knows what she's doing and is probably a good teacher. If she has only a few students, be a little bit wary. Don't hesitate to ask for references.

✔ **Personality:** Think about your favorite teacher in school and why you liked him so much. Having raw skills and teaching experience only goes so far. How much do you like the person you're taking lessons from? If you really like and respect your teacher, you'll want to continue to come to him to improve your skills, and you'll enjoy the process of learning. Although this is hard to tell at first, observe how the teacher interacts with you at the lessons and on the phone when you initially contact him.

✔ **Adjustability:** This is another trait that you really don't know is missing until you find yourself not wanting to come back to the lessons. Some things I'd put in this category are the ability of the teacher to be interested in your goals, encourage you when you're feeling discouraged, and adjust to your needs and wants. Some teachers have a set routine and get very anxious when you want to change it. Because you're paying for the lessons, you should be able to have the lesson tailored to your needs.

Knowing Your Goals

Everyone has a reason for wanting to play the fiddle, whether it's just for fun or to eventually get into a jam session/group. Some goals are more serious than others, but every goal is important because it's what motivates you to continue to progress. Knowing your goals is important when going to a teacher because she'll be the one helping you on your journey to reach those goals. Although the path to your goals may be muddy, the teacher will lead you on the path to success and help you along the way. Here are some possible goals to consider. Try to open up your mind to these possibilities!

- ✔ Being good enough to play in a jam session
- ✔ Playing in front of friends/family
- ✔ Being good enough to actually impress yourself
- ✔ Getting accepted into an orchestra or local group

Another big part of knowing your goals is understanding the type of music you want to learn. Although it's okay to just want to play "whatever," a particular style goal gives your teacher a clearer vision of how she can help you. Because the fiddle and violin are the same instrument, make sure you make it clear to your teacher that you want to learn fiddle or you may wind up learning classical violin!

Contacting a University/School

A good place to start looking for a private teacher is your local university, college, and/or high school. Most of these places have connections with instructors, and if you call and ask for a reference, they'll usually point you in the right direction. If you're looking for a low-price option, this can be the best way to find teachers who want to make extra money but don't have the experience to charge a lot. You can also ask the schools whether they know some of the best instructors in the area and those who have the most students.

Another resource is to contact a music school in your area to see whether it has any fiddle teachers or can recommend one. Remember, violin and fiddle are two totally different styles of learning; be sure to ask potential teachers whether they have experience playing fiddle!

Searching the Internet

Searching the Internet can be a great way to find fiddle teaching candidates. Although not every fiddle instructor is listed online, many of them have some sort of interest/exposure on the web. Here are some places to find teachers on the web:

- ✔ **Craigslist:** This is a very popular site where many fiddle teachers advertise. Just search for "fiddle lessons" on your local Craigslist page and see what comes up. Because violin and fiddle are the same instrument, you can also try searching for "violin lessons" and see whether the teacher also teaches fiddle.

- ✔ **Google search:** Many teachers list their services on various classified ad sites that you can only find by doing a Google search. Just type in "fiddle teachers in your area" and see what comes up.

- ✔ **Social media:** Searching for fiddle teachers is possible on Facebook and other social networking sites. This works best, though, if you're open to online lessons because you're more likely to find someone this way who is outside of your area but teaches online.

If you live in the middle of nowhere, you may be better off searching for general fiddle teachers and considering the option of learning fiddle online. I cover this option in the next section.

Considering Online Lessons

Many students think they can only take lessons face to face from a teacher. This way of thinking was fairly accurate years ago, but with the way technology is advancing, it's very possible to find a great teacher online and get effective online lessons. All you really need is a good Internet connection, HD webcam, and a teacher with the same professional setup.

This is an area I can attest to personally. I have a lot of online students and have great success with teaching online. I don't think every teacher can teach well online, but it's becoming more popular, and I think this is the way of the future. I highly encourage you to at least try out this method to see whether you like it or not. One way to find an online teacher is to search "online fiddle teacher" or "fiddle webcam lessons" on Google. You can also visit online forums and ask questions.

Getting Good References

A great way to narrow down teacher candidates is to ask for references of past or current students. If the teacher is able to give you many references, that's a good sign that he has his business in order. If the teacher is hesitant to give you a reference, that isn't a good sign; he may have something to hide, such as unhappy former students!

If you're looking for lessons for your child, you may want to consider running a background check on the teacher you're considering. If you're going to the teacher's house, make sure that it's in a safe neighborhood and that you feel comfortable going there.

Ask the teacher you're considering whether he holds any recitals. A good instructor may have one or two recitals a year; this is a way for him to showcase his students. The ultimate reference is for you to attend one of these recitals to really see how the parents interact with the teacher and what they have to say about their experiences. If the teacher doesn't hold any recitals, this may be a sign of an amateur teacher, although if the teacher lives in a small town, finding lots of students may be difficult. Still, I always feel that a teacher should hold a recital, even if he has only a few students.

Not Settling for the Least Expensive

I consider myself a very good instructor, and because of my experience, I generally charge $25 per half-hour session. In my area, this fee is considered to be on the higher side, and many students turn down taking lessons because the price is too high. My opinion is that if you think the price a teacher is asking is too high, ask why the teacher charges that rate. The worst thing you can do is settle for the lowest price because you aren't sure whether you really need a quality teacher (or you're not even sure whether you're going to like playing in general). Finding the right teacher should be the most important thing, and finding a good balance of price and quality should be next.

Here are the reasons why I charge what I do. See how your candidates respond and compare their answers to my credentials to decide whether you want to meet with them.

- ✔ I have an average of over 70 students at a time.
- ✔ I have experience teaching all styles of violin and fiddle.
- ✔ I'm a professional performer and get paid top dollar for local performances.

> ✔ I hold two recitals per year.
>
> ✔ I've run my studio for six years full time.
>
> ✔ I have excellent references and professional online resources.
>
> ✔ I've been playing the violin/fiddle for over 24 years.

In my area, the range for fiddle teachers is between $10 and $35 per half-hour session. People that charge $10 typically have only a little bit of playing/teaching experience. The ones who charge the most are those who have high educational credentials and have experience playing in orchestras or national touring acts. Finding something in the middle is what you should look for, but there are many possibilities.

Trying Out Different Instructors

Try to narrow your choice of instructors down to two or three and then ask them whether they're willing to do a free lesson/meet and greet with you. Most teachers are open to this because it gives you an opportunity to see how they teach, and they want to have you as a new student! If a teacher isn't willing to do this, that may be a sign that she won't really care for you as a student and just wants to make money. Nothing is better than a teacher who truly cares about her students and wants to establish a relationship with you first.

After going to each meet and greet, evaluate the teacher based on things I talk about in this chapter. Which teacher do you feel will inspire you the most, and whom are you most excited to learn from? Go with your instinct, and if you like a few of them, you can always try out multiple teachers for a few lessons to see how it goes.

Asking Potential Teachers (and Yourself) the Right Questions

It's always good to be prepared when going to a private lesson. This shows the teacher that you're serious about learning from him.

Here are some good questions to ask your potential teacher:

> ✔ How often do you think I should practice?
>
> ✔ What do you think are the areas I can improve in the most?

✔ Where do you think my progress should be at various points?

✔ What music should I be studying to help achieve my goals?

✔ Why am I struggling with a particular area?

Here are some good questions to ask regarding studio policy:

✔ Do you allow me to reschedule lessons if I give you enough notice?

✔ Will you charge me if I don't show up for a lesson?

✔ Do you give discounts if I pay for lessons ahead of time?

If any responses or experiences seem odd to you, definitely bring it up. Some teachers are really nice but have problems with punctuality or even showing up at a lesson (you go to their house and they aren't there).

Now a few questions to ask yourself:

✔ Am I practicing enough to continue paying for private lessons?

✔ Should I try out another teacher because I'm having trouble getting motivated?

✔ Is the teacher pushing me to achieve my goals?

✔ Do I feel encouraged after leaving the lesson and know what I need to practice?

Persevering

I've had more than seven teachers in my career, and each had good and bad qualities. Some teachers were way too serious, while others were way too laid-back. Some teachers knew a lot about the instrument, but I didn't feel encouraged to practice and almost felt intimidated to come to them. Some teachers are great with kids, but maybe not so great with adults. All these things can be reasons to continue to look for another instructor, but my advice to you is never give up. It may take you a while to find the right teacher, but I promise you that there are many great ones out there!

Hopefully, this chapter gives you some good insights, and I really hope you find a teacher who will inspire you to great lengths on the fiddle. It really is key to your success!

Appendix

Audio Tracks and Video Clips

• •

Sometimes, reading about a concept and trying to practice it just doesn't cut it — you need to see or hear it, too. Wherever you see the "PlayThis!" icon, you find references to audio tracks and video clips that demonstrate various musical techniques or show certain fiddle-related tools and accessories in more detail. This appendix provides you with a handy list of all the audio tracks and video clips referenced throughout the book.

If you've purchased the paper or e-book version of *Fiddle For Dummies,* you can find the audio tracks and video clips — ready and waiting for you — at www.dummies.com/go/fiddle.

Discovering What's on the Audio Tracks

Table A-1 lists all the audio tracks that accompany each chapter.

Table A-1		Audio Tracks
Track Number	Chapter	Description
1	1	Sound of an upslide
2	1	Sound of a downslide
3	1	Single notes versus double-stops
4	3	String pitches
5	6	Basic note pitches
6	6	Proper contact tone
7	6	Plucking basic notes

(continued)

Table A-1 *(continued)*

Track Number	Chapter	Description
8	6	Plucking "Mary Had a Little Lamb"
9	8	"Twinkle, Twinkle, Little Star"
10	8	"Cotton Eyed Joe"
11	8	Comparing the rhythm of a dotted eighth note and 16th note pair to a pair of two eighth notes
12	8	Easy rhythm line broken down
13	8	Clapping along thinking in eighth notes
14	8	Clapping along thinking in 16th notes
15	9	"Au claire de la lune"
16	9	Violin sound versus fiddle sound
17	9	Matching sounds of upslides and downslides
18	9	"Cripple Creek" with slides
19	9	"Bile 'em Cabbage Down" with slides
20	9	"Oh! Susanna" at medium speed with slides
21	9	The slur test
22	9	Slides and slurs in "Yankee Doodle"
23	9	"Home on the Range"
24	10	"Fiddlin' with Dynamics"
25	10	"Old Joe Clark"
26	10	"America the Beautiful"
27	10	"Amazing Grace"
28	10	"Little Brown Jug"
29	10	"Turkey in the Straw"
30	10	"Slurrin' Dixie"
31	11	"Swallowtail Jig" played slowly
32	11	"Swallowtail Jig" played fast
33	11	"Irish Washerwoman" with no ornamentation
34	11	"Irish Washerwoman" played quickly with ornamentation
35	11	Hearing the difference in sound between two notes played in the same bow stroke

Track Number	Chapter	Description
36	11	"Haste to the Wedding" played slowly
37	11	"Haste to the Wedding" played up to speed
38	11	Accent at the end of a quarter note
39	11	"Bill Sullivan's Polka" measure 1
40	11	"Bill Sullivan's Polka"
41	11	The grace note
42	11	"The Mason's Apron"
43	11	The triplet run
44	11	Swing rhythm in eighth notes
45	11	"The Derry Hornpipe" measures 6 and 15
46	11	Irish rolls in "The Derry Hornpipe"
47	11	"The Derry Hornpipe"
48	12	Difference between an Irish grace note and a Scottish grace note
49	12	"The Jig of Slurs"
50	12	"Cock o' the North"
51	12	"The Devil's Dream" slow
52	12	"The Devil's Dream" up to speed
53	12	"The Flowers of Edinburgh"
54	12	The Scottish snap
55	12	"Boyne Strathspey" slow
56	12	"Boyne Strathspey" fast
57	12	Driving up-bows
58	12	"Sally Air"
59	12	"Largo's Fairy Dance" version 1
60	12	"Largo's Fairy Dance" version 2
61	12	"Largo's Fairy Dance" version 3
62	13	Comparing standard and syncopated beat patterns
63	13	"Mississippi Sawyer" at moderate speed
64	13	Old-time accent pattern
65	13	"Wildwood Flower" at moderate speed

(continued)

Table A-1 (continued)

Track Number	Chapter	Description
66	13	"Angelina the Baker"
67	13	"Angelina the Baker" first measure with accents
68	13	"Martha Campbell"
69	13	"Bitter Creek"
70	13	"Liberty"
71	13	Droning measure 1
72	13	Droning measure 2
73	13	Droning measure 4 of "Betty Likens"
74	13	Droning throughout "Betty Likens" played slowly
75	13	Measure 1 of "Whiskey Before Breakfast"
76	13	"Bonaparte's Retreat" featuring alternative tuning
77	14	Bluegrass kick-offs
78	14	Simple bluegrass tags
79	14	Complex bluegrass tags
80	14	Rhythms in the Nashville shuffle
81	14	"Durham's Bull"
82	14	"Bill Cheatham"
83	14	"Blackberry Blossom"
84	14	"Ragtime Joe"
85	14	"Fire on the Mountain"
86	15	"Song of Christy"
87	15	Musical phrase with vibrato and without vibrato
88	15	Consistency versus inconsistency in vibrato
89	15	Vibrato sound
90	15	Vibrato sound over time
91	15	Vibrato line
92	15	"Au claire de la lune" with vibrato
93	15	Double-stop demonstration
94	15	Double-stop line
95	15	"Galesburg Tune" part 1

Track Number	Chapter	Description
96	15	"Galesburg Tune" part 2
97	15	"Cacklin' Hen"
98	15	Fiddle intro line with double-stops played slowly
99	15	"Fairview County"
100	17	DDGG progression examples

Looking at What's on the Video Clips

Table A-2 lists all the video clips that accompany each chapter.

Table A-2		Video Clips
Clip Number	Chapter	Description
1	2	Comparison of beginner, intermediate, and premium fiddles
2	2	Comparison of different types of bows
3	2	Overview of various fiddle accessories
4	3	How to tighten and rosin your bow correctly
5	3	How to replace fiddle strings
6	4	Preventing bad bow hold habits
7	5	The quarter drill
8	5	Moving the bow
9	5	Arm extension drill
10	5	Avoiding bad sounds
11	5	Motion of the index finger
12	5	The index drill
13	5	The pinkie drill
14	5	The wall drill
15	6	Setting up the left hand
16	6	Finger angles test

(continued)

Table A-2 *(continued)*

Clip Number	Chapter	Description
17	8	Demonstration of eighth notes, half notes, and quarter notes
18	9	Demonstration of down bow, up bow, and bow lifts
19	9	Fundamentals of using the 4th finger
20	11	Demonstration of Irish accents
21	13	Playing two strings at once
22	13	Tunneling with drones
23	14	Georgia shuffle blow pattern
24	14	Playing chops
25	15	Shifting in C and D major
26	15	Creating a beautiful vibrato, part 1
27	15	Creating a beautiful vibrato, part 2
28	15	Creating clear double-stops
29	17	Electric fiddle demo

Index

bridge
  collapse, dealing with, 55
  defined, 10
  location of when changing strings, 54
button, bow, 11
buying fiddle. *See also* accessories; bow
  beginner-level, 27–28
  fiddle versus violin, 27
  intermediate-level, 28–29
  left- or right-handed, choosing between,
    26–27
  overview, 21–22
  premium-level, 29–31
  quality, role in pricing, 24–26
  versus renting, 31
  sizes, 22–23
  sound qualities, 23–24

• C •

C major scale, 131–132, 253, 254
C natural key, 131
cables, electric fiddle, 293
"Cacklin' Hen", 265, 266
California Bluegrass Association Music
    Camp, 273–274
camps, 272–275
Cape Breton Scottish fiddling style, 206
carbon fiber fiddle bows, 33, 58
care, fiddle
  bridge collapse, dealing with, 55
  case, 61–62
  cracks and open seams, preventing, 51–52
  humid conditions, avoiding, 52
  overview, 39, 50
  polishing and cleaning, 50–51
  rehairing bow, 56–58
  sound post, 52–53
  strings, changing, 53–55
  strings, replacing, 59–61
  wear and tear, overview of, 56
Cascadia Irish Music Week, 274
case
  hygrometer in, 52
  putting fiddle into, 61–62
  quality, paying attention to, 27
  types of, 61

center-mount chin rest, 68, 69
Cheat Sheet, 5, 286
chin rest
  holding fiddle, 72–73
  overview, 65–66, 68
  replacing, 68–70
Chinese fiddles, 25
chips, in intermediate-level fiddles, 29
chops, in bluegrass fiddling, 237, 247–248
chord structure, 284–285, 286
chords, in improvisation. *See also*
    double-stops
  notes in, 285–289
  rhythms, 289–290
chromatic scale, 135
cleaning fiddle, 50–51
cleanliness of tone, 23
clefs, 129–130
closed jam sessions, 276
cloth, using as shoulder rest, 68
"Cock o' the North", 207, 209
coffee shops, performing at, 282
Colorado Roots Music Camp, 274
common (4/4) time, 148–149
compound, peg, 45
concert speed, 144
condition, in fiddle pricing, 26
confidence, building, 271. *See also*
    performing
consignment, fiddles on, 31
consistency, importance of to
    vibrato, 256
contact point
  drill for, 104
  finding, 82–83
cost
  fiddle, 24–26
  of lessons, 309–310
"Cotton Eyed Joe", 149, 151, 152
counting
  overview, 16
  by subdividing, 155–159
country of origin, in fiddle pricing, 25
cracks
  in fiddle pricing, 26
  intermediate-level fiddles, 29
  preventing, 51–52

• *P* •

Notes

Notes

Notes

Notes

About the Author

Michael Sanchez has been playing classical violin and fiddle for more than 24 years and teaching in his private studio for almost 10 years. He has taught more than 500 students during his teaching career and currently has more than 50 students weekly at his studio in Grand Rapids, Michigan.

Michael's instrument abilities include the violin, viola, fiddle, mandolin, and piano. He has played fiddle in many country music bands and for the "Medora" musical, a well-known and popular show that has been held each year in North Dakota since 1965. Michael has also lived and performed in Nashville, where he taught fiddle professionally.

Currently, Michael dedicates much of his time to teaching and performing in various special events and weddings. He's a popular online violin/fiddle teacher on YouTube (www.youtube.com/violintutorpro) with more than 15,000 subscribers and millions of viewers, and he has more than 80,000 followers on Facebook (www.facebook.com/violintutorpro). Michael provides a fun, interactive approach to learning the fiddle and violin and is reaching students all over the world with his innovative ideas using the Internet and online classes. He believes that a solid foundation in the fundamentals of fiddle and violin is crucial to helping students achieve that beautiful sound they're looking for.

Michael is CEO and creator of Violin Tutor Pro (www.violintutorpro.com), an online site established in 2009 where members can gain access to hundreds of Michael's video lessons on the violin and fiddle. He is also the CEO of Superior Violins (www.superiorviolins.com), a site dedicated to all his instrument and accessory recommendations. Michael plans on expanding this into a chain of stores in the future, focusing on the string instruments market.

Dedication

I would like to dedicate this book to my wonderful wife Christy, who has inspired me day in and day out. I'm thankful that God brought you into my life and literally to my doorstep for a music lesson that year. Thank you for your love and support!

Author's Acknowledgments

I must start by thanking my parents, who have been there for me throughout my life. If it wasn't for you both, I wouldn't be the man that I am today. Thanks for starting me on the violin/fiddle so young and for supporting me every year through private lessons. I'm also very thankful to my mom and stepdad, Randy, who allowed me to teach so many years out of their home. This is what lit the spark to help me become an entrepreneur and continue with my dream of becoming a worldwide teacher. Thanks also to my stepmom, Tracy, and in-laws, Dave and Peggy. You have all been such a wonderful support system for me. I'm so happy we all get along!

I'd also like to thank my assistant, Bernie, who has been a big part of my success since I started my online businesses. She has helped me in countless ways, from managing inventory, helping with emails, helping with this book, and, of course, moral support. Thanks for being not just a great assistant but also a great friend. A big thanks goes to all the teachers I've had over the years, including Christine Venn, Susan Belliel, Barbara Vanderheide, and Christina Fong. Thanks also to Gregory Maytan, who has been a great friend and supporter over the last few years.

Finally, I'd like to thank all the students who have molded me into the teacher I am today. I'm grateful for the opportunity to reach so many students worldwide and for the nice letters from those I've influenced. I hope to continue to help you all reach your dreams of learning to master fiddle!

Publisher's Acknowledgments

Acquisitions Editor: David Lutton
Senior Project Editor: Christina Guthrie
Copy Editor: Todd Lothery
Technical Editor: Carolyn Dutton
Art Coordinator: Alicia B. South

Project Coordinator: Melissa Cossell
Project Manager: Kathleen Jeffers
Producers: Shelley Lea, Eric Hurst
Illustrator: Rashell Smith
Cover Image: ©iStock.com/aloha_17

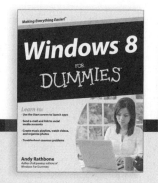

Math & Science

Algebra I For Dummies,
2nd Edition
978-0-470-55964-2

Anatomy and Physiology
For Dummies, 2nd Edition
978-0-470-92326-9

Astronomy For Dummies,
3rd Edition
978-1-118-37697-3

Biology For Dummies,
2nd Edition
978-0-470-59875-7

Chemistry For Dummies,
2nd Edition
978-1-118-00730-3

1001 Algebra II Practice
Problems For Dummies
978-1-118-44662-1

Microsoft Office

Excel 2013 For Dummies
978-1-118-51012-4

Office 2013 All-in-One
For Dummies
978-1-118-51636-2

PowerPoint 2013
For Dummies
978-1-118-50253-2

Word 2013 For Dummies
978-1-118-49123-2

Music

Blues Harmonica
For Dummies
978-1-118-25269-7

Guitar For Dummies,
3rd Edition
978-1-118-11554-1

iPod & iTunes
For Dummies, 10th Edition
978-1-118-50864-0

Programming

Beginning Programming
with C For Dummies
978-1-118-73763-7

Excel VBA Programming
For Dummies, 3rd Edition
978-1-118-49037-2

Java For Dummies,
6th Edition
978-1-118-40780-6

Religion & Inspiration

The Bible For Dummies
978-0-7645-5296-0

Buddhism For Dummies,
2nd Edition
978-1-118-02379-2

Catholicism For Dummies,
2nd Edition
978-1-118-07778-8

Self-Help & Relationships

Beating Sugar Addiction
For Dummies
978-1-118-54645-1

Meditation For Dummies,
3rd Edition
978-1-118-29144-3

Seniors

Laptops For Seniors
For Dummies, 3rd Edition
978-1-118-71105-7

Computers For Seniors
For Dummies, 3rd Edition
978-1-118-11553-4

iPad For Seniors
For Dummies, 6th Edition
978-1-118-72826-0

Social Security
For Dummies
978-1-118-20573-0

Smartphones & Tablets

Android Phones
For Dummies, 2nd Edition
978-1-118-72030-1

Nexus Tablets
For Dummies
978-1-118-77243-0

Samsung Galaxy S 4
For Dummies
978-1-118-64222-1

Samsung Galaxy Tabs
For Dummies
978-1-118-77294-2

Test Prep

ACT For Dummies,
5th Edition
978-1-118-01259-8

ASVAB For Dummies,
3rd Edition
978-0-470-63760-9

GRE For Dummies,
7th Edition
978-0-470-88921-3

Officer Candidate Tests
For Dummies
978-0-470-59876-4

Physician's Assistant Exar
For Dummies
978-1-118-11556-5

Series 7 Exam For Dumm
978-0-470-09932-2

Windows 8

Windows 8.1 All-in-One
For Dummies
978-1-118-82087-2

Windows 8.1 For Dummie
978-1-118-82121-3

Windows 8.1 For Dummie
Book + DVD Bundle
978-1-118-82107-7

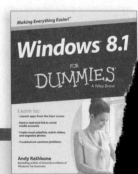

Take Dummies with you everywhere you go!

Whether you are excited about e-books, want more from the web, must have your mobile apps, or are swept up in social media, Dummies makes everything easier.

Leverage the Power

For Dummies is the global leader in the reference category and one of the most trusted and highly regarded brands in the world. No longer just focused on books, customers now have access to the For Dummies content they need in the format they want. Let us help you develop a solution that will fit your brand and help you connect with your customers.

Advertising & Sponsorships

Connect with an engaged audience on a powerful multimedia site, and position your message alongside expert how-to content.

Targeted ads • Video • Email marketing • Microsites • Sweepstakes sponsorship

21 Million Monthly Page Views & 13 Million Unique Visitors

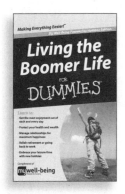

Dummies products make life easier!

- DIY
- Consumer Electronics
- Crafts
- Software
- Cookware
- Hobbies
- Videos
- Music
- Games
- and More!

For more information, go to **Dummies.com** and search the store by category